*Leaders have been taught how to
plan but not how to implement.
This has created a strategy
implementation skills gap.*

— Robin Speculand & Antonio Nieto-Rodriguez

ENDORSEMENTS

For too long there's been a gap in the market on how to implement strategy. That's why Thinkers50 has championed the important work of Robin Speculand and Antonio Nieto-Rodriguez at the Strategy Implementation Institute. This Playbook finally fills that gap and is essential practical reading.

—Stuart Crainer & Des Dearlove
Founders, Thinkers50

If you think the implementation of your strategy is a major issue, which few books address correctly, let yourself be charmed by the Playbook offered by Antonio and Robin, full of tools, techniques, and practical tips that you can immediately apply.

—Yves Pigneur
Co-inventor of the Business Model Canvas with Alex Osterwalder

This Playbook offers a healthy balance of big-picture explanation, immediate action steps, illustrative stories, and user-friendly frameworks. It's an essential companion for leaders who need to navigate the dangerous journey of crafting and implementing strategy. The material will guide you and make you glad you have this reference book by your side as you take advantage of Antonio and Robin's deep understanding and thought leadership on strategy implementation.

—Michael Netzley, PhD
Founder and CEO of Extend My Runway

Robin and Antonio have truly captured a formidable "body of knowledge" based on their extensive experiences and expertise in successful strategy implementation. Delve in to discover a practical step-by-step guide by practitioners, for practitioners. This Playbook, together with their Institute and live sessions combine the best of action learning, social learning, and digital learning—a great combination to drive meaningful and sustainable implementation.

—Lori Figueiredo
Change & Digital Learning Strategist, Shaping SYZYGY Development

Very few leaders have the necessary experience or tools to design and implement strategies. This Playbook provides the tools and frameworks for true leaders to develop the skills that allow them to successfully implement their corporate strategy. The Playbook also acts as a guide and monitoring model through their implementation journey.

—Francisco de Miguel
Former chairman of RPVL.BV and counselor to the CEO of Greif Bros.

Research reveals that very few leaders have the ability to both craft and implement strategy. This Playbook provides a clear and actionable framework and critical implementation tools and tips to help leaders guide their organization to strategy implementation success.

—Dr. Tony O'Driscoll
Fuqua School of Business, Duke University

Finally, an implementation-centred Playbook which recognises that executive leaders have traditionally been good at strategizing and planning, with many not focused enough on the implementation itself, the very stage where failure occurs more often than not. Antonio and Robin of the Strategy Implementation Institute have consolidated their vast knowledge and working experience to publish a Playbook that focuses squarely on the "how to," helping organisations and leaders successfully implement their strategies and plans. Complete with templates, tools, and an action-oriented strategy implementation road map, this book is the benchmark for success. I highly recommend this for executives, boards, and leaders everywhere.

—Jeremy Blain
Award-winning CEO and international #1 best-selling author
of *The Inner CEO: Unleashing Leaders at All Levels*

There are many frameworks and approaches for developing strategy in the business literature but very few for successful implementation. This Playbook provides the tools, tips, and techniques that all leaders need and is an invaluable resource for anyone involved in implementing strategy.

—Dharma Chandran
Chief People Officer, Australian Broadcasting Corporation (or
ABC) and Non-Executive Director, 7-Eleven Australia.

There are not many books that present these systematic ways of implementing the strategies that leaders embark on. This approach is easy to understand and gives the implementation a better chance to succeed.

—Patricia Enslow
Ex Managing Director of Credit Suisse and UBS APAC

CONTENTS

INTRODUCTION

The Strategy Implementation Institute (Institute) was founded in 2019 by Robin Speculand and Antonio Nieto-Rodriguez, two global thought leaders who share a passion for developing people to be implementation professionals.

> *Implementing strategy is a rare and highly appreciated skill set that sets apart the most influential and successful leaders in business.*
>
> – Antonio Nieto Rodriguez and Robin Speculand

The Institute brings people together from around the world who are passionate about implementation and is creating an online community for them to learn, share, and grow. It recognizes that implementing strategy is a rare and highly appreciated skill set that sets apart the most influential and successful leaders in business. People with the skill to implement strategy are in high demand from organizations all around the world, especially at a time when strategies are being formed and implemented at a more rapid pace than ever before.

To meet this increasing demand for skilled implementers, the Institute offers:

1. Membership to the online community—offers various benefits such as monthly meetings to discuss trends and best practices
2. Online Professional exam and certification in partnership with APMG International—test your knowledge and understanding
3. Fellowship certification—demonstrate your skill and ability

The Strategy Implementation Institute aims to become the global gold standard in implementation certification.

Leaders Challenge

Strategy implementation continues to be a crucial challenge for leaders, especially as the business landscape continues to rapidly change.

Part of the challenge is that the current generation of leaders has been taught how to plan and not how to implement, as reflected in the high strategy implementation failure rate.

Every participant studying a business degree is taught strategy, but very few are taught how to implement. The Institute is filling this skills gap among leaders.

How to Use the Strategy Implementation Playbook

This *Playbook* is designed to support you in implementing your organization's strategy. You can use it most effectively as both a guide to build and support your implementation and a reference book by going to each of the color-coded sections as you require.

Strategy implementation is not a linear journey, which is why our framework, the Strategy Implementation Road Map© that provides the structure for this Playbook, is circular. Your organization needs to dictate your starting point. If you need to change your measures, for example, you'd go to Track Performance, or if you want to nurture your communications throughout your journey, you'd go to Stakeholder Management.

Each section of this road map features related articles and refers you to useful videos and external papers.

At the end of each section, you will find 10 quiz questions to test your understanding and knowledge of the contents. Both the *Playbook* and the quiz questions support all participants in preparing for the Strategy Implementation Professional (SIP) online certification course. (See Appendix for more details.)

How the Institute Works

Our focus is to:

Create an implementation community—where people can connect, discuss, and learn about strategy implementation

Share knowledge—provide the platform and opportunity to discuss and debate key areas

Continually build a body of knowledge—establish an effective strategy implementation framework built and enriched by experts from the field

Support leaders—provide the implementation framework, best practices, and templates

Award Professional and Fellowship—to leaders who pass the accreditation and become a member of an exclusive group of highly sought-after implementation professionals

Volunteers participation—creates volunteering opportunities for strategy practitioners who want to contribute to the global continuous improvement of implementation

What We Offer

The Institute offers two levels of training and certification to members.

1. Strategy Implementation Professional (SIP)
2. Fellowship (FSII)

1. **Strategy Implementation Professional certified by APMG**

This course involves understanding what it takes to become a professional in the domain.

The seven-course module is open to anyone who wants to develop further in their career and wants to learn the fundamentals, best practices, and key tools about strategy implementation. It is based on the Institute's propriety body of knowledge, the Strategy Implementation Road Map© (SIR), that provides a step-by-step guide on "how" to implement strategy—see next chapter. It covers the key areas and outlines the required skills an implementation professional needs to know. The online course is based on its creators' years of experience as practitioners, authors, and teachers. It is designed to blend learning from presentations, articles, and videos.

The course consists of the following modules:

1) Leadership Excellence
2) Value Creation
3) Business Model
4) Culture Evolution
5) Stakeholder Management
6) Employee Engagement
7) Track Performance

Each module has four levels:

- Crafting
- Embedding
- Executing
- Sustaining

2. Fellowship

The Fellowship is the highest and most prestigious recognition from the Strategy Implementation Institute (Institute) for practitioners in the field of strategy implementation. "Fellows of the Institute" have successfully demonstrated a passion in the subject, success in demonstrating the skills they have learned as a Strategy Implementation Professional—our online course and certification and a desire to continuously learn and develop.

Recognition as a Fellow of the Institute enters you into an exclusive club of not only Fellowships of the Institute but also among leaders globally who have the skills and experience to successfully implement strategy. Recipients are accomplished leaders from a broad range of fields who have had the vision and passion to make significant and lasting contributions to the strategy implementation profession, community, and the Institute.

The Fellowship is a significant part of the Institute's purpose to develop implementation professionals around the world.

Implementing strategy is a rare and highly appreciated skill set that sets apart the most influential and successful leaders in business.

SIBoK Contributors

Developing a comprehensive body of knowledge requires support and feedback from our members. We would specifically like to thank the following members for their contribution and time: Sarmad Saghir, Gurpreet Rehal, Ricardo Sastre, and Robert King, MBA, Allan Samaroo, and Onajite Newton.

AUTHORS & CO-FOUNDERS

Antonio Nieto-Rodriguez

Author of the *Harvard Business Review Project Management Handbook*, the featured HBR article "The Project Economy Has Arrived," and five other books, Antonio is the creator of concepts such as the Project Economy. He is the most published author of project management articles in HBR. His research and global impact have been recognized and included in the top 50 most influential management thought leaders by Thinkers50. Fellow and Former Chairman of the Project Management Institute, he is the creator of the Brightline Initiative, founder of Projects&Co, and co-founder of PMOtto and the Strategy Implementation Institute. Born in Madrid, Spain, and educated in Germany, Mexico, Italy, and the United States, Antonio is fluent in five languages. He has an MBA from London Business School. He is a member of Marshall Goldsmith 100 coaches. You can follow Antonio through his LinkedIn Newsletter - Lead Projects Successfully, his popular online course Project Management Reinvented for Non-Project Managers, and his website.

He has advised and trained thousands of senior leaders on prioritizing and implementing strategic initiatives and leading transformational change in companies like Nestle, L'Oreal, Euronext, IMEC, Moet Hennessey, ING, ABInveb, Google, Metlife, Saudia Airlines, KLM, Moodys, Vision 2030 Office, Ageas, Knauf, RGP, Qatar Petroleum, Lonza, Aliaxis, Kinepolis, Cleary Gottlieb, etc.

Robin Speculand

Robin Speculand lives and breathes strategy and digital implementation. He supports C-Suite and Boards in transforming their organizations and is well known for his innovative approaches and passionate delivery.

He is one of the world's most prolific writers on the subject, having published eight books that includes, the Amazon number one bestseller *World's Best Bank—A Strategic Guide to Digital Transformation* that is available in seven languages.

This strategy and digital implementation specialist is an established consultant and keynote speaker who has founded and runs three companies. In 2000, he recognized that executives talked "strategy" with little focus on "implementation" and he started Bridges Business Consultancy Int to support leaders in their implementation journey. He later co-founded and co-runs the Strategy Implementation Institute and Digital Leadership Specialists.

Robin has pioneered a number of breakthrough methodologies and techniques that feature the Implementation Compass™, a proprietary framework built on the eight areas for excellence for execution; Ticking Clock© Model, a framework for creating a digitally driven organization; Digital Maturity Index, a self-assessment; and the Digital Best Practices Benchmark.

In 2014, Robin recognized while working with two of his clients who were early adopters of digital transformation, the world's best bank and the world's largest luxury company, that digital transformations presented different and sterner challenges from previous strategy implementations. In 2019 and again in 2024, he conducted research with over 4,000 leaders across four continents, resulting in the publication of the highly acclaimed business white paper *Business Transforming Your Company into a Digital-Driven Business* and *The Digital Leadership 2024 Perspective*.

Robin's innovations focused on supporting boards and executives on their perilous implementation journey have been featured in such media as BBC World, CNBC, and Forbes. A TEDx speaker, adjunct faculty at Singapore Management University and educator for Duke CE, IMD, National University of Singapore, he is also a Harvard-listed and award-winning case study writer.

In 2021, Robin was co-nominated with Piyush Gupta, CEO of DBS Bank, for the Thinkers50 Ideas into Practice Award. In 2021 and again in 2022, he was awarded the Business Strategist Singapore title. He is constantly and is included in the Top 10 list of Global Gurus and in 2023 he addressed the prestigious Global Peter Drucker Forum.

The First Minister of Scotland has named this Scotsman a GlobalScot for his passionate contribution to international business. Outside of work, Robin competes in Ironman events.

CHAPTER 1

Strategy Implementation Road Map©

STRATEGY
IMPLEMENTATION
INSTITUTE

Too often, leaders are asked to implement strategy but are not provided with the guidance or any kind of road map to do so. To this end, the Institute has developed the Strategy Implementation Road Map© (SIR) as part of its body of knowledge.

SIR is circular, which means you can start at any point in the model. This replicates the use of SIR by leaders when implementing their organization's strategy as they start from the most relevant area. It consists of the seven components required to be successful in strategy implementation (Figure 1.0).

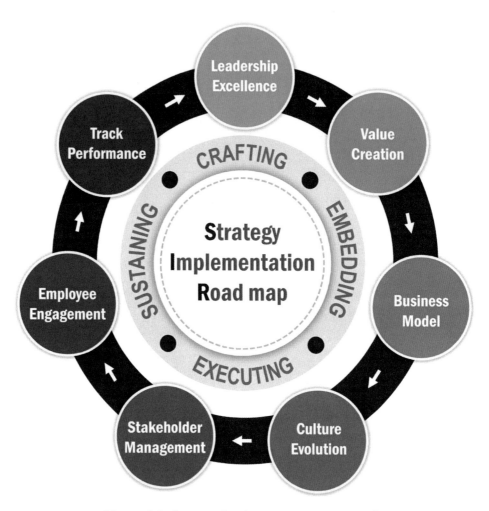

Figure 1.0: Strategy Implementation Road Map©

The Seven Components—Outer Circle

These seven components make up the Strategy Implementation course and the core of the SIBoK.

Leadership Excellence

As a leader, you don't *implement*. A leader's role in implementation is to drive the implementation forward and champion the strategy. The delivery team advances all of the implementation actions. You need to stay engaged throughout the implementation, offering continual inspiration and coaching the team while providing oversight and assuring the trajectory of the implementation.

Value Creation

The ultimate goal behind all strategy implementation is to develop and grow the value of the organization.

Business Model

Adopting a new strategy means changing the business model. Sometimes these changes are minor, and other times they require a complete business model transformation; for example, adopting digitization. Whatever the scale, the business model must change to support the implementation.

Culture Evolution

Culture drives the way an organization implements its strategy. Two organizations can have the same strategy, but how they implement any strategy will always be unique, as in every organization, the culture is different. Culture no longer always *eats strategy for breakfast* because of the speed at which we are working today. Strategy now drives the culture in many organizations, which, in turn, drives the implementation approach leaders need to adopt.

Stakeholder Management

The initial challenge is to present the new strategy to the whole organization. The launch of the strategy is only 15% of the overall implementation communication goals. Too frequently in stakeholder management, communication around the implementation dissipates after the first six months. This module places a heavy emphasis on nurturing the communications throughout the whole implementation journey.

Employee Engagement

The level of employees who are disengaged in their work is surprisingly high in many countries and industries. If your employees are disengaged, it is extremely difficult to inspire them to implement, which by its very nature requires *doing more*. This is why it's important to prepare employees with the right implementation attitude, knowledge, and skills.

Track Performance

Taking corrective actions along the way is critical for success. But how do you know where you are and what action to take if you are not diligently tracking your performance throughout the whole implementation journey? Too many leaders start off with the right intentions, but somewhere between thoughts and actions, they lose focus and commitment. Tracking performance is an essential discipline. The senior team needs to ensure the organization has the right measures in place to manage the implementation, as well as the discipline to constantly review its performance.

Four Stages—Inner Circle

The center of SIR shows the four stages associated with the seven components:

Crafting

You should start to prepare for the implementation by considering how to communicate and engage the whole organization. This includes focusing on generating awareness of the new strategy, explaining why the organization needs to change, aligning activities, allocating resources, assessing the organization culture, and identifying measures and any new skills people require.

Embedding

After the strategy has been launched, your focus is on gaining traction, building momentum, and changing the way the organization operates. You do this by synchronizing projects, allocating budgets to strategic initiatives, aligning roles and responsibilities, identifying resource requirements, adopting technology, and developing the discipline required, as well as taking any corrective actions.

Executing

This stage focuses on ensuring the organization continues to transform to the new way of working so as to deliver the strategy. By this point, the new strategy should increasingly be seen as business as usual. Key activities include ensuring key business decisions and financial investments are positioned to the strategy, reviewing external partners' performance, regularly reviewing actions internally, supporting middle managers, and leveraging measures to drive the implementation.

Sustaining

In this fourth stage, the financial benefits of the strategy start to flourish as the organization completes its implementation. The time this takes for each organization varies depending on the strategy, culture, and business. Activities in this stage include reviewing the business model, reviewing changes to the initial strategy, and recognizing and adapting to shifts in trends and culture.

CHAPTER 2

Leadership Excellence

STRATEGY
IMPLEMENTATION
INSTITUTE

> *Leaders don't implement.*
> *A leader's role in strategy implementation*
> *is to drive and champion it.*

The members of the delivery team are the ones taking the implementation actions every day.

As a leader, you, on the other hand, need to stay engaged throughout the implementation, coaching and inspiring your employees. You'll need to provide oversight on the trajectory of the implementation so that you can request pauses, tweaks, or more fundamental changes as the developing strategy meets the emerging reality of the external environment in which you operate.

Figure 2.0: Strategy Implementation Road Map©

Leadership Excellence addresses:

- Why and how to avoid repeating past mistakes
- Understanding the role of the leader in implementation
- The importance of consistent messaging
- Best practices for leading employees

CRAFTING

Introduction

There is plenty of evidence that you are likely to habitually repeat mistakes in strategy implementation. The challenge is to learn from past mistakes while maintaining best practices for the new implementation.

- Avoid Past Mistakes
- How Leaders Learn Lessons
- Establishing Right Leadership to Embrace Learning

Avoid Past Mistakes	
Goal	To ensure that organizations and leaders learn from previous implementation failures and achievements and that both are considered in the next implementation.
Implementation Challenge	One of the most frequent mistakes in implementation is that leaders show themselves unable to learn from failures and past mistakes. Various research shows that leaders have a good understanding of why implementation fails and yet, when rolling out a new strategy, they repeatedly forget about the past and fall into the same traps as before!
What Needs to Change	You need to develop the habit of continuous learning: adopting regular reflection moments, admitting mistakes, learning from them, and most importantly, not repeating earlier errors.

Fail Fast, Learn Fast.

The phrase "fail fast, learn fast" has become more popular as organizations adopt the agile methodology. Although it's counterintuitive to many leaders who were trained in the leadership model of the industrial era, iterating fast, making mistakes, and suffering failures (with the proviso that you learn from your setbacks at every stage) achieves a desired result faster than spending the necessary time aiming for the perfect solution or in our case the perfect implementation. The point is that in the environment of fast change and uncertainty, you cannot accurately define the perfect solution from the start because you are aiming at a moving target.

Failures, if accepted as lessons learned, become the stepping-stones to success. Such is the case with Thomas Edison, whose most memorable invention was the light bulb, which purportedly took him one thousand tries before he developed a successful prototype. "How did it feel to fail one thousand times?" a reporter asked. "I didn't fail one thousand times," Edison responded. "The light bulb was an invention with one thousand steps."

The prevailing school of thought in progressive organizations—such as Intuit, General Electric, Corning, DBS Bank, Alibaba, and Virgin Atlantic—is that great success depends on great risk, and failure is simply a common by-product. Leaders of such organizations don't mourn their mistakes but instead parlay them into future gains.

Failing fast requires a culture where the leadership allows teams and individuals the freedom to fail and the time to learn something from each failure that helps the team succeed faster the next time.

Why Strategy Implementation Fails

How many times have you seen a strategic plan launch to great fanfare and optimism, only to be forgotten within a few months? There are many studies explaining why strategy implementation fails (such as Strategy Implementation: What Is the Failure Rate? *Journal of Management & Organization* 21(2): 237–262, 2015; Five Reasons Most Companies Fail at Strategy Execution, INSEAD Knowledge, 2016; and Why Good Strategies Fail: Lessons for the C-suite, *The Economist* Intelligence Unit, 2013), and all offer numerous reasons.

From the list captured below, select the five top potential threats to a strategy being implemented in your organization.

Why Strategy Implementation Fails		
Poor execution planning Most of the planning time is spent crafting the strategy rather than preparing the execution.	**Not clear on how to implement** Leaders don't identify the right actions for employees to take, and they struggle to translate the lofty strategy into their day-to-day work.	**Leaders are not selling the strategy** Even though the strategy is right, it stalls as leaders are not vocally and visibly selling the strategy to the organization.

Strategy a mile wide and an inch deep

The launch of a new strategy causes confusion in any organization. This is compounded when individual leaders perceive the strategy differently. Leaders understand the impact of the strategy across the business (a mile wide) but not the implications on the vertical business (a mile deep).

Leaders underestimate the execution challenge

By doing so, leaders don't allocate the required resources such as budget, people, and time. Therefore, before the strategy is even launched, it is set up to fail!

Wrong people in leadership positions

People in key positions don't have the ability to succeed, and nothing is done by the organization.

Wrong measures are used

Leaders plan their new strategy and then launch it but fail to change the organization's success measures or to monitor progress effectively.

Not my job to execute

Leaders delegate the responsibility for the implementation.

Unrealistic targets

The timeline for implementation set by the leaders is unrealistic, and they expect a five-year strategy to be implemented in five months.

Strategy requires a long-term perspective, yet leaders run the business with a short-term view

Being driven by quarterly performance often conflicts with the required long-term strategic actions.

Overload of objectives

When people have to deal with too many objectives, they can become paralyzed. They don't know where to start and what to do. As a result, they end up making a lot of noise but achieving little.

Political interests are ignored

A new strategy means disrupting the current business model. When politics and struggles overpower and leadership are ignored, the implementation can fail.

Execution never goes according to plan

Whatever is planned in the boardroom changes in the execution.

Poor and infrequent communication

If employees don't know what the strategy is, they can never implement it. After leaders announce the new strategy, they do little communication beyond that.

Cultural disconnects

If the culture does not support the new actions required to implement the strategy, then the actions will not be taken, especially if the culture is one where employees fear making mistakes.

Culture does not support the execution

When there is misalignment between the culture of the organization and the essence of the strategy, then it fails to be executed.

No support given by bosses

People are willing to step up and take risks to support the new strategy. Yet, when they do, often they receive no encouragement or support from their immediate bosses. As a result, they stop taking the new actions, and the execution falters.

Employees are not engaged

The leaders do not take the time or make the effort to engage employees or merely do so for the first three months and then not again.

Top-heavy strategy

Time is spent thinking through the impact of the strategy at the top of the organization, but the top team only takes a short time to explain it to the rest of the organization.

The strategy does not resemble the current reality

The strategy is disconnected from what is currently happening in the organization, and the chasm is too wide to allow its implementation.

No buy-in before launch

Leaders make no effort or fail to leverage the opportunity to engage employees before the launch.

Strategy is bad

Employees are confused, as the strategy is unclear in what it is aiming to achieve, and no clear implementation route is explained.

How Leaders Learn Lessons

While setbacks and failure are a natural part of strategic change, it is important to act on failure and capture lessons learned. This involves 5 steps.

Step One: Discover

Explore why implementation has failed in the past by holding a brainstorming session with key stakeholders. Allow people to feel safe to speak openly and honestly in acknowledging past mistakes. Share the list in this building block on "Why Strategy Implementation Fails" and ask participants to select what is most relevant for your organization. Also allow them to suggest other reasons by asking, regarding the previous implementation:

- What went right?
- What went wrong?
- What could have been better?

If the organization culture doesn't naturally support this kind of postmortem, which is likely the case if the organization has not encouraged after-action reviews and reflection in the past, then you may need to start by casting forward. Asking people what they think might go wrong with the strategy, where the obvious challenges lie, and what obstacles are most likely to slow down or trip up the implementation doesn't require people to admit mistakes or own past failures and may start you off with a richer discussion.

Step Two: Recommendations

Identifying what the organization needs to do differently to succeed this time is important. This requires transparency and for people to be open and constructive. Participants brainstorm and then prioritize actions.

Step Three: Actions

Taking the right actions requires discipline. Talking about what to do is one thing, but making it happen is quite another. High-performing organizations have discipline as part of their culture. This ensures that what is discussed is acted upon.

Step Four: Documentation

The lessons learned and what needs to be done differently needs to be captured so that it can be shared with the rest of the organization and become a living document. In this process, the medium and timing of the sharing is as important as the lesson itself.

Step Five: Revisit

During the implementation, the document created in Step Four is constantly reviewed to ensure the organization is constantly learning and moving forward.

> ### If you're not making mistakes, then you're not doing anything.
>
> — John Wooden, basketball coach, University of California

Establishing Right Leadership to Embrace Learning

A powerful sign of an effective leader is an ability to unlearn old habits and change your mind when presented with convincing evidence or recognizing when you have made a mistake.

Many employees are used to a culture that doesn't tolerate failure, but failure is an essential ingredient for successful implementation. This is because no one knows the implementation road ahead. Employees need to experiment and try new things; naturally, not everything will work. What's critical is that you embrace these mistakes as learning opportunities in the organization.

To create a learning environment from mistakes, you should:

- Provide an environment where employees freely experiment and serendipitously come up with their own ideas (self-organization).
- Facilitate moderate (not too hard or too easy) challenges that employees need to work through.
- Tolerate—indeed, embrace—failure as a necessary input to radical innovation.
- Coach your people to learn from the experiences.

Pause—Reflect—Learn

The PRL Model (Figure 3.0) is a useful tool for leaders.

Pause—avoid rushing into the strategy implementation, and make sure you create the time and space to prepare properly.

Reflect—on past mistakes on why implementations have failed and have not delivered their full value. According to research by Michael C. Mankins and Richard Steele, companies deliver, on average, only 63% of the financial performance their strategies promise.

Learn—to maximize the pause and reflection and, more importantly, to deliver full value from lessons learned by diligently applying the lessons into the new implementation.

PRL Model

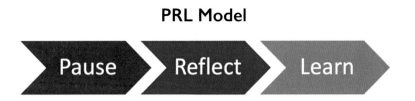

Figure 3.0: PRL Model

PRL Model Example

A CEO was recently rolling out a new strategy in India. The previous strategy by the predecessor had failed. While completing the new strategy, the CEO hosted an offsite with her 40 leading organizational change agents. The first item on the agenda was to ask everyone to share why the previous strategy had failed.

By personally facilitating the discussion, the CEO demonstrated her openness to listen and reflect on what her change agents had to say. She also provided the strategy with an appropriate level of importance and context.

More importantly, the organization identified what it should do differently to implement the new strategy successfully, and the CEO followed up after the meeting to ensure the lessons learned were being applied.

External Papers

- Strategies for Learning from Failure **by Amy C. Edmondson, HBR**

Video Links

- 3 Strategies for Becoming More Self-aware, **Tasha Eurich**
- Excellence in Execution, **Robin Speculand, Keynote**

EMBEDDING

Introduction

Your challenge is to find ways of sharing a consistent message across the organization while driving, coaching, and championing the implementation.

- Implementation Never Goes According to Plan
- Stepping Back to Implement
- Strategic Thinking as You Implement—Four Techniques to Adopt

Implementation Never Goes According to Plan

The best laid schemes o' mice an' men/Gang aft a-gley.

– Scotland's favorite poet, Robert Burns

Translated from Scottish, it means the best-laid plans of mice and men never go according to plan. Similarly, after you have crafted the implementation strategy, you need to recognize that whatever was planned will not be what happens in the execution.

There are few absolutes in business, but this is one. Considerable forces affecting the strategy also affect the implementation, and therefore it will change. That's why leaders have to remain agile and open-minded as they constantly review the implementation.

Here are a few highly visible examples of when the execution didn't go according to plan.

Example #1

Heathrow Airport learned an embarrassing and costly lesson when it opened its fifth terminal in March 2008. The airport had promised a sparkling new efficient terminal that would provide a "much-improved" experience for passengers. It was designed to handle 45 million passengers a year and 12,000 bags an hour. Before its opening, then British Airways CEO Willie Walsh went on global television declaring, "Three years of planning . . . we're waiting for the day . . . We have worked through every scenario . . . We believe we are ready."

The reality? On the second day of the terminal's opening, 70 flights were cancelled and 30,000 bags were mislaid. The terminal became known as a hotel for the stranded. The cost of this failure was £62 million. In the words of Walsh, "It was not our finest hour." A well-thought-out strategy was poorly executed.

> *Leaders need to be constantly engaged throughout*
> *the implementation journey, ensuring the*
> *actions are achieving the desired outcomes.*
>
> — Antonio Nieto Rodriguez and Robin Speculand

Example #2

In 2002, the German retail chain Metro became the first foreign distributor to enter Vietnam. The retailer promised a new kind of shopping experience for the country. Yet when the doors opened, hardly any customers came to buy. Metro had spent considerable time and money preparing to enter the market, but despite this, their execution faltered initially due to missteps.

Specifically, Metro stationed uniformed security guards at the entrance for security—not an unusual practice in retail stores in some countries. But in Vietnam, the practice evoked memories of the country's former totalitarian rule, and it prevented potential customers from entering. Those who did enter experienced an unfamiliar shopping experience.

For example, tomatoes were already packaged and not laid out for customers to select as they were used to. Some customers were suspicious of this new layout and tore open the packets, thinking the store was hiding rotten tomatoes beneath fresh-looking ones. Metro had to give up the plastic packaging and stack the tomatoes the way they usually were at a farm stall. Also, when the customers saw signs saying Fresh Chicken, they expected those chickens to be live, not dressed and packed!

Example #3

McDonald's initiated a growth strategy for China in 1992. At the time, it was playing catch-up with Kentucky Fried Chicken, which had already entered China. As part of the strategy to maximize customer revenue, McDonald's introduced the "drive-through" concept, and individual locations were refurnished to accommodate drive-through orders.

One day, a manager was outside watching to see how the new revenue-producing idea was performing. A customer drove up to the machine, placed his order, and drove forward to collect his meal and pay for it. The astonished manager then watched as the customer parked his car in the car park, picked up his brown bag, walked into the restaurant, and sat down to eat his meal.

McDonald's had not only introduced the first fast food drive-through but the very first drive-through in all of China. The strategy of maximizing revenue by having customers purchase their meal and eat it outside did not go according to plan.

Example #4

The French railway had a plan to improve their regional network and accessibility for the disabled to attract more passengers, including the purchase of 2,000 new trains. When the plan was implemented in 2014, the new trains that cost $20 billion were too wide for the platforms.

What happened? They had measured the distance between the platforms at the stations built around 30 years previously. But in the south of France and other areas, there were more than 1,000 stations that had been built 50 years prior to the upgrade at a time when the platform distances were less. The blunder cost over $70 million to correct, as 1,300 platforms had to be rebuilt. But worse was to come. The new trains were several millimeters too tall to go through the tunnels in Italy, forcing passengers to change to shorter trains at the border.

Stepping Back to Implement

Goal	Implementation involves you stepping back from the strategy and overseeing the rollout. As a leader, you are responsible for identifying the organization's strategy but relying on your employees to implement it. Your role in strategy implementation is to drive and champion the implementation.
Implementation Challenge	Strategy implementation involves moving from the thinking to the doing. This step triggers numerous actions across the whole organization, both in terms of day-to-day activities as well as projects and strategic initiatives. Employees should be the predominant ones taking these actions with the supervision and support of leaders; there needs to be a determined handover to the employees. It is sometimes hard for leaders to step back during the implementation and focus on overseeing and directing rather than doing the work or micromanaging. Once you step back, the paradoxical second challenge is to remain engaged because, although you have stood back, beware of the mistake of delegating the implementation and then not paying attention to it. When leaders stop paying attention to the implementation, so will their employees.
What Needs to Change	You need to be clear on your role in the implementation and that the employees are the ones who take the actions to deliver the strategy.

Leaders Step Back, Employees Step Up

What Does It Mean to *Step Back*?

To *Step Back* is to provide the space for others willing and able to *Step Up*. You need to see this as an opportunity for employees to grow and to feel part of the implementation. Encourage employees to take the right implementation actions, and provide them the space to do their work. This means supporting your employees' efforts but never overshadowing them.

Building an implementation culture that encourages others to *Step Up* means that leaders purposefully *Step Back* so employees have the opportunity to *Step Up*. In order to be in a position to *Step Back*, you need to have first identified the key person or people who are prepared to *Step Up*.

In the act of giving employees space to *Step Up*, you nevertheless provide the support, guidance, coaching, and resources to ensure that employees know that mistakes are part of the learning. Leaders in high-performing organizations encourage risk taking, which results, occasionally, in mistakes being made. High-performing organizations not only survive these mistakes but thrive because of them. It all depends on how they are handled and what learning is applied to the overall business.

What Does It Mean to *Step Up*?

To *Step Up* is to recognize the times in an organization during the implementation when someone else is required to do what needs to be done. This usually happens when something is extremely difficult and particularly challenging. The act of *Stepping Up* involves showing the courage to be vulnerable and do what needs to be done to achieve the strategic goals… regardless of the personal sacrifices. True leaders like to *Step Up* most of the time, yet their role is to encourage employees to do it. When an employee is brave enough to *Step Up*, they encourage those around them to do the same, which has a positive impact on the implementation momentum.

> ## *Leaders are responsible for Stepping Up to craft the strategy. Employees are responsible for Stepping Up to implement the strategy.*

Leaders Know When to *Step Up* and When to *Step Back*

The balance between *Stepping Up* and *Stepping Back* is all about leading by example and encouraging employees to think and act for themselves. You may find that you are the one who is doing most of the *Stepping Up* in the early days of implementation. But if this phase takes too long (more than a month), that means you are not effectively handing the implementation over to the employees and the organization.

That doesn't mean that you should completely ignore the organization. Besides overseeing, you need to support employees when they:

- Take the wrong action and require coaching
- Hit a roadblock in the implementation
- Need to change policy and/or procedures
- Need to be empowered
- Require training
- Are heading in the wrong direction
- Need to be inspired

On certain occasions, when a major unforeseen roadblock appears (for example, the competitive launch of a successful product), you should *Step Up* and drive the organization through it. Over time, however, it's your job to do more of the *Stepping Back* so that the employees can be the ones *Stepping Up*.

Implementation Tools

Leadership as Coaches to Engage Employees

Even if you can fire them up at the start, employees will not be inspired throughout the whole implementation journey, and it is during these stages of low motivation when you need to drive and champion the implementation. Your role is that of the coach and the mentor. These are not necessarily natural skills for everyone, and you may need to train yourself in the skills and behaviors of an effective coach.

Being a good coach involves:

- The right attitude
- Openness to sharing
- Being personable
- Identifying specific and well-defined issues to discuss
- Being accessible when required
- Treating employees as partners in the implementation
- Making expectations clear at the beginning of each coaching session
- Listening at least twice as much as you talk
- Recommending resources or training
- Holding people accountable
- Following up

The implementation is more effective when internal leaders are the coaches rather than the organization outsourcing the responsibility. This is because leaders are responsible for supporting, driving, and championing the implementation. You and your fellow leaders need to stay involved, be visible, and know what is going on.

> *Just because people understand what to do doesn't ensure that they will actually do it.*
>
> – Marshall Goldsmith

Strategic Thinking as You Implement—
Four Techniques to Adopt

As soon as you start implementing, you need to be conscious of the changes around you and keep adapting both the strategy and the implementation.

This session examines how you can be conscious of the changes.

If you cleared your calendar for an entire day to free you up to be "more strategic," what would you actually do?

> *A good thinker is always in demand. A person who knows how may always have a job, but the person who knows why will always be their boss.*
>
> – John C Maxwell

What strategic opportunity did they miss?

General Electric missed the computer industry that created...

IBM, who then missed the software industry that created...

Microsoft, who then missed Internet search that created...

Google, who then missed staying in contact online with friends that created...

Facebook, who then missed...!

How much time do you spend firefighting versus thinking strategically?

Where do you spend your time?

Running Your Company

- Preparing for tomorrow
- Attending meetings
- Managing strategic objectives
- Overseeing employees
- Reviewing strategic measures
- Day-to-day activities

Thinking Strategically

- Managing quarterly performance
- Building future competencies
- Conference calls
- Building long-term value
- Managing emails
- Operational excellence

> *Strategic people create connections between ideas, plans, and people that others fail to see.*
>
> – Liane Davey, HBR Article "Strengthen Your Strategic Thinking Muscles"

Four Techniques for Strategic Thinking in Organizations

1. Strategic Thinkers Analyze
2. Strategic Thinkers Consider
3. Strategic Thinkers Reflect
4. Strategic Thinking Pushes

1. Strategic Thinkers Analyze

Strategic thinking is about analyzing opportunities and problems from a broad perspective and understanding their impact.

Example 1:

In 2013, Tesla cars caught fire in both the UK and USA. But the company did not have to recall the car from all their customers. The engineers identified that the problem was that the battery pack became exposed at certain times. To solve the problem, the team thought strategically and, instead of a recall that would have damaged the brand and revenue, they sent an update to the computer on board every car and solved the problem.

Example 2:

The casino in Singapore has robotic servers to overcome the challenges from staff shortages.

2. Strategic Thinkers Consider

Strategic thinkers consider what might and could be.

Example 1: The Two Steves

If the role of a CEO is to increase sales, then Microsoft's Steve Ballmer was a success. He tripled sales to $78 billion and profits more than doubled. On a quarter-by-quarter review by the board, everything was good.

But when Ballmer stepped down in 2014, Microsoft was not prepared for the future. He had missed the five most important technology trends of the 21st century:

- Search
- Smart phones
- Mobile operating systems
- Media
- Cloud

(Apple under Tim Cook has doubled its revenue to $200 billion while doubling its profit and tripling the amount of cash it has in the bank—now a quarter of a trillion.)

Steve Jobs considered the future and created numerous opportunities for Apple, including:

- Apple stores
- iPhone
- App Store
- Mac computer

3. Strategic Thinkers Reflect

Strategic thinkers reflect that the business landscape is changing faster than any other time in history.

Example 1:

Students today, after graduating, will be applying for a job that doesn't yet exist, will be using technology that has not yet been invented, and will be asked to solve problems that we don't yet know!

Example 2:

In the 1950s the average tenure of a company in the S&P 500 (the average company size on the S&P is US$11 billion) was 61 years.

In 2021, the average tenure is 14 years, which is the same for the average life of a Fortune 500 company.

20 years ago, the five largest companies in the world were, on average, 93 years old (based on market capitalization).

In 2021, the five largest companies in the world are an average of 30 years old, and the youngest is 12.

4. Strategic Thinking Pushes

Strategic thinking pushes you to think above your day-to-day work.

Example 1:

For many years it was the army's policy to aim their cannons at the target and then wait eight seconds before firing. During its drive to improve work processes, the army hired an external consultant. He noted this peculiar pause and queried the process.

The privates responsible for firing the cannons told the consultant that they were just following the instructions in the manual. The consultant started researching the army archives for the reason of waiting eight seconds before firing the cannon.

He discovered that the policy was a well-established tradition stretching back to the 18th century. The reason for waiting eight seconds before firing the cannon? To give the soldiers time to move the horses away! What policies do you have in your company that have been around for too long and are now obsolete and add no value to the business?

We all know the Kodak story... But do we learn from it to make sure it does not happen to us?

> ## *Most business fail because they miss the future.*
>
> — Larry Page, CEO of Alphabet

External Papers

- To Help Others Develop, Start with Yourself, **Marshall Goldsmith, Fast Company**

Video Links

- Yes, Our Brain Is a Masochist, **Antonio Nieto-Rodriguez, TEDxULB**
- Everyone Needs a Coach, **Bill Gates & Eric Schmidt**

EXECUTING

Introduction

Your challenge is to stay true to the strategy and at the same time manage the business. This requires an ambidextrous leadership style.

- Leadership Engagement Is a Discipline
- Nine Uncommon Practices in Implementation
- Belief in Implementation Success
- Why Implementing Strategy Is Like Flying a Kite

Leadership Engagement Is a Discipline

Goal	To ensure that you remain fully engaged throughout the implementation and support your teams to achieve the strategic objectives.
Implementation Challenge	During the implementation journey, leaders often lose focus and/or are distracted by issues associated with running the business. When you stop paying attention to the implementation, so do your employees. Various studies show that a typical leader's engagement in implementing strategy starts to waver three to six months after it has been defined and launched. You may feel that your mission has been accomplished and that the responsibility lies now on your employees.
What Needs to Change	Continuous engagement throughout the implementation requires discipline from leaders and employees. Developing this discipline is not easy, but the payoff is likely to be both greater financial and nonfinancial benefits. You need to develop your own strategy for staying engaged during the entire duration of the implementation journey.

As an organization moves from Crafting to Embedding to Executing to Sustaining, your direct involvement reduces and employee engagement increases. To sustain the engagement, you need to build a culture of discipline.

Discipline, a Leadership Art

The difference between good and great strategy implementation often comes down to discipline. While subjecting yourself to the rigor of discipline is not easy, it is essential if you want to maximize your effectiveness as a leader. Top-performing leaders are extremely disciplined—they do the things others are not willing to do and they follow through on them.

Much material has been written about leadership strengths and weaknesses, but the truth of the matter is the mantra of "*playing to your strengths*" can be an excuse to avoid doing things you dislike or don't happen to be good at. It's much easier for most leaders to refine their areas of giftedness and revel in the admiration of being a high achiever than it is to be honest about your shortcomings. Being efficient is not always the same as being effective.

Disciplined leaders stand out because they're the ones who get implementation done—the ones you can count on to drive an organization to achieve its strategy. Real leaders don't accept mediocrity—they constantly seek improvement of themselves and their employees. If you want your organization to stand out, become intentional about bringing discipline to every area of your strategy implementation.

Develop a Culture of Discipline to Drive Engagement and Results

Jim Collins said in his *Good to Great* book that "a culture of discipline is not a principle of business; it is a principle of greatness." These words may resonate with you, particularly if you are feeling frustrated about aspects of accountability, attention to detail, collaboration, or some other area in their organization. The reality is that discipline must start with the habits, routines, and rigor of leadership. Therefore, the big question is, "What are the approaches that will set the tone for a deeper culture of discipline?"

Discipline Starts at the Top

Many leaders jump to conclusions about the source of potential cultural problems or frustrations in their organization. A good example is accountability. While a leader might be frustrated with the lack of follow-up, proactive action, and attention to detail of their employees, those same employees are often complaining about a lack of clear priorities, expectations, and support.

The following checklist can be used as a guide to assess your organization's cultural foundations:

Culture Core—Your Purpose and Values	Agree or Disagree

- The purpose and/or mission is clearly documented and consistently shared.

- Values are documented and further clarified with expected behaviors captured in stories, definitions, or examples.

Priorities and Measures	Agree or Disagree

- The top leader has clarified the top performance priorities and their vision for the focus of any improvement necessary (Note: John Kotter highlighted that most leaders undercommunicate their change vision by a factor of 10, 100, or even 1000X).

- The general strategy is communicated clearly to the organization with explanation of supporting strategic priorities (areas of focus).

- Top leaders use a consistent approach to engage the organization in defining the goals and related improvements that support the strategy.

- Goals or objectives are clearly documented and rigorously tracked in a standard format.

Day-to-Day Management	Agree or Disagree

- A regular management meeting (staff meeting, leadership team meeting, and so on) is held to track the status of goals and measures.

- Top leaders are not afraid to confront reality or to surface difficult issues for resolution during management meetings.

- Regularly scheduled group communication meetings, webcasts, or other approaches are consistently maintained.

- Top leaders check with individuals and subgroups periodically before, during, and after communication activities to confirm and/or improve clarity.

- There is accountability among top leaders for making and meeting commitments related to goals and measures.

- A disciplined process to hire for competence and cultural fit is rigorously followed.

Leaders' Responsibilities in Implementation

As a leader in implementation, you are responsible for the following:

1. Inspire employees to sustain them throughout the experience.
2. Drive and champion the organization in the right direction.
3. Model what is required.
4. Coach employees to make the right decisions and take the right actions.
5. Constantly clarify what to focus on (and what not to focus on).
6. Empower people to take the right actions.
7. Ensure resources are available.
8. Hold people accountable for taking the right actions.
9. Provide feedback as required.
10. Constantly review performance.
11. Make tough decisions when needed.
12. Adjust strategy when needed.

> *The only discipline that lasts is self-discipline.*
>
> – Bum Phillips

> *Talent without discipline is like an octopus on roller skates. There's plenty of movement, but you never know if it's going to be forward, backwards, or sideways.*
>
> – H. Jackson Brown Jr.

> *Mastering others is strength. Mastering yourself is true power.*
>
> – Lao Tzu

Nine Uncommon Practices in Implementation

Goal	To share "uncommon practices" that high-performing leaders adopt in successful implementations.
Implementation Challenge	Many leaders habitually repeat past mistakes, and this contributes to the high failure rate.
What Needs to Change	You need a different thinking and approach to stop repeating past implementation mistakes.

Numerous articles and blog posts list various reasons why leaders fail to implement strategy. The good news is that most leaders have not only read these articles, but they have taken them to heart. They now appreciate the need to have a balance between strategy and its implementation. The question they ask is "how" to achieve that balance.

The statement that leaders have taken implementation to heart is not made lightly. Bridges Business Consultancy Int has been researching leaders' thinking on implementing strategy since 2002. That's when Bridges first published research that nine out of 10 implementations were failing. At the time, this was a wake-up call for all leaders. The research supported a global movement toward a greater understanding of what it takes to successfully implement strategy in an organization.

In its latest research, Bridges has identified that for the first time, more implementations succeed than fail. This is a steady improvement from 90% in 2002 to 67% in 2016 and 48% in 2020. But it still begs two questions:

1. Why are we still failing?
2. What do leaders need to do differently?

Early indicators also show that implementation failure rates are becoming higher as organizations struggle to implement a digital strategy—a necessity in today's world.

The following nine uncommon practices highlight what the top-performing leaders are doing to succeed.

1. Less Is More

When you have too many objectives on your agenda, you typically end up doing less, not more. This is because you become overwhelmed with the amount of work and end up paralyzed. More work ends up with less being done.

Organizations that succeed in implementing strategy recognize this and limit the number of objectives they focus on each year.

> *There must be a certain balance to the number and type of goals and objectives: too many goals and objectives are paralyzing; too few, confusing.*
>
> – Professor Kathleen Eisenhardt, Stanford University

So how many strategic objectives should a leader focus on each year?

Sheena S. Iyengar from Columbia University and Mark R. Lepper from Stanford University conducted a famous experiment on selling jam, recorded in their paper titled "When Choice Is Demotivating: Can One Desire Too Much of a Good Thing?"

Their jam experiment involved an upscale grocery store displaying 24 jams for customers to view and purchase. Subsequently in the same store, only six different jams were available. From the customers who visited the 24-jam selection, only 3% made a purchase.

However, from those who had six jams to choose from, 30% made a purchase—10 times more than those who had 24 choices. This experiment was also tested for choices of chocolate. Once again, the group offered the six choices versus 24 choices had a higher level of satisfaction.

Research has demonstrated that an excess of choices, called option overload, often leads us to be less, not more, satisfied once we actually decide. This is because we're often left with a nagging feeling we could have done better.

The ideal is to have five (plus or minus two) strategy objectives to focus on each year.

A study from New York University titled "Restricted Choice Can Increase Creativity" also found that restricting the choice of creative inputs actually enhances creativity.

We can conclude that having too many choices in implementation leads to lower engagement and satisfaction. Having five (plus or minus two) strategic objectives each year allows everyone to recognize what is important and understand on what to focus. It also allows for effective resource allocation and results in a focused organization. Any other strategic objectives remain in view and will be addressed in 12-month cycles.

2. Magic of 90 Days

Why take action over 90 days? There's something magic about 90 days in business. If an action is not completed within that time frame, then:

- It might not have been important enough, or
- It was too complicated.

If something requires more than 90 days, it needs to be broken down into smaller actions.

By consciously ensuring the actions can be completed within 90 days, you make the actions manageable. As a result, you can start to gain traction. Taking action in 90-day compartments also makes the long-term strategy feel realistic to the people responsible for implementing it, and creates quick wins that people can see.

People identify the actions they should take by asking this question: "What can I do in the next 90 days to implement the strategy?"

Some people struggle with this question because they don't see how their work contributes to the overall strategy or because they don't believe they should do anything differently. These people will need the support of their immediate supervisor—the person they listen to most. At the start of every quarter, provide them with an opportunity to discuss what right actions they should take toward implementing the strategy.

During the 90 days, they should constantly check in with the supervisor to see how they are progressing, while receiving support and guidance. The agreed-upon actions are captured by supervisors to make sure there is a sense of achievement and accountability.

Not all possible actions will be the right ones or create the expected outcome. This is another reason why supervisors constantly need to review what is happening.

The aim of insisting on one action every 90 days is to have as many people as possible taking the right actions. They can be small and easy to achieve, as the aim is to "boil the pot" and not to try and "boil the ocean." These small steps create traction and teach the discipline of taking the right actions.

To demonstrate the importance of the new strategy, always remember to identify and allocate the required resources that will support the right actions.

3. Adopt a Framework

When you return to your office after crafting a new strategy, are you confident you have a framework to guide everyone through their implementation journey? Without it, you will be unsure of where to start. The lack of a framework results in teams executing the strategy differently across each business and even needlessly replicating research and methodology.

Having a framework guides both you and the whole organization through the implementation journey. It also ensures the right actions are being taken consistently throughout. Not every framework is right for every organization. In recognizing this, we recommend the Institute Strategy Implementation Road Map©. You may also wish to review the Implementation Compass™ (Bridges framework), the Execution Premium from Kaplan and Norton, and Kotter's 8-Step Process for Leading Change.

4. Allow People to Choose the Right Actions Themselves, as Everyone Works Best When Self-Directed

People commit to taking the right actions when they perceive they will benefit. This is partly why so many leaders in the initial launch highlight the expected benefits from the new strategy. This may be enough to capture the interest of the early adopters, but to engage everyone to take the right actions, you will need to continually reiterate the benefits and offer ongoing encouragement and feedback.

We know, people are more committed to outcomes they set themselves, by a ratio of almost five to one. This claim is made by Carolyn Dewar and Scott Keller from McKinsey and Company in their paper titled "The Irrational Side of Change Management." The authors cite a famous behavioral experiment in which half the participants are randomly assigned a lottery ticket number while the others are asked to write down any number they would like on a blank ticket. Just before drawing the winning number, the researchers offer to buy back the tickets from their holders. The result: no matter what geography or demographic environment the experiment has taken place in, researchers have always found that they have to pay at least five times more to those who came up with their own number.

People commit more easily to taking the right actions when they feel empowered rather than taking instructions.

5. Nurture Communication

After the strategy kickoff, leaders are often polarized when talking about operations or implementation because they are typically held more accountable for short-term performance than long-term results. Short-term objectives tend to dominate your agenda. Any discussion about implementation dissipates with alarming acceleration.

When people attend meetings and hear no mention of a new strategy—no updates, no questions or discussions—they resort to focusing on what is being addressed: operations. All their best intentions for the implementation and their planned actions fall by the wayside. Before long, the whole process has failed.

What is required is a balance between discussing operations and setting in motion the implementation, focusing constantly on both.

After the launch of the strategy in any organization, when discussion on the implementation dissipates, so does the interest among people. Applying the discipline of constant communication is a best practice among organizations that achieve excellence in implementation. Communication requires you to provide updates on, for example, the progress toward achieving objectives, what's not working, customer feedback, best practices, lessons learned, milestones achieved, and strategy deviations.

6. Abandon Yesterday

With today's accelerated pace of doing business, you need to abandon thoughts about what has worked in the past. You can no longer plan the future as an extension of yesterday. As agonizingly difficult as it is, it's necessary to extinguish any belief that what worked yesterday will also work tomorrow.

Consider also that in 1985, 35% of stocks on the S&P were considered high risk (risk being based on the ability to achieve long-term stable earnings growth), 24% were average, and 41% were low risk. By 2006, only 13% were low risk, 14% were average, and a whopping 73% were high risk. These percentages were reported just before the global financial crises of 2008–9.

Or consider that in the 1950s, the average tenure of an organization in the S&P 500 was 61 years. By comparison, in 2013, the average tenure of an organization was only 18 years. As a result, you must design new strategies more frequently than ever and thus implement your strategies more frequently.

Achieving success in implementation enables you to manage the accelerated pace of business and beat your competition. To do this, you need to be prepared to release the past and seize the future while ensuring the organization's culture supports the transformation.

7. Create a "To-Stop" List

Part of achieving successful implementation is telling people what to stop doing and empowering them to kill off non-value-adding work.

To achieve business implementation success, Drucker coined the term "purposeful abandonment." That means if you want to grow your business, before you decide where and how to grow, first stop doing what's not working and get rid of the outgrown, the obsolete, and the unproductive.

Everyone who has a "to-do" list should also have a "to-stop" list of the actions that don't contribute to the new strategy. At the same time, they can't afford to stop talking about the strategy and the implementation. When you empower your people to stop doing non-value-adding work, they become more engaged and accomplish more in less time. In effect, you are creating the right conditions for achieving excellence in implementation.

8. Create a Review Rhythm

The frequency of implementation reviews is one of the main activities to carve out, leading to a successful implementation. Yet, as Bridges research reveals, 85% of organizational leaders spend fewer than 10 hours a month discussing their implementation.

Conducting regular reviews creates a review rhythm—a pattern and expectation that progress is checked. Every week, you need to ask your people what they're doing to contribute to the implementation. Diarize reviews every two weeks to examine the different components of the implementation in each business vertical. By the end of every quarter, you will have a complete assessment of how the implementation is progressing. All of this activity prepares the organization for an overall performance annual review.

It takes discipline for leaders to change the dialogue across the organization. You are responsible for creating space for the reviews on the calendar. Unfortunately, many leaders don't do this; they get swept along by the current of everyday activities and never find the time.

It's important to keep the reviews succinct. A meeting that exceeds two hours is not a meeting but a workshop.

At Amazon, Jeff Bezos insists that those who call a meeting must provide a three-page briefing on the objectives of the meeting and the content for the discussion. Everyone is expected to spend one-third of a scheduled one-hour meeting reading the notes, leaving 40 minutes to discuss the agenda issues.

Organizations that implement change successfully adopt the following review rhythm:

Weekly questions from immediate boss	Biweekly reviews across every business vertical	Quarterly strategic implementation review	Annual leadership review

Weekly reviews hold people accountable and ensure they are taking the right actions. These reviews also tell employees they will be asked how they're progressing against the actions they have identified to take every 90 days. Finally, they allow time for support and coaching.

Biweekly reviews across every business vertical ensure the organization is applying the discipline needed and is taking the right actions. They allow for immediate corrective action and support such as resource allocation as well as reinforcing the right actions.

Quarterly strategic implementation reviews involve top leaders and invited employees. These reviews encapsulate the discussions and actions from the biweekly reviews across all the business verticals and provide a summary of the progress being made across the whole organization. They also may identify flaws in the strategy that need correction, and they enable a collective examination of the feedback from the biweekly reviews.

The annual leadership review is a learning opportunity to reflect on performance, share best practices, review lessons learned, and embed changes. It brings the key players together and is leveraged to celebrate successes.

9. Implementation Planning—Part of Strategy Planning

You can demonstrate the depth of your appreciation of implementation by moving the implementation planning into the strategy planning.

Leaders are responsible for decoding the implementation challenge by explaining what needs to be achieved and then guiding the organization through the whole implementation journey. This means you need to know, before the implementation starts, exactly what's involved and what's required.

It's better to postpone the launch of a strategy until you've developed a solid implementation plan rather than to launch it without having a good plan in place. When there's no implementation plan, you will find yourself struggling after the launch. What do you do first? Where should you allocate resources? How should you communicate the new strategy? Do you need to provide new skills training? Should you put in place new progress or performance measures?

Feeling uncertain about how to answer these typical questions breeds discontent and lack of confidence. That in turn undermines any opportunity for the new strategy to gain traction.

So, to achieve a successful implementation, it's important to make planning the implementation part of planning the strategy—and to do it before the new strategy is communicated through the organization. This requires taking time to develop a detailed and rigorous implementation plan to ensure a smart start. The plan needs to guide the organization by allocating resources, providing direction, and maintaining momentum. It also helps demonstrate the leaders' authentic commitment and sincerity. Above all, you should ensure the implementation is discussed in great detail early on.

Former CEO of GE Jack Welch stated this point succinctly when he said, "In real life, strategy is actually very straightforward. You pick a general direction and implement like hell." Yet most leaders need to learn how to "implement like hell."

Taking time to develop your implementation plan doesn't dilute from the strategy planning, as some leaders think. Rather, it adds tremendous long-term value. Enriched conversations among the leadership result in:

- Further defining the strategy to all the leaders
- Stating what needs to be done in more detail to achieve excellence in implementation
- Detailing the expected timeline of implementation
- Clearly articulating the strategy outcomes
- Specifying individual responsibilities
- Starting the implementation journey with the right resources and capabilities
- Building belief and confidence across the organization

A good strategy, well implemented, transforms the experience from one that is challenging, confusing, and complicated to one that is engaging, enjoyable, and even exhilarating. It decodes the tough challenge, gives people focus, and dramatically increases the odds for success—especially when it's developed with the same intensity and energy as the strategy itself.

Belief in Implementation Success

Albert Bandura, a psychologist at Stanford University, postulated that self-efficacy was important for individuals, organizations, and societies to be successful.

> *Self-efficacy is the belief we have in our own abilities, specifically our ability to meet the challenges ahead of us and complete a task successfully.*
>
> – Albert Bandura

Leaders need to believe in the strategy if they are to be authentic and sincere in implementing it. This is not always the case, and the organization needs to prepare leaders to stay true to the strategy.

If you don't create the time to oversee the implementation journey, change the agenda, and explain why the organization needs to transform, then employees will sense the lack of commitment and not step up; the implementation will fail.

Why Implementing Strategy Is Like Flying a Kite

Contribution by Rita Gunther McGrath (Institute Board of Advisor)

How can you tell, in advance, whether a strategy is positioned to be well-implemented? It's a challenge. Our judgment is often influenced by the halo effect[1]—the attribution of excellence to organizations after their success is known.

Let's take business school case studies as Exhibit A. If you piled up the case studies written about Enron, Nokia, Dell, The Body Shop, Toys R Us, and of course General Electric, you would have the makings for a very impressive bonfire.

Five Minutes of Alignment

Were all those companies excellent? Of course, they were. For a moment, all the elements of their strategies were deeply aligned. Dell, for instance, was lionized for its operational excellence. As Erik Brynjolfsson observed in its heyday, "They're inventing business processes. It's an asset that Dell has that its competitors don't."[2] One can't get more implementation savvy than being praised by Brynjolfsson for process depth!

And yet, by 2013, the strategic underpinnings of Dell's business had eroded badly. Competition had improved. Selling standardized boxes to enterprise customers had given way to the bring-your-own-device movement at work. Innovation had moved to consumer devices. The advent of the cloud era meant corporate spending on things like servers fell drastically. Even longtime partner Microsoft went into competition with Dell in hardware.

Dell eventually went private, in order to take a new direction, providing digitization services to enterprise clients. Dell now embraced an idea that former CEO Kevin Rollins had proposed (but which Michael Dell rejected), to acquire EMC[3] to offer a suite of services as Dell renamed itself "Dell Technologies." As of the date of writing, Dell is once again trading on the public markets and enjoying a bevy of flattering articles about how well it pulled off the integration and how bright its prospects are.

The Dilemma of Alignment in the Context of Transient Advantage

Firms at the peak of their success achieve that high-performance holy grail: alignment between all the essential elements of their business model. Those are the periods when they can seemingly do no wrong, and observers credit the high degree of alignment in their activity systems as the reason.

This is true, but importantly, it isn't true forever.[4] As we see with Dell, systems that are well designed to deliver high levels of performance in one context can be a tremendous barrier when that context changes.

Consider the life stages of a competitive advantage. It starts with insight and innovation. In Dell's case, the famous dorm-room flash of insight was that since personal computers were more or less off-the-shelf items, they could be made and sold far less expensively than extant practice. There is then a growth or scale-up phase. Successfully surmounting this phase leads you to the "exploitation" period. This is the nirvana of steady-state advantage beloved of strategy scholars. This is the point at which business school cases get written! However, technologies change, customer needs change, competitors catch up, offerings become commoditized, and eventually the system starts to erode in its ability to deliver results.

The central leadership challenge is to pull apart the carefully designed and aligned systems, to replace them with different ones that are capable of supporting the next-generation competitive advantage. The period in between advantages is a fraught one—the old aligned system is no longer there, but the new one is not yet in place. Having a simple way of thinking about what new form the alignment will take can be helpful in navigating through this period.

Keeping It Simple: The Kite Framework

For the purposes of this chapter, let's assume that a choice of strategy in a changing context has been made—as Dell has done in becoming an enterprise services provider. Next up: realigning the organization.

Think of it in terms of flying a kite. A kite isn't going to respond to yelling, incentives, or your levels of charisma. To fly, a kite needs to be built with its various elements in balance. It needs to be launched into the right environment. And it can be guided, but not driven. As you can see in the figure (4.0), you may think of the discrete elements that need to be aligned in terms of building a kite that can fly. It is important here to think holistically—getting only one or another of these elements right but leaving out the others won't get you an implementable strategy, just as leaving out an element of a kite's structure will inhibit it from flying.

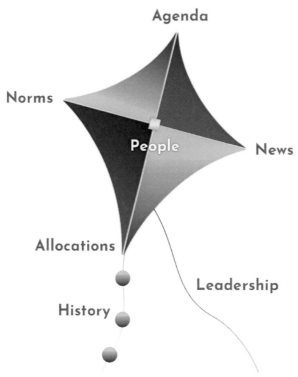

Figure 4.0: The Kite Model

Agenda: Aligning the organization literally starts with your agenda. Your agenda, meaning how you spend your time, is how you marshal energy, demonstrate to others what your priorities are, create focus, and otherwise direct the attention of the organization. It's incredibly powerful. And yet, we see leaders all the time who leave their agendas to chance, filling in their diaries willy-nilly with requests, travel, events, and other activities that dilute the impact of their time.

If you think of organizations that are excellent implementers, you will see proactive agenda management at the center. Alan Mulally famously used his weekly "business plan review" meeting to keep his management team on track as they turned around Ford. General Stanley McChrystal used a daily Operations and Intelligence (O&I) briefing that eventually connected thousands of people every day in real time as the US Army battled Al Qaeda. Sharon John used the principle of regular meetings to harmonize her turnaround team at Build-A-Bear Workshop.

The way to start is with the clear strategic choice that informs your point of view about the future. Now—look at your meetings and your calendar. If you have really thought it through, your top priorities at every meeting and in every conversation will be #1, #2, or #3. And they will be there consistently. Eventually, the organization will learn that you really mean it. Even better, the agendas of those around you will begin to respond.

Norms: Norms, or culture, represent the unspoken beliefs that inform action. You know the old phrase—culture eats strategy for breakfast! What culture do you need in the new environment?

For example, when Satya Nadella was named CEO of Microsoft (only the third CEO in that company's history), the culture was routinely lampooned as being internally hyper-competitive. A cartoon circulating at one point showed Microsoft's culture as a circle with people pointing guns at one another. Nadella's strategy, however, was to shift the focus for Microsoft from the declining PC business and away from its unsuccessful efforts in phones to the Cloud and to devices users would love. Profits, he explained to his team, were the outcome, not the goal. A prime leading indicator was "customer love." This in turn required empathy—a radical shift in attitude that Nadella has been demanding throughout employees' relationships, not only with customers but with one another.

News: The news part of the kite refers to what information (news) you gather, how you interpret it, and how you communicate your conclusions to others. If you can't measure it, you can't use it to drive the future. The more you can get others on track with the news you are paying attention to, the better.

For instance, Jack Stack, a well-regarded CEO and author of *The Great Game of Business*, evangelizes teaching everyone in his organization to learn about the numbers that make a business work—or don't—and apply them. As he says, if people can learn the rules and draw conclusions about their favorite sports teams, they can do the same about business. He has been well known for the practice of "open book" management, which lets employees self-manage those parts of the operation they can influence.

Allocations: The allocations portion of the kite has to do with where your resources are being spent. Those could be how you allocate resources across a portfolio of opportunities. It can also be how you provide incentives to your people. If there isn't alignment between the budget and the strategy, you can guess what is going to happen.

I was recently at a management meeting of a group of senior leaders in a firm whose top leadership is hungry for innovation. They've been encouraging their executives to send people to innovation boot camps and training classes. "No way am I going to do that," one of their middle managers said to me later, privately. "Given the way my bonus is calculated, 20% of that expense will come right out of my pocket at the end of the year." Sad, but true—you can imagine where the innovation efforts are going to end up.

People: At the center of the kite, we have the formal and informal structures into which people are organized. A big mistake is to try to implement a new strategy with a structure that was built to support the old one. Structural transformation is almost always necessary in light of a strategic inflection point.

Further, the formal organizational structure provides often quite limited information about how real work gets done. In most organizations, the informal structure, the "who knows and talks to whom" is where real flows of influence reside. Angela Ahrendts famously put her informal, authentic style to work in the informal organization in a turnaround at Burberry and continues to do so now as the head of retail at Apple.

History: You can think of your organization's history like the tail of the kite. An organization with no tail flails around. A bit of history is valuable—it provides balance. But history that is too big and heavy—that will almost certainly hold you back. So a key element of leadership is determining which parts of your history you want to keep and then to honor what needs to be left behind.

Although the brand has suffered recently, Wells Fargo's logo, featuring a stagecoach, recalls its early days delivering mail throughout the American West, offering a distinctive brand positioning for the firm.

Leadership: Just as with the string of a kite, leaders guide and influence where the organization flies, without necessarily being able to make it go in any particular direction. With respect to this influencing activity, perhaps the most important element of leadership is the realm of symbolism.

Symbols give meaning to activities in organizations. Everything you do as a senior leader has both substance (the rational reason you're doing something) and symbolism (the meaning people make of observing your activities).

Indra Nooyi, the outgoing CEO of PepsiCo is brilliant at marshaling effective symbolism. Confronted with an organization that had long focused on fun and snack activity, she sought to introduce a shift toward what she calls "performance with purpose," moving the company toward healthier options that are also more popular with younger consumers than Pepsi's traditional brands. To illustrate the importance of purpose, she uses the example of growing up in an environment in which water was scarce, because a local company was using the bulk of the water supply. She tells this story to reinforce the importance of corporations being not only about profit but about good corporate stewardship.

Flying the Kite

When your organization is in the exploitation phase of a competitive advantage, you should strive for tight alignment across all the elements of the kite. As the situation shifts, however, you will need to start shifting the way the elements are aligned. This is likely to feel uncomfortable, as change will take place unevenly across kite elements, across people, and over time. You'll feel out of alignment while undergoing a shift. This is one of the reasons why fundamental transformation can be so difficult—having built and aligned a system, it is quite natural for people to prefer to stay in it, particularly since the changes you'll be making in the early days feel like a drop in performance.

Having a simple framework to use to make choices both about how and where your kite should be aligned and how it might need to be changed can accelerate your own thinking and help you bring others along on the journey.

Notes

This material is taken in part from Rita McGrath's book, *Seeing Around Corners: How to Spot Inflection Points Before They Happen.*

References

1. P. Rosenzweig, *The Halo Effect . . . and the Eight Other Business Delusions That Deceive Managers* (New York: The Free Press, 2007).
2. D. M. Fisher, *Optimize Now (or Else!): How to Leverage Processes and Information to Achieve Enterprise Optimization (and Avoid Enterprise Extinction)* (iUniverse, 2003).
3. K. Benner, "Michael Dell's Dilemma," *Fortune* (June 13, 2011).
4. R. G. McGrath, "Transient Advantage," *Harvard Business Review*, 91(6), 2013: p. 62–70.

External Papers

- Creating a Cohesive Team for Corporate Transformation Projects by Kate Duchene and Antonio Nieto-Rodriguez
- Scenario Planning, MIT
- Ten unsung digital and AI ideas shaping business, McKinsey

Video Links

- Scenario Planning–A Tool for the Future, Shell

SUSTAINING

Introduction

As the organization is celebrating the successful implementation, leaders are responsible for already starting to ask, "What next?"

- Adaptive and Proactive Leadership

Adaptive and Proactive Leadership	
Goal	In order to achieve long-term success, leaders need to adapt their strategy and implementation as and when required, especially in today's fast-changing competitive landscape.
Implementation Challenge	Previously the average strategy life cycle was seven years. This is no longer the case. In some industries, strategies can now last a year or less. This new landscape requires organizations to respond faster than ever before. The challenge is that leaders miss changes in the strategic landscape and/or marketplace and remain steadfast with their current strategy and its implementation.
What Needs to Change	To make strategic choices, you rely on different analysis: market, financials, customers, competition, economic trends, etc. This should not be a one-off exercise. You need to be in close relationship with your customers, and constantly assessing market changes. If faced with strong evidence, you need to have the courage to revisit the chosen strategy and its implementation to ensure it remains relevant.

Agile Leadership

Part of leadership is the ability to envision powerful futures and to influence and empower others to work in alignment toward the realization of those futures.

Agile leadership capability includes:

- The ability of leaders to let go of fixed, static perspectives and to embrace perspectives that empower the new landscapes
- It is the capacity of leaders to avoid being blinded by limiting beliefs and established strategies; to be able to see things clearly and to respond effectively to what they are seeing
- The ability of a leader to envision futures that genuinely challenge people and organizations to move beyond familiarity and into realms of higher performance
- The capacity of leaders to work with people in ways that leave them utterly clear that they are the ones who own the implementation of the strategies of their organization
- Making the entire organizational apparatus more resilient and able to adapt effectively to changing conditions

Case Study

Kodak Collapse

One of the most famous examples of inagility is the collapse of Kodak. Why did Kodak make the poor strategic decisions they made? In 1993 they brought in a technology expert from outside the business to be CEO. George Fisher was believed to be almost as good as Jack Welch or Lou Gerstner. Even with a great CEO and people buried in the hierarchy who had all sorts of good ideas, poor strategic decisions and implementation were the result.

The organization overflowed with complacency. In the late 1980s, Kodak was failing to keep up even before the digital revolution, when Fuji started doing a better job with the old technology, the roll-film business. With their complacency so rock solid and no one at the top even devoting their priorities toward turning that problem into a huge urgency around a huge opportunity, of course the organization went nowhere. Strategy sessions with the CEO went nowhere. The people buried in the hierarchy, who saw the oncoming problems and had ideas for solutions, made no changes to the strategy, as their bosses and peers ignored them.

How can CEOs learn from Kodak's failure? Historically, Kodak was built on a culture of innovation and change. It's the type of culture that's full of passionate innovators, already naturally in tune to the urgency surrounding changes in the market and technology. It's these people—those excited about new ideas within your own organization—who keep your company moving ahead instead of falling behind. One key to avoiding complacency is to ensure these innovators have a voice with enough volume to be heard (and listened to) at the top. It's these voices that can continue to keep a sense of urgency in your organization. If they are given the power to lead, they will continue to innovate, help keep a culture of urgency, and affect change.

Expert Advice

Leaders should establish quarterly strategy reviews to ensure the strategies are being rightly and timely implemented. The reviews provide a forum where any unexpected challenges and competitive trends can be analyzed, discussed, and acted upon. No matter how good the annual strategy planning was, the strategy never rolls out as expected, because there are too many variables that impact its implementation.

The quarterly strategy review is also when leaders examine the shifting strategic landscape by revisiting:

- *The principles of the strategy*
- *Application of lessons learned from previous implementations*
- *The assumptions made during the planning*
- *Impact of micro trends, e.g., employee turnover*
- *Impact of macro trends, e.g., aging population*
- *Technological trends, e.g., AI*
- *Alignment of the organization culture and the implementation*
- *Geopolitical shifts*
- *Social factors, e.g., demographics*
- *Competition analysis*

Other factors that may impact an organization's strategy include legal, unions, ethical, and environmental.

Implementation Tools

Adaptive Leadership

Adaptive Leadership is a practical leadership framework that helps individuals and organizations adapt and thrive in challenging environments. It emerged from thirty-plus years of research at Harvard University by Dr. Ron Heifetz and Marty Linsky, defining the frontier of leadership training and development.

Adaptive Leadership involves being able, both individually and collectively, to take on the gradual but meaningful process of change. It is about diagnosing the essential from the expendable and bringing about a real challenge to the status quo and implementation strategy.

When you realize that your organization's aspirations cannot be attained through the current strategies, you can use adaptive leadership to diagnose, interrupt, and innovate to create the capabilities and strategies that will match the organization's vision. Adaptive Leadership is purposeful evolution in real time.

> *People in any organization are always attached*
> *to the obsolete—the things that should have*
> *worked but did not, the things that once*
> *were productive and no longer are.*
>
> – Peter Drucker

External Papers

- Closing the Strategy-to-Execution Gap **by CEB**
- Transformation Starts with Agile Leadership **by McKinsey**

Video Links

- Adaptive Leadership Explained in 4 Minutes, **Adriano Pianesi**
- Leading Digital: Turning Technology into Business Transformation, **George Westerman, MIT**

IMPLEMENTATION QUIZ QUESTIONS

1. A leader's role in strategy implementation is to drive and champion it. After launching the strategy, which of the following statements is true?

   A   Leaders can delegate all responsibility to employees

   B   Leaders only need to review the implementation once a year

   C   Leaders stay engaged throughout the whole implementation journey

   D   Leaders can ignore mistakes from previous implementations

2. Some organizations have adopted the motto, "Fail fast, learn fast." Which one of these is not one of the five steps for leaders to learn from failure?

   A   Discover the reasons the implementation failed

   B   Punish employees for making mistakes

   C   Take the right actions

   D   Document learning to share across the organization

3. It's becoming more critical than ever to create a culture that encourages learning. Leaders can make this happen by?

   A   Avoiding all forms of experimentation

   B   Coaching employees to learn from experiences

   C   Calling people out in meetings for making mistakes

   D   None of the above

4. Implementation involves you stepping back from the strategy and overseeing the rollout. Leaders can step back by?

   A   Providing the space for others willing and able to step up

   B   Building an implementation culture that encourages others

   C   Providing the support and resources to ensure that employees know that mistakes are part of the learning

   D   All of the above

5. Many digital initiatives are driven by employees. To encourage bottom-up and aligned initiative, leaders should:

   A   Empower employees

   B   Encourage regular two-way conversations

   C   Engage employees by understanding what inspires them

   D   All of the above

6. **When leaders stop paying attention to implementation, so do their employees. To overcome this, leaders should:**

    A   Continuously stay engaged throughout the whole implementation

    B   Develop the discipline of implementation within the culture

    C   Clarifying performance priorities

    D   All of the above

7. **Focusing on fewer rather than more objectives every 12 months is a powerful best practice. The reason why this is, is because it?**

    A   Allows people in the organization to understand and focus on what's most important

    B   Reduces external investments

    C   Allows leaders to attend more meetings

    D   All of the above

8. **People are more motivated to take actions when they choose them themselves. Therefore leaders should allow employees to choose their actions because it can increase engagement by:**

    A   2X

    B   5X

    C   10X

    D   100X

9. **Agile methodology is a popular best practice. To encourage the agile methodology in an organization's culture, leaders should?**

    A   Know how to facilitate design-thinking

    B   Be open to changing the way the organization operates

    C   Be a qualified scrum master

    D   Know how to facilitate customer journey mapping

10. **Customers notice an organization's implementation, not its strategy. To sustain the implementation, leaders should?**

    A   Ensure the right measures are in place

    B   Develop the discipline to take the right actions

    C   Constantly nurture the communications

    D   All of the above

Answers to the quiz questions can be found on page 314 in the Appendix.

CHAPTER 3

Value Creation

Welcome to the module on how to identify and maximize the return on your implementation investment.

The focus is to develop and grow the creation of value of the organization. Strategy implementation is tough, but the payoff from the organizations that succeed is excellent.

Figure 5.0: Strategy Implementation Road Map©

This section addresses:

- Prioritizing strategic investments and projects
- The importance of the budgeting cycle for keeping control of the investments and returns through the implementation
- Assessing your value creation and financial performance
- Realizing benefits from project investments
- Rewarding leaders and employees

CRAFTING

Introduction

This module focuses on ensuring the investment exercise happens after the crafting of the strategy and focuses on providing budgets to the value creation initiatives.

- Resource Readiness
- Drawing Up a Budget

Resource Readiness	
Goal	Once an organization has set its new strategy, it's essential to ensure that the investment is set after the strategy and that it is fully aligned to the strategic objectives. The budgeting cycle is the most effective way to keep the business—and its finances—under control while implementing strategy.
Implementation Challenge	Leaders involved in defining investment targets often struggle to determine the appropriate level of aggression as well as the level of resources dedicated to day-to-day activities versus strategic initiatives. Day-to-day activities tend to be a priority, but they are short term–focused, while strategic initiatives are longer term. This dilemma on budget allocation often translates into friction between departments, priorities, and goals, which ends up with strategic initiatives that are insufficiently funded and strategic goals not met.
What Needs to Change	It's essential to ensure that the budget is set after the strategy so that the organization is prepared for success. On too many occasions, budgeting is done before or with no reference to the strategy, contributing to its failed implementation.

Benefit of Financial and Business Planning

The key benefit of financial and business planning is that it allows the leadership team to create a focus for the strategic direction of the business and provides targets that will help the business grow. It will also give the opportunity to stand back and review performance and the factors affecting the business. Business planning provides:

- A greater ability to make continuous improvements and anticipate problems
- Sound financial information on which to base decisions
- Improved clarity and focus on strategy implementation
- A greater confidence in your decision-making

When you're running a business, it's easy to get caught up in the day-to-day problems and forget the bigger picture—the strategy implementation. However, successful organizations invest time to create and manage budgets, prepare and review business plans, and regularly monitor finance and performance.

Expert Advice

Structured planning can make all the difference to the growth of your business. It will enable you to concentrate resources on improving profits, reducing costs, and increasing returns on investment of the chosen strategic projects.

In fact, even without a formal process, many businesses carry out the majority of the activities associated with business planning, such as thinking about growth areas, competitors, cash flows, and profit.

Converting this into a cohesive process to manage the business's development doesn't have to be difficult or time-consuming. The most important thing is that financial plans are made, they are dynamic, and they are communicated to everyone involved.

The main aim of the annual business plan is to set out the strategy and action plan for the business. This should include a clear financial picture of where you stand—and expect to stand—over the coming year, including key assumptions. The annual business plan should include:

- *An outline of changes to make to the business*
- *Potential changes to the market, customers, and competition*
- *Key objectives and goals for the year*
- *Key performance indicators*
- *Any issues or problems*
- *Any operational changes*
- *Information about management and people*
- *Financial performance and forecasts*
- *Details of investment in the business*

Business planning is most effective when it's an ongoing process. This allows management to act quickly where necessary, rather than simply reacting to events after they've happened.

Implementation Tools

Budgeting

Creating, monitoring, and managing an investment budget is key to business success. It helps allocate resources where they are needed, so that the business remains profitable and successful. It starts with working out what you are likely to earn and spend in the budgeting period.

Begin by asking these questions:

- What are the **value creating initiatives** that will keep our organization in business and growing?
- What are the **projected sales** for the budget period? Be realistic—if you overestimate, it will cause you problems in the future.
- What are the **direct costs** of sales—i.e., costs of materials, components, or subcontractors to make the product or supply the service?
- What are the **fixed costs** or overheads?

You should break down the **fixed costs and overheads** by type; these include:

- cost of premises, including rent, municipal taxes, and service charges
- staff costs—e.g., wages, benefits, extras
- utilities—e.g., heating, lighting, telephone
- printing, postage, and stationery
- vehicle expenses
- equipment costs
- advertising and promotion
- travel and subsistence expenses
- legal and professional costs, including insurance

Your business may have different types of expenses, and you may need to divide up the investments by department.

Your business plan should help in establishing projected value creation, sales, cost of sales, fixed costs, and overheads, so it would be worthwhile preparing this first.

Expert Advice

Instead of evaluating employees as achieving or not achieving a budgetary goal, leaders can evaluate them with a straightforward tiered system. An employee who misses a budget target by a large amount would be considered off-target, one who achieves the budget goal would be on-target, and an employee who exceeds expectation would be considered above target.

Once you've got figures for value creation, income, and expenditure, you can work out how much money you're making. You can look at costs and work out ways to reduce them. You can see if you are likely to have cash flow problems, giving yourself time to do something about them.

When you've made a budget, you should stick to it as far as possible, but review and revise it as needed. Successful businesses often have a rolling budget so that they are continually budgeting, e.g., for a year in advance.

Drawing Up a Budget

There are a number of key steps you should follow to make sure your budgets and plans are as realistic and useful as possible. These include:

Make time for budgeting: If you invest some time in creating a comprehensive and realistic budget, it will be easier to manage and ultimately more effective.

Use last year's figures (but only as a guide): Collect historical information on sales and costs if they are available—these could give you a good indication of likely sales and costs. But it's also essential to consider what your sales plans are, how your sales resources will be used, and any changes in the competitive environment.

Create realistic budgets: Use historical information, your business plan, and any changes in operations or priorities to budget for overheads and other fixed costs.

It's useful to work out the relationship between variable costs and sales and then use your sales forecast to project variable costs. For example, if your unit costs reduce by 10 percent for each additional 20 percent of sales, how much will your unit costs decrease if you have a 33 percent rise in sales?

Make sure your budgets contain enough information for you to easily monitor the key drivers of your business such as sales, costs, and working capital. Accounting software can help you manage your accounts.

Involve the right people: It's best to ask staff with financial responsibilities to provide you with estimates of figures for your budget—for example, sales targets, production costs, or specific project control. If you balance their estimates against your own, you will achieve a more realistic budget. This involvement will also give them greater commitment to meeting the budget.

> *A budget tells us what we can't afford, but it doesn't keep us from buying it.*
>
> —William Feather, American author 1889–1981

External Papers

- How to Do Strategic Planning Like a Futurist **by Amy Webb**
- Turn Your Budgeting Process Upside Down **by Robert A. Howell**
- Is Your Budgeting Process Killing Your Strategy? **by Tony Golsby-Smith**

Video Links

- Value Creation Model **at RaboBank**

EMBEDDING

Introduction

The focus now shifts from the macro organization budgeting to managing the finance for strategic initiatives and projects.

- Investing in Implementation

Investing in Implementation	
Goal	The purpose of this process is to identify the strategic initiatives and projects that will lead to delivering the strategic objectives and creating the expected value. Before investing in any project, an organization needs to be aware of the effort to implement the strategy. This understanding is needed before deciding to continue with the strategic initiative or selecting another one better suited to achieve the organization's goals.
Implementation Challenge	The main challenge in this phase is for leaders to ensure that the most valuable projects are being selected and carried out. There are often too many project ideas from which to choose, in addition to a large number of projects still being carried out. Having enough and the right capacity to deliver all the projects is another of the biggest challenges organizations face. Managers should consider graduated levels of activity to avoid overwhelming their teams.

What Needs to Change

Focused organizations select the right strategic initiatives and projects in which to invest and carry them out in a defined order of importance. Investing in strategic initiatives requires decisions about where to allocate resources based on a solid understanding and the best use of the organization's core competencies and current resources. Because you cannot invest in everything, choosing which strategic initiatives and projects to fund can be a gamble. You must also prioritize the initiatives, which can involve challenging decision-making.

Project Selection and Prioritization (PSP) Process

Investment in strategic initiatives and projects starts by identifying both the projects that are currently running in the organization, as well as those value creation ideas in the pipeline. Obtaining accurate data tends to be a very time-consuming activity (but is becoming easier as data analytics mature), yet it is necessary to make informed and fact-based decisions.

Initiating a project can involve a large investment for an organization and sometimes a leap of faith in what's achievable, but it's a necessary investment to plan and run the implementation. In any project there are a number of important items to assess, and so there are a number of questions to ask:

- What are the reasons for doing the project (the "why")?
- What is the return on investment and payback period? Any other benefits?
- Do we have enough resources to deliver the project successfully?
- How does the project support the implementation?

Project Portfolio Management (PPM) Framework

This triage process is part of the implementation of the Project Portfolio Management (PPM) framework. Implementing a standard-based, structured, and organization-wide PPM framework in a large organization is a significant challenge, as it will change the way the organization operates in many areas. This is why, at first, it's important to focus on the project selection and prioritization process and to limit the scope to those projects that have a significant impact on technology and engineering.

The selection and arbitration focuses leaders on the budget of IT, engineering, infrastructure, etc., taking into account the financial and operational capacity of those entities. These are the most demanded, as most of the projects need this kind of expertise and often become a bottleneck.

A fair and objective allocation of resources to new or existing projects relies on a proper and objective knowledge and assessment of their main properties. That is the objective of the Project Selection and Prioritization (PSP). Each new project idea or project needs a simple form that is produced through a standard process involving all the entities contributing to the potential project. The form should be designed to provide the requisite data to enable a "go" or "no-go" decision to launch a project and to prioritize that project among the other new requests as well as the ongoing projects.

It is important to remember that a project is a dynamic concept. As it progresses along its life cycle, the initial parameters (costs, benefits, duration, scope), used when deciding to launch it, will usually change over time. These changes may have an impact both on the profitability of the project (either because the costs appear higher than expected or because the benefits appear lower than expected) and on the other projects (because of overall budget and capacity constraints). To manage those changes, ongoing reviews of existing projects are an important part of the PSP process.

1. **Qualification** kicks off the cycle with an idea-generation process managed by the division requesting a project, along with the involvement of all the entities whose collaboration will be necessary to realize it (contributors).

2. **Prioritization**—A first level of prioritization and arbitration belongs within each division, which should rank the ideas it requests, depending on the relative importance of the projects.

3. **Arbitration**—The third layer is called transversal portfolio management. The project ideas from all the divisions are collected, challenged, and finally arbitrated on by a governance body called (in the model) the Investment Decision and Strategy Execution (IDSE) Board. The IDSE Board is chaired, ideally, by the vice president of the organization who gathers the heads of all the business lines and main functions, the CIO, the CFO, and the secretary general, representing the smallest functions. The decisions of the IDSE have to be approved by the executive committee. Following ratification by the executive committee, the decisions are translated into budget allocations by the management accounting team.

Project Selection and Prioritization (PSP) Lessons Learned

Here is a summary of the most important concepts that should be retained from the PSP process as part of the PPM framework implementation:

- PSP has to remain a high-level and a light-touch process. PSP should not become overly complex (which will mean it loses transparency) nor overly prescriptive (which will limit the organization's agility).

- You'll need a communication and training plan to support the change across the entire organization to ensure consistency in the application of the new processes.

- PSP should involve all parties from the very beginning. The aim of the PSP is to encourage people, departments, and organizations to work together from day one of an idea that is worth looking at.

- PSP requires that all entities contributing to a project are involved in the estimation of the project cost.

- PSP advocates an initial high-level estimation of potential projects to enable comparison and selection of the best ideas in your organization. As such, it is not a checklist for certain defined, early steps in the projects (e.g. preparation or elaboration) that follow the prioritization process.

- Arbitration in PSP must include the entire portfolio of projects. Effective PSP also implies that projects that are already running will be subject to arbitration and thus potentially cancelled.

Organizing Resources to Support the Implementation

Once the strategic initiatives have been selected and prioritized, the next step is to organize resources to support the strategy execution. You need to determine, early on, the right balance between change-the-business and run-the-business activities and whether the organization has sufficient resources and the necessary capabilities to carry out the selected strategy.

This stage is similar to what the coaches of football teams have to do at the beginning of the season. The team chairmen and the fans set the objectives for the year, but the coaches need to establish whether they have the right players to achieve those objectives. If they do, then they need to determine how to organize the players on the field. If they do not, then the coaches need to invest in bringing in the necessary skills from the outside. Once the season starts, making significant changes to the teams is difficult. The coaches will need to use their knowledge and leadership skills to guide their teams to success.

Once the organization's structure and resources are aligned to the strategy, the key question is whether the organization is sufficiently focused to deliver the intended results. If not, chances are that the strategy will not be successfully executed. Successful strategy execution is not so much about how well the strategy is defined; success, instead, depends on project selection, effective organizational alignment, and focus.

Implementation Tools

Checklist of Strategic Initiatives in Which You Should Invest

It is hard to know precisely which strategic initiatives to invest in and how to allocate your scarce resources. You may well be missing accurate or relevant data or be relying on too many assumptions. Here is an example checklist that will help you and your leadership team with the decision-making process:

- **Value**: Opportunities that generate $50 million in annual revenue.
- **Growth**: Opportunities that generate at least 15% continuing growth rate.
- **Competitive Position**: Opportunities where our organization can be first or second in the market.
- **Products**: New products that can be sold into the mass market, that can be mass produced, or that offer consistently superior direct-client service and performance features.
- **Sustained Market Position**: Opportunities that put products or services in a distinctive position, that include plans for adding a significant number of new clients, and that offer a high payback for clients.
- **Sustainability**: Opportunities that reduce our organization's environmental impact.
- **Diversity**: Opportunities that increase the diversity in our organization.

Project Portfolio Management to Support Strategy Implementation

Executives generally have a poor understanding of project portfolio management (PPM). The first thing that comes to their minds is that this concept is about financial portfolio management (stocks, shares, investments). Few, if any of them, relate PPM to their projects and change initiatives. Therefore, we decided to develop a short guide to explain the benefits of PPM to senior management using business terms with which they are comfortable.

- Which projects should you select for the best interest of your organization and higher value creation?
- What is the best use of its existing and future financial and operational capacities?
- Alternatively, what are the projects to stop, suspend, or delay in case of a sudden economic downturn?

Providing the means to answer those questions rationally and consistently is the objective of project portfolio management.

Project portfolio management is the layer that rests on top of all project and program management activities. It is the cockpit of the change-the-business activities. Project portfolio management is composed of its own set of processes, templates, techniques, roles, and responsibilities, which are different from those involved in the project and program management processes. The most important aspects of project portfolio management are:

1. A standard and structured process for **collecting** all of the new project ideas. This organization-wide process must be applied consistently, which makes the next step—comparing project ideas—much easier. Every proposed idea requires a business case and some common qualitative criteria, such as strategic alignment, assessment of risk factors, and determination of interdependencies. The ideas for the most significant strategic projects, such as acquisitions, often will come directly from top management, but they too should follow the same common process. It is important to note that projects are not only about business ideas or research and development; projects also have to deal with organizational improvements; cost reduction; risk management; regulation, both national and international laws; and asset obsolescence (software, hardware, premises, etc.).

2. A procedure for **prioritizing and selecting** the new project ideas. Ongoing projects must also be prioritized, particularly when the prioritization process is implemented for the first time. The selection process has to be fair and transparent, based on criteria against which the new proposal is assessed. Some common criteria for analyzing the new ideas are net present value (NPV), return on investment (ROI), payback period, strategic alignment, risk, complexity, and interdependencies. One very important selection criterion involves ensuring that the organization has the right competencies to deliver the project. This is determined by performing a capability check. Although some theorists suggest that you should develop formulas that automate the process of prioritizing and selecting the projects, our recommendation is to not use such a systematic approach. The exercise is mainly to provide management with different orientations and viewpoints, but the ultimate decision has to be made by management based on human intelligence.

3. The strategic road map lists the change-the-business projects (both new and running) for the next two to three years. The organization's strategic objectives and goals should be clearly reflected by this road map, and the project list should be prioritized so that the top three projects are clearly identified. These top three projects usually do not change and are the focus of most of management's attention. The strategic road map is communicated and explained throughout the entire organization.

4. A governing body (the Investment Decision and Strategy Execution IDSE Committee) decides which ideas and initiatives the firm will invest in and which will be stopped or delayed. IDSE also approves the organization's strategic road map for the next two to three years. The positioning and the members that participate in the committee correlate directly to the success of this initiative. We recommend that the chair should be the organization CEO or one of the senior vice presidents, and the committee should be composed of N-1 directors. It is important to note that few companies manage to implement a PPM framework across all the departments but rather limit them to IT, R&D, or technical departments. We have decided to implement an organization-wide decision body, with the aim of breaking many silos and working together more closely as one organization.

5. A gate-approval process allows for effective portfolio monitoring and control of project funding. This process consists of establishing three to five standard phases for a project's life cycle—for example, feasibility, initiation, planning, execution, and close. At the end of each phase, project feasibility is evaluated and funding is released for the following phase (only)—if a project is not progressing according to plan, if priorities of the business have changed, or if the market has evolved. The gates provide top management with an opportunity to adjust or to cancel the project before more resources are wasted.

6. Monitoring the execution of the strategic road map consists mainly of regular reports to top management on the progress of the prioritized projects. If the strategic road map is following the plans, the strategy side of the change-the-business dimension is on track. These regular reports also help management to react quickly to market changes and to supervise the pipeline of new projects.

7. Finally comes a process for capturing the synergies and the benefits of the change-the-business dimension. One of the major issues with projects is that the benefits are difficult to track due primarily to their lack of ownership, the difficulty of measuring them, and the long time span (for some projects, benefits can be achieved only five years or more after the project has been completed). During an acquisition, synergies are linked to specific milestones in the integration plans. When a milestone is reached that has synergies attached to it—for example, the closure of some retail units—then the benefits can be calculated and compared to the plans. The strategic road map has to include these "synergies delivering" milestones that are attached to specific returns even if the project has been completed. By using this approach, you create a way of monitoring the benefits of the change-the-business dimension.

External Papers

- How to Prioritize Your Company's Projects **by Antonio Nieto-Rodriguez**
- Winning through Project Portfolio Management: The Practitioner's Perspective **by Perry Keenan, Jeanne Bickford, Jennifer Bratton, Annabel Doust, and Jennifer Tankersley**
- Linking Strategy to Planning and Budgeting **by Kaplan & Norton** (No longer available online)
- The Value of Digital Transformation **by Eric Lamarre, Shital Chheda, Marti Riba, Vincent Genest, and Ahmed Nizam**

Video Links

- What Are the Project Selection Methods? **Kavin Kumar**
- Triple Bottom Line Approach (What It Is and Why It Matters to YOU!), **Barbara Heffernan**

EXECUTING

Introduction

As the strategy implementation evolves, the organization needs to capture the value created and financial benefits.

- Monitor Benefits and Budget Consumption
- Strategy Implementation Office

Monitor Benefits and Budget Consumption	
Goal	The purpose of this process is to ensure that the right means are in place to monitor the value created, benefits achieved, and ongoing consumption of budget and resources to implement the strategy.
Implementation Challenge	There are several challenges in monitoring value creation and benefits, as well as resource and budget consumption. First, obtaining data and establishing the right tracking systems can be costly (although it is becoming less expensive) and time consuming. Second, some of the benefits of strategic initiatives are hard to quantify and therefore difficult to monitor and measure.
What Needs to Change	There are a number of ways you can monitor the budget performance of day-to-day operations and strategy implementation using available data. By using benefit management, you can assess where your business is underperforming, and judge the effects changes in one area of the business will have elsewhere.

Traditional financial reporting is done through the budgeting cycle, monthly reporting, and annual accounts. Investments in strategic initiatives and projects are covered by the young science of benefits management, described in the implementation tools section.

Monitoring reports are often requested without considering the time, effort, and relevance of the information provided. Before developing any monitoring system, you need to be pragmatic about the kind of information and level of detail you need in order to oversee the status of the investments, report benefits, and take appropriate decisions when the investment doesn't go according to plan. Remember: Reports enable decisions, and any report that doesn't do that is simply a waste of time and resources.

Cost Monitoring of Strategic Initiatives

Start with the estimates and projected budget. Having accurate estimates and a robust budget is fundamental to the delivery of strategic initiatives and projects. If you are unable to keep an eye on the actual costs while the project is being implemented, how can you hope to deliver on budget? There are several techniques used to monitor and control the cost of strategic initiatives and projects:

- Earned Value Management
- Forecasting
- To-Complete Performance Index (TCPI)
- Variance Analysis

Earned Value Management or Analysis

Earned Value Management (EVM) is a mathematical method by which you can measure the actual performance of a project. You will use EVM to monitor your project in terms of timeline and costs. For example, suppose your project is on track as per the timeline; through EVM, you will be able to understand whether the project is also on budget. If it is not, you can take corrective action.

Forecasting

EVM provides formulae to forecast the future performance of a strategic initiative. The forecast is based on the current actual performance. As a project leader, having the ability to tell whether your project will be delivered on time and on budget is critical.

Let's take an example to understand this. Suppose you have completed 25 percent of your project. You are on track according to the schedule. Subsequently, however, by the time you have completed 50 percent of the project, you realize your project is running toward a delay. By using forecasting formulae, you can determine the degree of delay. This will also enable you to investigate the cause of delay and the corrective action required to get the project back on track. In addition to the schedule delay, you can use EVM forecasting formulae to determine the actual cost of the project upon completion and take measures to rectify any anomaly before it is too late.

To-Complete Performance Index (TCPI)

If the project is delayed or overbudget, you can use TCPI to determine the project performance required to complete the project as budgeted or estimated. TCPI also leverages the EVM formulae.

Variance Analysis

Variance analysis is the comparison of expected strategic initiative performance to the actual cost performance. This analysis helps you understand the causes of variance, if any. Preventive and corrective actions are determined based on the variance analysis.

Benefits Management

Benefits management is a way to maximize outcomes from your strategy implementation by describing how value is generated from the projects. Thus a benefits management plan maps how the outputs of a transformation are translated into outcomes and impact through changes in behavior among the target audience.

This important process in strategy implementation involves identifying, planning, measuring, and tracking benefits from the start of the strategic initiative until realization of the last benefit. It aims to make sure that the desired benefits are specific, measurable, agreed, realistic, and time bounded.

Benefits management provides the common thread between project delivery and successful strategy implementation. The approach to strategic initiatives and project implementation needs to be benefit and value driven to ensure maximum value from the investment and resources allocated.

Benefits Management and Business Cases

A business case provides the formal justification for the existence of a strategic initiative and project. The senior leader owns the business case and is responsible for its development, maintenance, and progress. In developing a business case, a senior leader is also responsible for ensuring that the strategic initiative objectives, costs, and benefits are correctly aligned with the business strategy. Of particular importance, even at an early stage, is the identification of value and benefits, and how these will be realized.

The business case should:

- Assess or estimate the benefits that the program or project should deliver.
- Document the process for identifying, monitoring, and realizing the benefits.
- Ensure plans and processes are in place to achieve the benefits.
- Define the baseline benefits position to allow comparison with projected benefits.
- Define the boundaries with other programs and projects to ensure benefits are not double counted.

Some of these may be worked into an early version of the benefits and value realization plan. If a business case is being submitted for approval, evidence of plans for managing and realizing projected benefits will be requested.

Common pitfalls that may arise in relation to benefits management and business case development include:

- The initial work of identifying strategic benefits has not been expanded or developed
- A lack of early engagement with, or commitment from, key stakeholders to realize the benefits
- A lack of clear ownership of benefits beyond the business case
- The lack of robust processes to manage, monitor, and realize benefits
- Failure to update the business case due to changes in circumstances

Including a structured set of benefits with as much detail as possible in the business case will help clarify the underlying reason for investment and provide a firm foundation for initiating a project. Early-stage benefit identification and quantification can help identify a preferred option for investment (i.e., selecting the one that has the potential to deliver best against expected benefits). As benefits are further developed and defined, it is important to keep the business case updated.

Benefits Management Process

Managing the delivery of strategic initiatives and project benefits can be broken down into four distinct stages. Each high-level stage has a number of key objectives, activities, and deliverables associated with it. The four stages are:

1. Identifying and structuring benefits
2. Planning benefits realization
3. Realizing and tracking benefits
4. Evaluation of benefits

While this process will offer a structured approach to managing program and project benefits and value, it should not imply that benefits management is simply a mechanistic activity, or a one-off paper exercise. Focusing on the ultimate outcomes of any investment, and proactively putting in place a framework to manage and realize benefits, should be at the heart of all project delivery, driving the change and helping to retain focus on the end goals. Figure 6.0 shows the steps from benefit identification to post mortem review.

Figure 6.0: Benefits Management Process

Sources

- Project, Programme and Portfolio Management, Praxis Framework, PMI The Standard for Portfolio Management, Antonio Nieto-Rodriguez

Adhering to budgeting rules shouldn't trump good decision-making.

— Emily Fair Oster, American Economist and Author

Strategy Implementation Office

In some organizations, an office dedicated to implementation assists in ensuring the organization has a balance of both short-term and long-term objectives in its approach. It also ensures the organization adopts the discipline and best practices required to succeed, while coordinating plans and communication.

Setting up a Strategy Implementation Office is not necessarily the right approach for every organization. Some leaders argue they need an additional focus on structure and discipline that a dedicated office can provide. The opposing argument is that implementation is the responsibility of everyone, not simply one office. Just as noted for strategy planning and quality improvement, everyone must own the implementation.

General Electric (GE) famously dissolved its strategic planning (originally called long-range planning) under Jack Welch's stewardship because its leaders wanted everyone to be responsible for strategic planning. Jack Welch threw out GE's elaborative five-year planning documents and replaced them with a simple statement of business challenges and proposed action plans.

The same debate surfaced again around quality improvement. Should organizations set up a Central Quality Office, or is everyone responsible for quality? The question for strategy implementation is: should there be a specific office to drive and champion the process? After all, isn't implementation the responsibility of everyone? With a Strategy Implementation Office in place, there's a deep concern that people will say, "It's not my responsibility" and expect those in the office to do everything.

Take a look at the following list of typical responsibilities for the Strategy Implementation Office and form your own judgment:

1. Connect the corporate strategy to the lines of business (e.g., communicate and explain what needs to be achieved).
2. Report directly to the CEO.
3. Develop and champion the strategy management process and system.
4. Close any gaps between crafting strategy and implementation.
5. Manage organizational alignment with the strategy.
6. Assist in implementation planning (e.g., provide standard templates).
7. Keep implementation on the leaders' radar, e.g., influence meeting agendas.
8. Provide guidance and support throughout the whole process.
9. Ensure regular implementation reviews are conducted.
10. Champion, standardize, and manage strategic measures.
11. Prepare regular assessment meetings.
12. Ensure implementation governance is in place.
13. Share best practices and lessons learned across all lines of business.
14. Review the strategic landscape outside the organization.

If an organization decides to create a Strategy Implementation Office, then it should aim to make it obsolete within a few years. By then, the knowledge, skills, and discipline should be transferred to those in various lines of business.

External Papers

- 6 Questions to Ask Before Starting a Big Project by A. Nieto-Rodriguez and W. Johnson
- What Is Benefits Management? by APM
- Organize Your Change Initiative Around Purpose and Benefits by Antonio Nieto-Rodriguez
- Why Do So Many Strategies Fail? by David J. Collis
- Fred Krupp on the Benefits of Monitoring Resource Use

Video Links

- Accenture CEO Julie Sweet Discusses Diversity in Business and in the Boardroom

SUSTAINING

Introduction

Leaders at this stage need to decide the best use of capital investment, often balancing between investing in future growth and leveraging savings.

- Capture Strategic Value

Capture Strategic Value	
Goal	To ensure that the value created through the implementation activities and strategic decisions is captured and reflected in the performance and financial records of the organization.
Implementation Challenge	While a focus on shareholder value and value creation can benefit the owners of the organization, it does not provide a clear measure of other important strategic aspects such as employment, environmental issues, or ethical business practices. Short-term focus on shareholder value can be detrimental to long-term strategy implementation; the acquisition of a company will briefly boost a stock's value but often has negative effects on its long-term value.
What Needs to Change	Shareholder value is the value delivered to shareholders because of the leadership team's ability to implement its strategy (e.g., grow sales and earnings and free cash flow over time). A company's shareholder value depends on strategic decisions made by senior leaders, including the ability to make wise investments and generate a healthy return on strategic initiatives. In addition, organizations also need to look at stakeholder value creation.

Expert Advice

Value creation can be measured in two main ways—by looking at either past performance or future estimates. Past performance information is obtained through the organization's accounting, financial reports, and strategic outcomes. Future performance (as noted in the next sections) is based on strong assumptions and benchmarking data.

Implementation Tools

Economic Value Added (EVA)

EVA measures the effects of leaders' strategic decisions as it focuses on leadership effectiveness in a given year. These measures estimate an organization's true economic profit for the year and differ substantially from showing accounting profit.

This method's growing popularity reflects a realization that performance metrics used in the past (notably, return on equity and others based solely on accounting figures) are wanting when it comes to measuring the creation of value and strategy implementation.

EVA was introduced in the 1920s by the General Motors Corporation. But it was forgotten until Stern Stewart & Company, a New York-based consulting firm, reintroduced it in the 1980s as a replacement for the traditional measure of value creation. This approach has been trademarked by Stern Stewart.

Knowing that EVA helps managers understand the real drivers of strategy implementation and business performance, many organizations use it as a guidepost for making strategic decisions and measuring the resulting benefits and value created.

Expert Advice

Measures that attempt to value a company based on its prospects in the future are not easy. The popular idea that a company is no more than the net present value of its future cash flow depends on guessing first what that cash flow will be and then what future interest rates will be.

A measure developed to overcome these problems is called EVA (Economic Value Added). This is the measure of output (taken as operating profit after tax and some other adjustments) less input (taken as the annual rental charge on the total capital employed, both debt and equity). Leaders have all the elements of this equation (costs, revenues, debt, and capital expenditure) in their hands. So, when the numbers increase or decrease, leaders have no one to praise or blame other than themselves.

I'm committed to increasing long-term value for shareholders and am confident we will continue to do so through the successful execution of our core strategic priorities: the creation of high-quality, branded content and experiences, the use of technology, and creating growth in numerous and exciting international markets.

— Bob Iger, CEO, Walt Disney

"If you are committed to creating value and if you aren't afraid of hard times; obstacles become utterly unimportant. A nuisance perhaps; but with no real power. The world respects creation; people will get out of your way."

— Candice Carpenter Olson, Co-CEO of Fullbridge.

Expternal Papers

- Perspective on Value Creation and Synergies **by McKinsey**
- Unleashing value from digital transformation: Paths and pitfalls, Deloitte

Video Links

- How Are Creating Value and Capturing Value Different? **IMD**
- Paul Polman, CEO of Unilever, **The 3 Steps for Businesses to Be Successful in Sustainable Development**

IMPLEMENTATION QUIZ QUESTIONS

1. Organizations successful in implementation of their strategy can see tremendous payoff. The budgeting cycle is the most effective way to?

    A   Keep the business and its finances under control when implementing strategy

    B   Ensure CFO is aligned to the CEO

    C   Manage capital expenditure across the whole business

    D   Ensure spending alignment between departments

2. Organizations are creating new ways of identifying value more frequently than ever before. In business planning, which two statements are true?

    A   Guarantees successful implementation and sound financial information

    B   Creates a clear road map and leader confidence

    C   Improves clarity and ensures everyone keeps within budget

    D   Improves clarity and focus while creating greater confidence in decision-making

3. A number of organizations leverage annual business plans. The main aim of an annual business plan is to?

    A   Prepare the leaders for the year ahead

    B   Set out the strategy and action plan for the business

    C   Ensure alignment in the budget process

    D   Prepare a document to share with all employees

4. Projects are a critical part of implementation. When selecting and prioritizing projects, the three most important factors are?

    A   Time, cost, and qualification

    B   Cost, arbitration, and people

    C   Qualification, prioritization, and arbitration

    D   Prioritization, people, and process

5. Earned Value Management is one of the methodologies for monitoring the cost during implementation. It is a mathematical method by which leaders?

    A   Measure the actual performance of a project

    B   Calculate the value to management

    C   Identify increase in shareholder value

    D   All of the above

6. Developing a business case for a strategy initiative is a best practice. This is because?

   A It assists in identifying where to invest

   B Provides the formal justification for the existence of a strategic initiative

   C Aligns the different strategy initiatives and projects across the organization

   D All of the above

7. Benefits management is a way to maximize outcomes from strategy implementation. It can be described as?

   A A means for identifying resources for projects

   B A means for maximizing people's time

   C How value is generated from projects

   D All of the above

8. Some organizations create a Strategy Implementation Office. In any organization this should be?

   A A permanent part of the organization

   B Only part time responsibility for people involved

   C A full-time office that should aim to make itself obsolete

   D None of the above

9. To be effective, part of the Strategy Implementation Office responsibilities include?

   A Championing the strategy management process and system

   B Championing, standardizing, and managing strategic measures.

   C Championing implementation governance

   D All of the above

10. Project portfolio management is a popular implementation best practice. It can be used to?

    A Properly allocate resources and time among their portfolio projects

    B Make effective course corrections

    C Maximize value delivery

    D All of the above

Answers to the quiz questions can be found on page 314 in the Appendix.

CHAPTER 4

Business Model

STRATEGY
IMPLEMENTATION
INSTITUTE

Adopting a new strategy translates to changing the current business model. Sometimes the changes are minor, and at other times they require a whole business model transformation, e.g., when adopting digitization. But the business model must change to support the implementation.

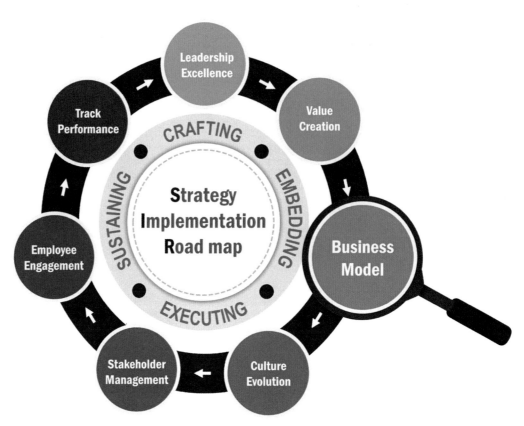

Figure 7.0: Strategy Implementation Road Map©

In this module you will:

- Understand why and how business models must change
- Realize the importance of thinking strategically
- Be aware of changing technologies
- Know how to digitize the business
- Learn how to execute projects with excellence
- Learn how to sustain engagement and resources

CRAFTING

Introduction

By default, a new strategy translates to changing the way the organization operates. This requires a new business model to support and enable employees.

- Why Do Business Models Need to Keep Changing?

Why Do Business Models Need to Keep Changing?

The Strategy Life Cycle replicates a Product Life Cycle.

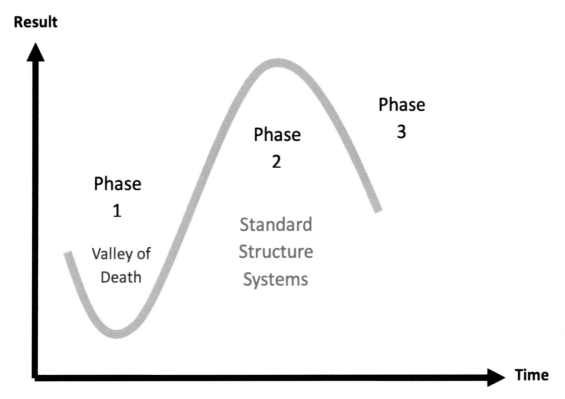

Figure 8.0: Strategy Life Cycle

In Phase 1 a product is being tested and sales dip while it is being refined. For a new organization, it is struggling to find the success model, and four out of five fail to reach Phase 2, thus the name "Valley of Death" between Phases 1 and 2.

In Phase 2 the product sales are taking off. An organization now wants to replicate its success by creating standards, consistent structure, and systems.

In Phase 3 the product sales are in decline. If an organization does not change, then eventually it will disappear.

> *If the rate of change on the outside exceeds the rate of change on the inside, the end is near.*
>
> — Jack Welch

Strategic Inflection Point

In the middle of Phase 2, the leaders of the organization are required to create a new strategy designed to drive growth, requiring significant shifts in the organization's business model.

> *A strategic inflection point is a time in the life of business when its fundamentals are about to change. That change can mean an opportunity to rise to new heights. But it may just as likely signal the beginning of the end.*
>
> — Andy Grove, former CEO of Intel

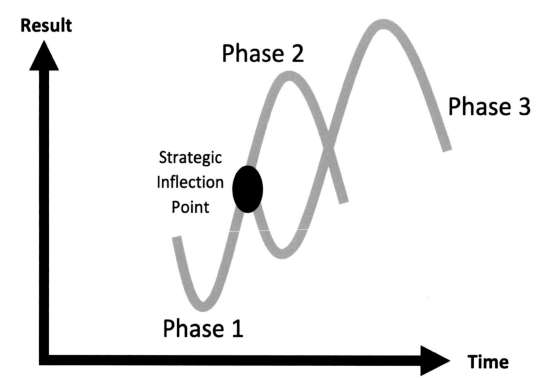

Figure 9.0: Strategic Inflection Point

> *The average large firm reorganizes every two to three years, and the average reorganization takes more than 18 months to implement. Wait and see is not an option; it's a death sentence.*
>
> — McKinsey & Company

We know from behavioral psychology that individuals tend to stick to an existing course of action, and the same is often true of organizations. Consider how HMV continued to expand its shops in the early 2000 during the rise of digital. It went into receivership in 2013.

> *One of the things that I've come to realize is that in companies that have been successful, one of the things that happens is the original idea or the concept that became a hit, the capability you built around it, and the culture that implicitly grew as you were growing the business all get into this beautiful, virtuous cycle.*
>
> *But there's no such thing as a perpetual-motion machine. At some point, the concept or the idea that made you successful is going to run out of gas. So, you need new capability to go after new concepts.*
>
> — Satya Nadella, CEO, Microsoft

What is the impact of decreasing strategy cycle times?

There are four main impacts:

1. New strategies are introduced more frequently.
2. Implementation happens more frequently.
3. Employees suffer greater change fatigue and have to get comfortable with it.
4. Organizations have to abandon yesterday more rapidly.

We can no longer plan the future as an extension of yesterday. As excruciatingly difficult as it is, we must shatter the belief that it worked yesterday, therefore hopefully it will work for . . . tomorrow.

External Papers

- The Quest for Sustainable Business Model Innovation **by BCG**
- Transforming beyond the Crisis with Head, Heart, and Hands **by BCG**
- 10 Principles for Modernizing Your Company's Technology **by strategy+business**
- How to Build a Data-Driven Company **by MIT**

Video Links

- The Project Economy **by Antonio Nieto-Rodrigue**
- Digital Transformation Series: Satya Nadella on Digital Transformation for Microsoft

EMBEDDING

Introduction

Synergizing the way employees work to drive the implementation requires focus and energy within the organization. You need to remain observant of both external and internal trends in your selection of the best methodology for transforming the business.

- How Digital Execution (DT) Differs from Traditional Strategy Execution (TSE)
- To-Stop List
- Digital Transformation Model
- Introduction to Robotics and AI

How Digital Transformation (DT) Differs from Traditional Strategy Execution (TSE)	
Goal	Leaders need to be conscious of the subtle differences in implementing different types of strategies. There are unique challenges for implementing Digital Execution (DT) versus Traditional Strategy Execution (TSE).
Implementation Challenge	The failure rate for implementing strategies in the digital world is 67 percent. The failure rate has gone up because digital transformation involves both transforming the business while also adopting and embedding the right technologies.
What Needs to Change	The pace and components you need for adopting and executing digital depends on the sense of urgency for your business, which is driven by your market and strategy.

The pace and components leaders need for adopting and executing digital depends on the sense of urgency for their business, which is driven by their market and strategy. But not adopting digital is not an option.

As leaders globally are recognizing the need to espouse digital, the critical question becomes "How do we successfully execute a strategy in a digital world?"

DT is even more challenging than previous strategy implementations. It involves the identification and adoption of the right digital technologies while simultaneously transforming the organization. Previously these would be two different initiatives.

Yesterday's success no longer guarantees tomorrow's results. Leaders are required to identify new strategies to remain competitive and change their modus operandi in a digital world. In DT, organizations cannot build on top of their current business model; they need a whole business model transformation to adopt digital.

Just like the Internet, digital is revolutionizing the way we conduct business— except with a much greater impact. Organizations must respond faster than ever to customer requirements. To be more customer and operational centric. To develop agility by leveraging short experiments as part of their strategy. To adopt the credo to fail early, fail fast and fail forward. To leverage data analytics and data visualization for business optimization. To identify ways to adopt and leverage artificial intelligence and to identify opportunities from the Internet of Things.

Understanding and acting on how DT differs from TSE can make the difference between success and failure, due to seven key dissimilarities in the approach needed..

> *It is not about having a digital strategy*
> *but a strategy in a digital world.*
>
> – Robin Speculand

Just as the internet did 18 years ago, digital is revolutionizing the way we conduct business—except with a much greater impact. Organizations must respond faster than ever to customer requirements: to be more customer and operational centric to develop agility by leveraging short experiments as part of your strategy; to adopt the credo to fail early, fail fast, and fail forward; to leverage data analytics and data visualization for business optimization; to identify ways to adopt and leverage artificial intelligence; and to identify opportunities from the Internet of Things.

Understanding and acting on how DT differs from TSE is fundamental to successful delivery due to seven key dissimilarities in the required approach.

1. Whole-Business Transformation Comes from the Core

Although some organizations initially adopt digital from the edges, eventually all must transform from the core. TSE does not always require the business to transform from the core; it's possible to adopt some strategies, such as cost optimization or overseas growth, that don't need to change the fabric of the organization.

In DT, however, the critical difference is that it requires a whole business model shift that will, eventually, transform the business from the core. As digital is woven through every component of the business, it alters the DNA of the organization. This is because DT encapsulates various initiatives that have an effect across the organization's value chain. The initiatives include artificial intelligence, big data, and human design-thinking.

Some leadership teams question whether adopting a digital strategy should be from the core or the periphery. Adopting from the edges typically involves creating a separate team to do experiments, often from a remote location. They start producing small successes that eventually build traction to transform the whole organization. By comparison, other organizations that have failed tinkered with their business model but did not commit to a full-scale transformation.

There's no right approach—a truth that can frustrate leaders. You need to determine what will work in your organization by considering the sense of urgency, culture, strategy, market, competition, and customer characteristics.

Key Mistake: Expecting DT to succeed while leveraging the organization's current business model.

Critical Digital Success Factor: DT affects every part of the business and requires a complete business model transformation.

2. Culture—Back with a Bang

An organization's culture has always been important in strategy implementation; today, it's even more significant. With DT, almost all organizations require a culture change. This is because transformation of the whole business model translates to changing the fundamental way the organization operates. For almost all, this means changing the culture.

Failing to change the culture is among the top three reasons for high failure rates in DT. The culture must support DT. As the late Peter Drucker said, "Culture eats strategy for breakfast." But in DT, this is not always true and, in fact, can be the other way around. With the accelerated pace of change in business today, strategy now eats culture. Allow me to elaborate.

The landscape has altered dramatically since Drucker made this famous statement. With businesses moving faster than at any time in history (and yet this is the slowest pace we will now ever work), the accelerated pace has dramatically reshaped the relationship strategy, culture, and execution.

In Drucker's era, a strategy for an organization could typically span for years while assuming a decade of stability and growth. During that period, an organization strived for stability.

Today, most organizations are working at a faster strategy cadence (speed of execution) than ever. On average, that means the strategy has to change every three years. This fast pace of transformation translates to the organizational culture being in a constant state of flux to keep pace with the rapidly changing strategies.

Key Mistake: Assuming the culture that got you here will make you successful tomorrow.

Critical Digital Success Factor: Recognizing that culture drives the way an organization executes its strategy.

3. Failure Is a Necessity

With DT, your organization must fail before it can succeed. To transform the whole business, recognize there will be failures. How leaders respond to them and to their employees can dictate the success of DT.

We know from behavioral psychology that *negative reinforcement* stops a behavior. That means if employees try and then fail and are punished for their efforts, they will stop trying. Therefore, leaders must create a culture in which failure is acceptable and encouraged, but within certain parameters. This is because DT requires testing followed by new ways of working while adopting new approaches, tools, and techniques.

When leaders say they want to create a "start-up" culture, that partly means having a structure that allows employees to try, fail, and learn. The parameters ensure that the organization learns from the failures and is able to move on rather than repeating earlier missteps.

Expert Advice

To succeed in DT, leaders need to create an environment that allows employees to try, fail, and learn.

The mantra within many organizations today is "fail early, fail fast, and fail forward." For example, Google's X—The Moonshot Factory[1] was created in 2010 as a new division to work on: "Moonshots: sci-fi sounding technologies that aim to make the world a radically better place." Inside the division, people are rewarded for stopping experiments that aren't working. This frees up essential resources with time to focus on projects that might work. In Google's office, employees are reminded by a sign on the wall that reads Fail Well.

Due to the rapid growth of FinTech, one industry that has to adopt digital to survive is banking. Prior to starting Bridges (one of Robin Speculand's companies) in 2000, the author was a regional VP in Citigroup. At that time, the bank's culture was unforgiving—that is, anyone who made a big mistake was out, no second chances. Fast-forward to today, and all banks now *encourage* failure. This requires a complete change in leadership thinking and how they manage the business.

Transformation needs to happen in both the leaders' and the employees' minds as well as the culture.

Key Mistake: Employees are punished for failing.

Critical Digital Success Factor: Leaders embrace failure as a stepping-stone to success. They coach employees through decisions that don't work so they can learn the right lessons and take the right actions.

4. Digital Speedometer

It's common for leaders to assume they have to transform by tomorrow, and all parts of the organization have to achieve DT at the same speed. Not so. The speed at which an organization executes its strategy is called its Strategy Cadence. While crafting the strategy, they decide the best Strategy Cadence, which has three gears of execution:

- Slow: more than five years
- Medium: less than five years and more than three years
- Fast: less than three years

Slow Strategy Cadence

If you intentionally select a slow strategy cadence, it may be because the sense of urgency for DT is not urgent. Businesses in certain industries such as mining, agriculture, or aircraft manufacturers have up to 15 years to execute their strategies.

One of the authors' clients, LVMH, is adopting digital with Ian Rogers, previously from Apple, who is driving the transformation. LVMH has chosen a slow strategy cadence because the barrier of entry to most of their markets is high. This allows them the luxury (excuse the pun) of time to transform. Having failed at their initial approach to digital in 2009 (called ELuxury.com), a different approach was required. Today, the leadership team has time to ensure the success of this DT, which goes across the 70 prestigious brands and a retail network of more than 4,370 stores worldwide.

Medium Strategy Cadence

Most organizations have a medium strategy cadence. That means every three to five years, they keep revisiting the need for change and crafting a new strategy.

During the medium strategy cadence, leaders have only a few years to execute a new strategy. They are forced to drive the new strategy forward before products and/or services become obsolete and revenue streams vanish.

The high number of organizations falling into the medium strategy cadence is a direct result of the fast-changing strategic landscape. This applies, for example, to construction and manufacturing. These industries have had to develop agility to adjust to the accelerated pace of change, hence the growing sense of urgency.

Fast Strategy Cadence

For some organizations, a five-year strategic plan—or even a three-year one—is a thing of the past. As a result of disruption or loss of market share, revenue, and/or customers, they may be under pressure. The situation requires immediate corrective action, which carries a high risk without the luxury of time to study circumstances and involve a variety of people. These organizations have an extremely high sense of urgency and a need for speed.

Samsung is an example of an organization that executes fast, using a fast strategy cadence to its advantage. For the last few years, its leaders have had a "fast market follower" strategy. That means they continually scan their industry for innovative new products that either threaten Samsung's current business or offer new revenue opportunities. Then they design their own product for the market.

Consider the success Samsung has had with its Galaxy smart phone. This strategic approach became possible because of the speed and excellence at which Samsung's culture enabled its people to work.

Samsung's "fast market follower" strategy keeps changing as the organization strives to be first to market in certain product areas. It's a strategy that emphasizes the need for agility. As an example, in 2013, Samsung launched the Android-powered Galaxy Gear smart watch. The following year, Apple's iPhone sales eradicated Galaxy Gear's end-of-year profits. In response, Samsung is looking to develop wireless charging.

Key Mistake: Not recognizing the business's sense of urgency to transform.

Critical Digital Success Factor: Identifying the strategy cadence for your organization—slow, medium, or fast.

5. Board Support

Because DT affects the whole organization, the board needs to fully support the organization's transformation. But before starting to transform, the board and the leadership team must discuss and collaborate on key decisions, creating the digital vision for the organization. This includes changes to products and services offered to customers, potential changes in customer segments, and required changes in operations.

It also includes allocating investments for adopting new technologies and expanding current ones as well as training employees and hiring external support, if required.

The leadership team and the board must also agree on the road map for transformation and assign new metrics to track performance. To keep the board's support along the journey, board members should be kept fully informed.

Key Mistake: Surprising your board with DT initiatives.

Critical Digital Success Factor: Projecting the cost of DT and the returns as well as managing board members' expectations.

6. Customer Centricity, for Real

For many years, leaders have adopted a strategy that involved being more customer centric than ever. They trained their employees in customer service, adopted customer centricity as a core value, and found ways to integrate the *voice of the customer* into the business. But many of the organizations failed to make the substantial changes required to sustain a permanent customer centric culture.

A manufacturing organization, for example, focused on creating an omnipresent customer experience. The leaders enabled their sales team with digital tools so they could connect with their customers and respond faster to them. But they did not address how operations would deliver on the salespeople's promises to customers. As a result, promises were made that the operations team could not fulfill, leading to customer dissatisfaction rather than satisfaction.

In DT, customer centricity is an essential component. It depends on an organization-wide understanding of customer problems that need to be solved as well as the different customer experience that can be created. Many leaders start their DT journey with customer centricity. They adopt techniques such as human-centered design so their employees can integrate digital solutions that create better customer experiences. This approach also results in significantly reduced costs, which can be passed on to customers and has the potential to foster a flawless end-to-end customer experience. As McKinsey and Co reported,[2] digitizing customer service can increase customer satisfaction by 33 percent and reduce costs by as much as 35 percent.

Key Mistake: Applying transformation predominantly to only one part of the organization, as too many previous customer service initiatives have done.

Critical Digital Success Factor: Creating a customer-centric digital experience involves examining the process end-to-end and transforming it across the organization.

7. Employee Empowerment, a Non-Negotiable

In TSE, it is not always necessary to adopt a management style of employee empowerment. One of the authors' Chinese clients, for example, was losing market share and revenue at an alarming rate. The new CEO dictated the changes that needed to happen, knowing the organization had to transform immediately to survive. Employees were told what to do—a necessary approach in this situation to plug the leaks and start to rebuild.

In DT, however, employee empowerment is non-negotiable. Why? *Transforming the whole business cannot be done by dictating details from the top.* Leaders need to point their employees in the right direction, set the parameters for empowerment, and then step back, allowing them to take the right actions. And when they make mistakes, leaders must support them in learning from their experience.

DBS Bank in Singapore has not only been awarded the title Best Digital Bank in the World but also that of Best Bank in the World (the first Asian bank to achieve either award). When Piyush Gupta, the CEO, started to transform the bank, he adopted *situational leadership*. Initially that translated into attending all key meetings to ensure what he wanted was being done, but now he goes to the meetings simply to find out what's going on! The employees have been empowered to execute digital. Between the start and now, they were trained in what digital means. This included participating in hackathons and using the right tools for DT, including human design-thinking and how to use big data.

Key Mistake: Leaders trying to control every aspect of DT.

Critical Digital Success Factor: After the initial launch of DT and training employees in the new skills required, employees are empowered to translate DT into their work. As an organization achieves this, decision-making moves down the hierarchy.

Conclusion

Leaders are repeating the same mistakes from TSE all over again in DT. To further complicate the situation, because DT is a larger transformation than TSE, mistakes made by the organization are now magnified.

Both TSE and DT require discipline and focus throughout the organization. The goal is to understand what's required in the approach and drive the right actions that will lead the organization to success in this digital world.

References

1. X, the Moonshot Factory, accessed April 6, 2022, https://x.company/
2. Raffaella Bianchi, Gergely Gacsal, and Daniel Svoboda, "Overcoming Obstacles to Digital Customer Care," McKinsey, August 1, 2015, https://www.mckinsey.com/business-functions/marketing-and-sales/our-insights/overcoming-obstacles-to-digital-customer-care?utm_source=mta&utm_campaign=10023&utm_term=vanditagrover

To-Stop List

As implementation happens at ground level, people need to be empowered to take the right actions to improve their work. This includes being able to eliminate non-value-adding work (sometimes referred to as "Toil," a term coined by Google). Examples of non-value-adding work include sending out reports people don't need, redoing work, being on a conference call unnecessarily, or checking work that's already been checked. Some will be excited because leaders are finally providing the opportunity to focus on more value-adding activities.

Everyone has used "to-do" lists, but employees also need "to-stop" lists of actions that don't contribute to the new strategy.

When you provide the opportunity, empowerment, and methodology for employees to eliminate unnecessary tasks, they will stop doing non-value-adding work, improve what they are doing, and rise to the occasion.

In a large organization, it's estimated up to 33% of people's work can be non-value-adding. When people eliminate non-value-adding work, they critically create space and free up resources to take the right actions.

Example: Procter & Gamble

As a leader, when you empower your people to create and follow a "to-stop list," they become more engaged and accomplish more in less time.

A. G. Lafley, in his turnaround of Procter & Gamble, established a portfolio of performance initiatives that gave priority to four core businesses. At the same time, he created a "not-to-do" list that included projects driven by technology rather than customer needs. What's more, he ensured every initiative—whatever its focus—included building mindsets and capabilities focused on customers and external partnerships.

Example: Apple

In a dramatic example, when Steve Jobs returned to Apple as CEO in 1997, he made a decision that shocked everyone from the frontline to the board members. He announced he was devoting all of Apple's resources to only four products. That stopped more than 70% of the hardware and software product development going on, canceling over 300 projects.

At the time, Apple was manufacturing dozens of different Macintosh desktops, laptops, and servers in a range of variations. It was also designing and manufacturing lines of printers, digital cameras, and other ancillary items. Very few of these products were making a profit.

Jobs's decision focused the organization on developing only two consumer desktops and portables and two professional desktops and portables. Jobs walked into a special board meeting where two dozen Apple products were displayed.

Dramatically, he began taking them down one at a time until only four products were left. Those were the ones, he said, that would give Apple new life by differentiating it in the marketplace.

> *We believe in saying no to thousands of projects*
> *so that we can really focus on the few that*
> *are truly important and meaningful to us.*
>
> – Steve Jobs, founder, Apple Computers

Encourage your people to adopt a "to-stop" list. Invite them to present the work they want to kill off to their immediate boss and/or the leader of the specific business, either in person or electronically. He or she should review the request and respond to it within three working days.

If it's refused, make sure employees are given a transparent and valid reason. This might include the fact that their proposal conflicts with an ongoing or planned strategic initiative. This step ensures any changes align with the strategy. But if this is the case, you should probably review your corporate communication to redouble your efforts to inform and involve everyone in the strategy.

Agree on a time and a means for them to follow up and see if these changes have produced the expected outcomes.

Digital Transformation Model

The Digital Transformation failure rate is shockingly high, no matter which consultancy's statistics you follow:

- 70%—McKinsey
- 67%—Boston Consulting Group
- 67%—Genpact

But why do they fail?

- Senior Leaders' Mindset—Leaders have not changed their thinking and attitude to embrace digital.
- Culture—Digital transformation requires a culture change.
- Whole Business Transformation—Digital transformation requires changing the fundamental way you operate.

> *Yesterday's performance no longer*
> *guarantees tomorrow's success.*
>
> – Robin Speculand

Key Message: It's not about having a digital strategy but strategy to compete in a digital world.

Digital transformation is not about tweaking your business. It's a whole new way of working.

> *The only way you survive is you continuously transform*
> *into something else. It's this idea of continuous*
> *transformation that makes you an innovation company.*
>
> – Ginni Rometty, former CEO of IBM

Digital Transformation Model: 11 Operational Steps

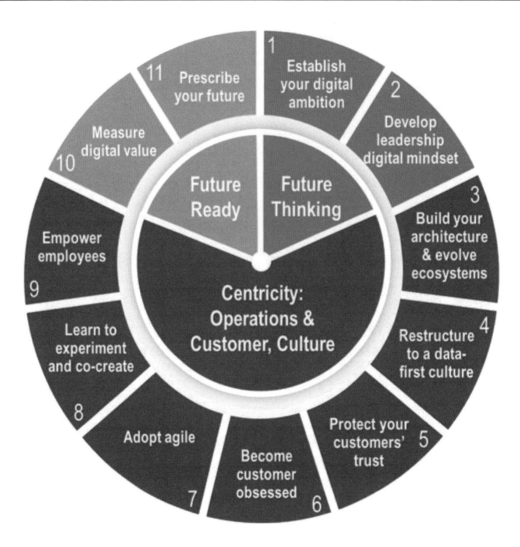

Figure 10.0: Ticking Clock© Model (Digital Leadership Specialists)

Strategy Cadence: What Speed Should You Transform At?

Some industries have up to 10 years to execute their strategies, such as:

- Aircraft manufacturers, hotels, high-end luxury, real estate, mining, and agriculture. Competitors are moving slowly, and there is typically a high barrier of entry to your industry.
- This allows them the opportunity to discuss the execution with various people and potentially engage them in crafting the strategy.

YOUR SPEED: SLOW

The sense of urgency is low.

Other industries function at a medium cadence. Leaders have only a few years to execute the new strategy.

- This applies to construction and manufacturing.
- With a Medium Strategy Cadence, leaders drive the new strategy forward before products and/or services become obsolete and revenue streams vanish.

YOUR SPEED: MEDIUM

The sense of urgency is medium.

For organizations who focus more on experimentation than strategy, for example, start-ups, immediate corrective action is often required, which carries a high risk without the luxury of time to study circumstances and involve a variety of people.

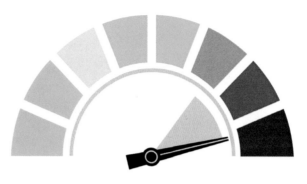

YOUR SPEED: FAST

The sense of urgency is high.

> *The pace of change has never been this fast,*
> *but it will never be this slow again.*
>
> – Justin Trudeau, Canadian Prime Minister

Disruption: is what happens *when you are slow.*

Digital Transformation: is what happens *when you are fast.*

Speed is more important today than size.

If you want to compete you must embrace technology.
Which means not just technology change but:

- *A culture change*
- *Take risk*
- *Being willing to experiment*
- *Be nimble*
- *Be focused on the customer*
- *Be data driven*
- *Be obsessed with continuous change*

– Piyush Gupta, CEO of DBS Bank

Introduction to Robotics and AI

The term *Industry 4.0* refers to the combination of several major innovations in digital technology, all coming to maturity right now, all poised to transform.

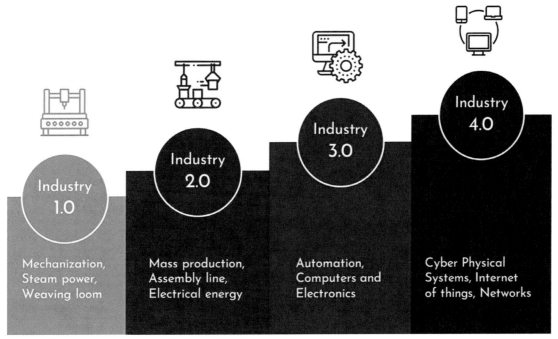

Figure 11.0: Types of Industry

Every technology follows the path of moving from discovery to engineering to transformation.

Consider these examples.

Electricity

In 1831 Michael Faraday discovered electricity. Fifty years later, after understanding the principles, Edison engineered and opened his first power plant. It took another 40 years before we transformed electricity to everyday household compliances, and in 1921 the first electric washing machine was introduced.

Computers

In the 1960s IBM discovered mainframe computers. In 1997 IBM engineered Deep Blue that beat Garry Kasparov at chess. It was the first time a world champion had been beaten by a computer, and then 14 years later Apple transformed computing into AI called Siri.

The impact of new technology is that it shapes us. We shape our technologies at the moment of conception, but from that point forward, they shape us.

We humans designed the telephone, but from then on, the telephone influenced how we have communicated, conducted business, and conceived of the world.

We also invented the automobile, but then rebuilt our cities around automotive travel and our geopolitics around fossil fuels.

Today robotics has rapidly evolved, and many organizations are integrating robotic-process automation and robotics in manufacturing.

> ## *AI is not replacing jobs. It is replacing tasks.*
>
> – Eric Schmidt

The impact of AI is:

- Laborious work is being automated.
- The need for finely tuned social and emotional skills is rapidly growing.
- There is a shift in demand toward higher cognitive skills.
- Only 6% of leaders in Europe and the US expect the workforce to shrink due to AI.

Integration is becoming more common and frequent. Consider these examples:

Self-Driving Cars

It's anticipated that with self-driving cars on the road there will be 90% fewer accidents, and the technology will potentially reduce the number of cars on the road by up to 75%. Smart traffic lights will reduce wait times by 40%.

Facebook Photo

When you upload photos to Facebook, the service automatically highlights faces and suggests friends to tag, as Facebook uses AI to recognize faces. They also use AI to personalize your newsfeed and ensure you're seeing posts that interest you.

Amazon Purchases

When you purchase on Amazon, in another example, you automatically see recommendations for other products you may be interested in as "customers who viewed this item also viewed" and "customers who bought this item also bought." Amazon uses artificial neural networks to generate these product recommendations. This has resulted in up to a 30% increase in sales.

External Papers

- Organizational Ambidexterity **by Antonio Nieto-Rodriguez**
- World Economic Forum: The Digital Enterprise: Moving from Experimentation to Transformation
- External Paper: Generative A.I.: How to future-proof your company's strategy

Video Links

- A Guide for Designing a Successful Corporate Transformation, **strategy+business**
- New Rules in the Age of AI, **Karim R. Lakhani**

EXECUTING

Introduction

At this stage, the new strategy starts to be imbued into the organization and is becoming the new norm. However, the business model must remain fluid.

- Integrate a Project-Driven Organization
- The Project Canvas

Integrate a Project-Driven Organization	
Goal	To establish a project-driven organizational business model that will accelerate transformation and support the implementation.
Implementation Challenge	The main challenge of building a project-driven organization business model is shifting away from the legacy and inertia of the existing model. People (especially leaders) unwilling to let go and still think in silos are another challenge to be addressed.
What Needs to Change	Adapting the business model to become a project-driven organization requires strong leaders who can challenge the status quo and will take steps to transform the organization's hierarchy, structure, process, and systems.

In his 1962 book *Strategy and Structure*, Alfred Chandler argues that an organization's structure should be driven by its chosen strategy and that if it isn't, inefficiency results.

Taking this one step further, the degree to which project activities are reflected in the organization's business model determines its implementation success. When executives underestimate or ignore this fact, organizations fail to evolve or adapt as quickly as the markets do. As a result, a large proportion of strategic projects fail, and organizations disappear.

Today, organizations need a strategy to help their people make decisions independently. Leaders must react at the level of where things are happening, which is typically at the operational level.

Cross-departmental—or company-wide—projects in a traditional functional organization all face similar difficulties. Many are linked to the following questions:

1. Which department will lead the project?
2. Who will be the project manager?
3. Who is the sponsor of the project?
4. Who gets rewarded if the project is successful?
5. Who owns the resources assigned to the project?
6. Who will pay the project's costs?

The Chinese Way

Interestingly, faced with a silo mentality, a lack of agility, attachment to the status quo, innovation paralysis, and all the downsides of traditional organizations, Chinese companies have frequently managed to reformulate their organizations. Let's look at three successful Chinese organizational models: Xiaomi, Alibaba, and Haier.

Case Study

Xiaomi

Xiaomi is a mobile internet company focused on smart hardware and electronics. It is one of the most valuable Chinese unicorns (a start-up company with a value of over $1 billion) with a market capitalization of $50 billion. It has been included in the MIT Technology Review's list of the 50 "smartest companies," and founder Lei Jun has appeared on the cover of Wired, claiming, "It's time to copy China."

The company, which started in 2010, has emerged at a rapid pace. It outstripped Apple's smartphone sales in China within four years. Then it introduced new products to the market at breakneck speed, disrupting—or at least surprising—market incumbents virtually every time. By 2018, Xiaomi had successfully launched more than 40 products ranging from smart rice cookers and air purifiers to robot vacuum cleaners and smart running shoes.

The silo mentality adds to this complexity, with managers often wondering why they should commit resources and a budget to a project that, although important, would not give them credit for being successful. Rather, they believe a management colleague (often a direct competitor) would benefit.

Within the traditional organizational structure, completing a project execution quickly is not possible. If managing only one project in such a complex structure presents a challenge, imagine the difficulty of selecting and executing hundreds of projects of varying sizes!

Xiaomi has gained a lot of attention for its unusual marketing strategy, which relies completely on digital technology. It uses online sales channels and social media platforms rather than heavy-asset retail shops and distributors. The result is low-cost sales channels that meet the demands of targeted customers. However, the truly innovative aspect of Xiaomi is how its organizational model is driven by projects. Its

40-plus products in the market are not organized in strategic business units and have not become part of the organizational hierarchy.

In fact, the company has a relatively flat organizational structure, with the seven co-founders only one line of management away from the engineers and sales teams. The latter make up the largest part of the employee base. Moreover, the co-founders are required to be directly involved with projects and new product development. They participate in user interaction, such as on Xiaomi's own platform, and keep up to date with products and projects. Each Xiaomi employee (including the founders) has a contractual responsibility to directly deal with a certain quota of customer requests. A sophisticated digital problem distribution system allocates questions to any suitable employee. Customer proximity has not only become a performance assessment criterion for employees but also a driver for customer-driven projects. Each new product development is treated as a project that can be achieved by mobilizing resources inside and outside Xiaomi.

Two features of Xiaomi stand out:

- *Iteration of product development and customer-driven projects*
- *Leveraging an ecosystem of external resources to speed up project execution*

First, Xiaomi uses a new product development approach that focuses on getting prototypes into the market as soon as possible (i.e., with good-enough products) and actively involves users in fine-tuning and updating the technology and design. It results in a product that is largely co-developed by the community (i.e., closer to the market need and with a more efficient R&D process).

Xiaomi also uses highly qualified suppliers for components and focuses on integration and design rather than production and hardware R&D. The key competence of Xiaomi is a project-driven structure in which the business model, marketing, promotion, and design are centered on customer interaction rather than manufacturing. That means the company can deliver good-quality products that customers want without the investments in production and R&D that a traditional organizational model requires.

Second, customer-driven projects gain speed in Xiaomi by leveraging external resources. Following its three original designs—smartphone, router, and TV set top box—all other Xiaomi products were developed as projects in collaboration with other companies or entrepreneurs. For example, Xiaomi identified a market need for air purifiers but could not find a suitable producer. So it suggested to Su Jun, former associate professor of industrial design at North China University of Technology, that he develop an air purifier and Xiaomi would invest in the start-up.

Within nine months (by December 2014), the product was developed and launched at a killer price of 899 RMB, which was one third of the average market price at that time.

Case Study

Alibaba

Alibaba Group is the world's largest and most valuable retailer operating in more than 200 countries. With over 50,000 employees and a market cap of $520 billion (as of early 2018), it is one of the top 10 most valuable and biggest companies in the world.

The success of Alibaba can be largely attributed to its innovative organizational structure, a business ecosystem that has fostered the rapid growth and transformation of its businesses since the company began in 1999. A business ecosystem refers to "a new organizational form where the businesses are interdependent through a variety of equity relationships combining product and service offerings into a customer centric offering."

Alibaba's business ecosystems consist of hundreds of companies, ventures, and projects across at least 20 different sectors. But the majority of these are independently run operations, neither part of strategic business units nor subject to reporting structures. In fact, many of the players in Alibaba's business ecosystem are fairly small.

Alibaba is widely characterized as a dynamic system of companies, ventures, and projects enabled by digital technology. Instead of directing the development of new products and implementing projects from the top down, Alibaba functions as what is known as a gravity provider and network orchestrator.

For instance, Alibaba's core is composed of four e-commerce platforms (Alibaba.com, 1688.com, Taobao.com, and Tmall.com) that are home to 700 million users. Moreover, the interdependence among the companies, ventures, and projects is not only based on finance and equity, although these are prerequisites to be part of the business ecosystem.

The interdependence is found in growth strategies, investment approaches, and complementarities among the offerings, business synergies, and resource sharing. In this ecosystem, entrepreneurial projects are allowed to fail without severe consequences for the sustainability of the whole ecosystem—or the careers of top management.

Employees in Alibaba's ecosystem are selected and managed according to an alignment of values rather than rules. The key values of Alibaba include putting customers first, teamwork, embracing change, integrity, passion, and dedication. The result of such a value-driven approach is encouragement of taking risks and a strong organizational culture and competition.

Employees are assessed on a quarterly basis and rated in terms of performance and value, which are seen as equally important. There is no HR guidebook, only a set of strong principles that guide the employees to operate in a highly dynamic environment. They can initiate any project they like without regard to their current company or department. In fact, the ecosystem of Alibaba provides a safe marketplace of resources in which project initiators can implement their ideas without organizational boundaries and complex hierarchical and vertical reporting structures.

Alibaba has made considerable efforts in keeping its business ecosystem entrepreneurial. While the majority of Chinese entrepreneurs are grassroots entrepreneurs who start from zero, a significant number in Chinese internet businesses have spun off from the large technology companies.

Alibaba itself has been, by far, the most active generator of new CEOs. By the beginning of 2016, more than 450 individuals had emerged from Alibaba to start their own ventures. In total, over 250 ventures have been established by former Alibaba employees. Many of these new projects begin within Alibaba's ecosystem, leveraging its rich resources and opportunities.

New project initiatives and implementation stay within the ecosystem and do not suffer from bureaucracy, department silos, or managerial limitations.

Case Study

Haier

Haier Group is today the world's leading brand of major household appliances. Founded in 1984, it has been the number one white goods supplier since 2009, with 10% global market share and more than 78,000 employees (in 2016). The World Brand Lab's listing of the 500 most influential brands ranked Haier at the top of the global white appliances list. In 2016, Haier reached revenues of over 200 billion RMB and acquired GE's appliance division for $5.4 billion, a feat previously unimaginable given its humble beginnings only three decades ago. Haier is also one of the first Chinese companies to continually bring new products to the market.

It has many products that satisfy special needs in China—for instance, washing machines with quick washing cycles and 15-minute nonstop washing. Haier's Crystal washing machine series is the outcome of several series of user observations, surveys, and innovations in terms of spin speed and operating noise.

At Haier, ideas for new products do not only come from the minds of the engineers and managers. Many come from the front end of the company, including repair people and salespeople.

Since 1998, the company has experimented with new organizational forms to reduce hierarchy and control and increase autonomy using self-organizing work units and internal labor markets. But it wasn't until 2010 that Haier put in place a unique project organization platform throughout the company. To create it, leaders had to fundamentally reorganize the company's structure.

First, they eliminated strategic business units and managerial hierarchies so there would be zero distance from the users of its products. The company reorganized into three project units, each with a specific focus. The first unit focuses on new product development, marketing, and production; it is the closest to the user. A second set of project units includes corporate support functions such as HR, accounting, and legal. The third unit is the executive team. Interestingly, the third unit, the smallest, is positioned at the bottom of the inverted pyramid with its role redefined as a support function for the customer-facing, self-organizing project organizations.

Today, Haier has thousands of work units, more than 100 of which have annual revenues in excess of 100 million RMB. More recently, the platform has evolved to let work units of noncore products spin off. Since 2014, external investors have been allowed to invest in promising new products jointly with Haier's investment fund. For instance, a furniture maker invested in one of the e-commerce platforms (Youzhu. com) that spun off into a work unit relating to house decoration. To date, 41 such spin-offs have received funding, with 16 getting in excess of 100 million RMB.

Through measures such as decentralization, disintermediation, and eliminating internal communication barriers, Haier has decreased its staff by 45% while creating more than 1.6 million job opportunities.

Implementation Tools

Succeeding in today's fast-changing world requires an agile, lean design-thinking and project-driven business model.

Large organizations with strong top-down leadership and fast implementation, Chinese companies are both highly innovative and adaptive to changing markets through swift project implementation. The cases of Xiaomi, Alibaba, and Haier illustrate how these companies organize and expand their businesses by combining lean, agile, and design-thinking approaches with project-driven structures.

Agile: With the arrival of the internet and the subsequent digital technology revolution, the pioneers have been quick to adapt, surprising many international enterprises. Not only the digital natives BAT and Xiaomi but traditional manufacturers such as Sony and Haier have embraced digital technologies and created competitive advantages. By embracing digital technologies and deeply embedding them in their structure, these companies have been able to adapt to changing market conditions through repetitive product development.

Lean: Operating in the complex, dynamic Chinese market, these companies have designed their organization as a system of work, rather than a system of control. Their approach focuses on making decisions by experimenting, learning, and empowering the people closest to the customer. Key features of lean manufacturing such as zero waste, continuous quality, and process optimization are found in novel ways of organizing. Alibaba's value-driven (rather than control-driven) management and Xiaomi's iterated development and swift product upgrades are based on the logic of experimentation and fast learning cycles.

Design-thinking: The ultimate goal of reaching zero distance to the customer is shared by these Chinese success stories. Besides increasing responsiveness, this allows organizations to deal with ambiguity and explore solutions customers want to buy. In fact, Chinese companies are, by necessity, design thinkers—that is, given the dynamic market, the continuous emergence of new customers, and the limited loyalty and maturity of the average customer, Chinese companies have to get as close to consumers as possible. Much of the new product development projects (e.g., Haier's Crystal washing machines and most of Xiaomi's consumer electronics products) are exclusively customer driven, rather than product driven or technology driven.

Project-driven structures: The three organizational models of the Chinese companies Xiaomi, Alibaba, and Haier represent entrepreneurial business ecosystems built around customers with structures that thrive in the project-driven world. They have three common attributes. First, they have no strategic business units as the dominant organizational structure and means of management governance; second, there is entrepreneurial motivation and dedication; and third, they have relatively simple organizational structures. Moreover, risk taking and new project execution are not limited by the burdens of bureaucracy but come from resources within the organizational framework of the business ecosystem.

The Project Canvas

From the book *The Project Revolution* (LID 2019) by Antonio Nieto-Rodriguez

Leaders' Responsibilities in Implementation

Projects are timeless and universal. The construction of the pyramids in Egypt, the development of modern cities, the Marshall Plan, the Apollo space program, the creation of the European Union—all these achievements were the result of ideas being turned into reality through projects. Project-based work is the engine that generates the major accomplishments of our civilization; it has stimulated society to advance and often go beyond long-established scientific and cultural limits.

After studying hundreds of successful and failed projects ranging from small individual ones, I have developed a simple tool—the Project Canvas—that can be applied by any individual, team, organization, or country.

The framework can be used by leaders and organizations at the beginning of a project to assess how well it has been defined and whether it is worth starting right away or needs further refinement. It can be applied to programs, strategic initiatives, and any other activities that can be considered projects.

It is composed of 14 dimensions grouped into four major domains.

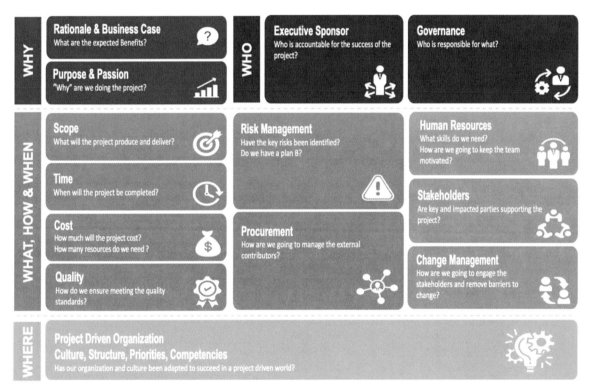

Figure 12.0: Project Canvas

Domain 1

The *Why* dimension covers the triggers and actual meaning of a project (the rationale and business case, and the purpose and passion), which will become the drivers once the project gets underway.

Dimension #1: Rationale and Business Case

All project management methodologies demand that projects always have a well-defined business case. Experience shows, however, that business cases have biases and subjective assumptions, especially concerning the financial benefits from the project, which often get inflated in order to make the project seem more attractive to the decision makers. Have you ever seen a project with a negative or meager return being presented?

Dimension #2: Purpose and Passion

Two of the newer elements in the Project Canvas are purpose and passion. Besides having a rationale, a project should be linked to a higher purpose.

Domain 2

The *Who* domain relates to the executive sponsor and governance, and it addresses the elements of accountability and allocation of responsibilities.

Dimension #3: Executive Sponsor

Many projects start without it being decided who is ultimately accountable for their successful delivery. As projects tend to go across departments, business units, and countries, they are often prone to "shared accountability and collective sponsorship." As a result, many executives feel responsible, yet no one is really accountable for driving the project to completion.

Dimension #4: Governance

The executive sponsor, together with the project manager, should define the project governance. The governance in a project is represented by a project chart in which the various contributing roles and decision-making bodies are defined.

One of the most important bodies in a project is the steering committee, which is chaired by the executive sponsor and run by the project manager. The members and the frequency with which they meet often determine the importance the project has for the organization.

Domain 3

The *What, How, and When* cover the fundamental elements that constitute the project. They can be split into technical areas and people-related elements.

Dimension #5: Scope

Understanding and agreeing what the project will consist of and deliver—the scope—is one of the raisons d'être of project management. Other terms for scope include specifications, detailed requirements, design, and functionality. The scope is the most important element in making an accurate estimation of the cost, duration, plan, and benefits of the project. Various tools can be used to try to determine what the outcome of the project will look like, yet this remains one of the most difficult tasks.

Dimension #6: Time

"Time is money": this famous phrase, attributed to Benjamin Franklin, is an absolute in projects. Time is one of the major characteristics of projects in that, unless there is an articulated, compelling, official, and publicly announced deadline, there is a good chance that the project will be delivered later than originally planned.

Delays in projects mean, besides extra costs, a loss of benefits and expected revenues, both having a tremendous negative impact in the business case of the initiative. A project without a deadline should not be considered a project—better call it an experiment, an exploration, or daily business activity.

Dimension #7: Cost

Budget in projects is composed mostly of the time dedicated by the project resources. These mainly include the people working on the project plus all other investments (consultants, material, software, hardware, etc.) required to develop the scope of the project. Budget is, together with time and scope, the third main constraint in traditional project management. Without budget, there is no project.

Dimension #8: Quality

Ensuring that the outcome of the project meets the quality expectations is an integral part of project management, yet it is often overlooked or not a priority. Often teams focus on doing the work and leave the quality part to the end of the project, when adjustments are most expensive.

Dimension #9: Risk Management

This is one of the most important techniques in project management and an essential duty of the project manager. Bluntly, if a project fails, it is because the risks that caused the failure were either not identified or not mitigated on time by the project team.

Dimension #10: Procurement

Projects tend to have a novelty component; therefore, the need to hire external capabilities to deliver the project is much higher. As projects are temporary assignments, it is cheaper to engage external capacity during the project than to hire internal resources.

Dimension #11: Human Resources

Today, project managers need to be project leaders too, especially for the more complex and cross-functional projects. These require pulling resources across the organization and changing the old status quo. In fact, we can argue that the best project managers are leaders but also entrepreneurs—they are the CEOs of their projects.

Dimension #12: Stakeholders

These are individuals and groups (entities, organizations, etc.) that are impacted by, are involved in, or have an interest in the outcome of a project. The larger the project, the more stakeholders there will likely be. The more stakeholders, the more efforts required in terms of communication and change management activities.

Dimension #13: Change Management

Aim to communicate what needs to be done clearly and accurately, ensuring that the organization and its employees are ready to embrace the changes introduced by a project. According to PMI's Guide to the Project Management Body of Knowledge, about 75–90 percent of a project manager's time is spent formally or informally communicating during the implementation phase of a project.

Domain 4

The *Where* domain covers the external elements that can have a positive or negative impact on the project.

Dimension #14: Project-Driven Organization

Most Western companies have a hierarchical, functional structure, which is ideal for running their daily business activities. Budgets, resources, key performance indicators, and decision power are "owned" by the heads of business units, departments, and functions.

However, the largest and most critical projects—the strategic ones—are cross-functional and cross-hierarchical by nature: they cut across the organization. The most successful organizations today have adjusted their structure to facilitate and support the execution of projects. They have become project driven.

> *There are few ways of working and collaborating that are particularly motivating and inspiring for people than working on a project.*
>
> — Antonio Nieto-Rodriguez

Case Study

Netflix

Founded in 1997, Netflix has a stock market value of nearly $165 billion, greater than that of Disney.

Netflix received 112 Emmy nominations, the most of any network or streaming service, toppling HBO (when written). Its reputation is so strong that a simple PowerPoint slideshow about its culture and HR policies has been viewed more than 18 million times.

If you aim to disrupt an industry, you must be willing to be disrupted.

Netflix grants its people the freedom and trust to make decisions, and information is shared across the organization so all employees are involved in each aspect of the company's strategy. Netflix has a "no vacation" policy—employees choose when and how often they take time off work. It also:

- *Doesn't reveal its viewership (as others do)*
- *Buys a whole program season without a pilot (as others request)*
- *Releases full seasons in one go (others don't)*
- *No ads, as because people pay a subscription rate*
- *In 2015, the company's stock rose 134%, which was the best performance of any Fortune 500 organization*

Big data is powerful, but big data plus big ideas is transformational. Netflix is a technology juggernaut whose analytics, algorithms, and digital-streaming innovations have changed how customers watch movies and TV shows. Its aim is to build a platform that shapes what customers watch, not just how they watch.

The company has vast amounts of data on the viewing habits of its 125 million subscribers, from which movies and TV shows they liked or disliked to how long they watched an individual episode or how much they binged a new series.

This powerful data system creates a rich social system that influences the movies and shows members see, based in part on which shows they've liked in the past and what other subscribers see and like.

Netflix could be the dictionary definition of a Silicon Valley disruptor, a new entrant that reshaped the logic of an entire industry.

Yet what's truly remarkable about the company's trajectory over the last two decades is how dramatically it has disrupted itself in service of its mission. Netflix began, of course, with a pretty simple innovation—crushing Blockbuster by shipping DVDs by mail and abolishing late fees. It then transitioned from mailing content to streaming movies and TV shows digitally. Today, Netflix is most noteworthy as a creator of content; it will spend a staggering $12 billion this year alone on programming.

The idea behind Netflix came in 1997 after the CEO was charged $40 for a late VHS copy of Apollo 13.

Reed Hastings, CEO, and his colleagues think just as rigorously about people and culture as they do about digital streaming and content. When it comes to who it hires and what it promises them, how it makes decisions and shares information, even what it does about vacations, Netflix has invented (and reinvented) a range of practices that are designed explicitly to connect what the company aims to achieve in the marketplace to how it organizes the workplace.

The average Netflix subscriber streams around 90 minutes a day.

In 2000, Netflix was offered to Blockbuster for $50 million. The now practically dead video rental company declined the offer. Netflix is currently worth $20 billion and is very much alive.

External Papers

- 8 Steps eBook to Accelerate Change **by Kotter**
- Discovery-Driven Digital Transformation **by Rita McGrath and Ryan McManus**
- Selling Products Is Good. Selling Projects Can Be Even Better **by Antonio Nieto-Rodriguez, HBR**
- Competing on Platforms **by MIT**
- The impact of agility: How to shape your organization to compete, McKinsey
- Five Truths (and One Lie) About Corporate Transformation **by BCG**

Video Links

- Project Management Conversation, **Brightline**
- Flipping the Odds of Digital Transformation, **BCG**

SUSTAINING

Introduction

This is almost a contradiction in terms because as the organization is sustaining the implementation success, you must already be preparing the next strategy and the next step in the organization's transformation.

- The Future of Strategy Implementation, White Paper
- DBS Bank Case Study

The Future of Strategy Implementation

A White Paper from the Strategy Implementation Institute

By Antonio Nieto-Rodriguez, Robin Speculand, Randall Rollinson, Ricardo Sastre, Joe DeCarlo, Gurpreet Rehal, and Michele Manocchi

The Current State

Strategy implementation is rapidly growing in importance for three key reasons:

1. Strategy cadence is increasing, requiring organizations to implement more frequently.
2. Many organizations are transforming to compete in a digital market, which requires implementing new strategies.
3. The global pandemic requires organizations to rethink and redesign their strategy.

When strategy planning first became popular in the 1960s as a business discipline, it was not unusual to plan 10-year-long strategies or even longer. By the turn of the millennium, the average strategy lasted five to six years.

Today, the average strategy life cycle is only three years. Considering it can take 18 months before a large organization starts to implement its strategy successfully, what does this mean?

Just as the organization is implementing its current strategy, leaders need to be identifying the next strategy. This increase in strategy cadence—plus the high failure rate of implementations—has added to their increased importance. More than that, these factors have contributed to strategy implementation becoming its own business discipline.

> *Leaders need both the ability to craft the right strategy and the skills to implement it.*

According to various research, for years organizations were planning new strategies but not successfully implementing them. (Succeeding in this context is defined as achieving at least 50 percent of the strategic goals.) To address this failure, the Strategy Implementation Institute (the Institute) was founded in 2020.

Dramatic Need to Improve Implementation Performance

The increase in strategy cadence and the high failure rate have firmly put the spotlight on this discipline *and* the need to dramatically improve implementation performance globally.

Another contributor to the high failure rate is that leaders have been taught how to *plan* but not how to *implement,* thus creating a strategy implementation skills gap. Every business school teaches how to *create* strategy; however, very few teach how to *implement* the strategy.

The strategy implementation challenge has further been complicated by the pressing need to compete in the digital world. Digitalization had already started to transform the way organizations operate. This was dramatically accelerated by the Covid-19 pandemic that has forced some organizations to change their operating business model. Digital implementation requires every leader to understand both technology and ways to transform their organization and its culture.

Action Taken by the Institute

In February 2021, the Institute held a virtual conference to discuss the future of strategy implementation. Distinguished speakers included Professor Rita McGrath from Columbia University and Professor Tony O'Driscoll from Duke University as well as senior leaders from APMG and Singapore Airlines. Conference delegates not only heard presentations from the speakers but also discussed their impact in breakout sessions where they identified future trends for strategy implementation.

The conference became the catalyst for crafting this white paper, which highlights these six future trends for strategy implementation:

1. Implementation Prioritization
2. Shift in Leadership Style to Implement in a Digital World
3. Leverage AI in Implementation
4. Increasing Importance of Middle Managers in Strategy Implementation
5. Purpose-Driven Strategy Implementation
6. Culture of Flexibility

The Future of Strategy Implementation

Members from the Institute have collaborated with the co-founders in writing this white paper, which highlights why these six future trends are significant for the future of strategy implementation

1. Implementation Prioritization

In organization terms, prioritization sets the agenda for what really matters. It is reflected by the allocation of resources—especially the scarce resources of time and money. Many organizations fail (in part) due to a lack of sensing what is urgent. Or they simply select the wrong priorities to work on.

If your organization's priorities are wrong, the effects can be calamitous. Let's look at two corporate failures in recent times: Toys R Us and Blockbuster.

Toys R Us identified the internet as a new business opportunity, but it failed to implement its online strategy fast enough. That resulted in a decline in its reputation and cash flow returns for almost 15 years straight. It had created www.toysrus.com to have an internet presence. At the time, it had a strong following and brand—a perfect mix for going online. It already had warehouses stocked with inventory and relationships with multiple suppliers. But Toys R Us failed in implementing its strategy because it was used to shipping large quantities of products to single stores for restocking. It was not set up to ship single products to multiple addresses. So, in the 1999 holiday season, the number of orders overwhelmed the organization, and it failed to deliver children's toys on time for Christmas. The resulting damage proved devastating to the brand. Customers abandoned not only its online shopping service but its physical stores, too.

Similarly, Blockbuster failed to prioritize the importance of the internet in its business model. The leadership team remained focused on a brick-and-mortar approach that became irrelevant in the changing video-rental marketplace around them. Repeating the mistakes of organizations such as Kodak, Nokia, and Toys R Us, its leaders failed to see what was urgent and what needed to be prioritized. They stuck to their guns as everyone around them transformed to meet their changing customer needs.

Alignment of Projects and Programs with Strategies

If the executive team doesn't set priorities, middle management and employees will, based on what they think is best for the organization. At first, we might think that's a good practice. Empowering people to make decisions has been promoted since the times of Peter Drucker. Yet, without decision-makers following a prioritized set of strategic objectives, the consequences are often disastrous.

> *A well-communicated set of priorities aligns most of an organization's projects and programs with its strategies.*
>
> — Antonio Nieto Rodriguez and Robin Speculand

This alignment is often championed by business thinkers. But the reality of how an organization works is more complex than many suggest. Sometimes, the strategic objectives are not clear or don't even exist. A gap and lack of alignment often exists between the corporate strategic objectives and the ones from the different business units, departments, or functions.

To address the challenges of prioritization Antonio confronted over his executive career in several multinationals, he developed a simple tool he calls "Hierarchy of Purpose." Members of both the board of directors and executive team can use this tool to rank priorities and select strategic initiatives.

Hierarchy of Purpose

1.1 Purpose:

Vision and mission are often mixed up, and their differences misunderstood. Therefore, they are hardly ever used when strategic objectives are set. For clarity, it's best to use purpose instead—that is, state the purpose of your organization and the strategic vision supporting this purpose. The stated purpose has to be sharp and easily understood by everyone working in your organization. For example, Amazon's purpose—"to be earth's most customer-centric organization"—is so clear and compelling that it avoids ambiguity among people within the organization.

1.2 Priorities:

The number of priorities admitted to by an organization is revealing. If the risk appetite of the executives is low, then they tend to set a large number of priorities. They don't want to risk not having the latest technology, missing a market opportunity, and so forth. On the other hand, if the executives are risk takers, they tend to have a laser-like focus on a small number of priorities. They know what matters today and tomorrow. Therefore, it's best to define the priorities that matter most to your organization—now and in the future. Amazon's purpose clearly puts the customer in the center; everyone working there knows that. That means when making decisions, those most closely related to customers always come first.

1.3 Projects:

Strategic initiatives and projects, when successfully executed, bring the organization closer to its purpose and its strategic vision. These days, organizations have a large number of projects running in parallel, mostly because it is easier to start projects than to finish them. Very often capacity, not strategy, determines project launches. Therefore, if people are available, a project gets launched; if not, it is dismissed. Who wants to risk missing a big opportunity? But in which projects should organizations invest in and focus on? When executives employ the answers to the first two points of the Hierarchy of Purpose, they identify which strategic initiatives and projects align best with their purpose, vision, and priorities. It also helps them identify those that should be stopped or scrapped. Some theorists suggest developing formulas that automate the process of prioritizing and selecting ideas, but that's not recommended. The exercise is to provide management with different orientations and viewpoints; however, the ultimate decision has to be based on the human intelligence of the executives.

1.4 People:

Prioritizing at an organization level is incredibly difficult. Large organizations are made up of individuals who have their own strong sense of what matters. Every person in an organization has his or her own list of priorities. By their nature, the priorities are self-serving and informed as much by personal ambition and aspiration as any sense of alignment with the organization's strategy. Yet, employees are the ones implementing organization strategies as they perform day-to-day activities and deliver projects. They also have to make minor decisions and trade-offs every day. Creating clarity around priorities and the strategic projects of the organization will ensure that every employee works in the same direction. It is important to allocate the best resources to the most strategic projects and liberate certain employees from day-to-day operational tasks. Projects are delivered more successfully when they are run by a fully dedicated team and a strong, committed, proactive sponsor.

1.5 Performance:

Traditionally, performance indicators don't measure priorities and seldom indicate progress toward implementing an organization's strategy. Project metrics tend to measure inputs (scope, cost, time) instead of outputs because inputs are easier to track than outputs (benefits, impact, goals). You want to identify indicators linked to the organization's priorities and to the outcomes expected from the strategic projects. In this case, less is more, so stating one or two outputs for each area will do the job. It is better if people know by heart how performance is measured with outcome performance indicators embedded in their minds. Management should have the right information at hand to quickly react to market changes and supervise the pipeline of new priorities.

Think of your organization's purpose and priorities. Do all your employees work according to those priorities? Are the activities prioritized in the best interests of the organization as a whole? How would your priorities change in case of a sudden economic downturn?

Overall, prioritizing increases the success rates of the most strategic projects. It also increases the alignment and focus of senior management teams around strategies while creating a crucial implementation mindset and culture.

2. Shift in Leadership Style to Implement in a Digital World

At hyper speed, digitalization has gone from awareness among leaders to almost being a hygiene factor in the way organizations operate today.

Fueling the accelerated transformation was the recent pandemic, which forced businesses worldwide to rethink their operating model. For example, insurance organizations could no longer depend on agents visiting customers; universities could no longer bring students onto the campus; restaurants became dependent on takeaway meals.

> *The combination of the pandemic and the restructuring of business models to compete in the digital world has dramatically affected how implementations are led, resulting in fundamental shifts in the way leaders operate today.*
>
> – Antonio Nieto Rodriguez and Robin Speculand

To implement in a digital world requires a style that differs from the past. For example, leaders used to walk into meetings and tell attendees what they wanted done. Today, they go into a meeting to find out what's happening in their organization.

Why? *Crafting strategy is driven from the top down while implementation in a digital world is driven from the bottom up.*

Employees participate in activities such as hackathons, customer journey mapping, and design-thinking. To implement the outcomes of these activities, they are empowered and supported by incubators and accelerators. They no longer need to go around asking for signatures of approval or budget funds.

To support this new way of implementing, leaders need to:

2.1 Go Back to School

Implementing digitalization requires learning new skills that were unknown a few years ago. They need to go back to school to learn, for example, how to use machine learning or analyze data or understand agile.

As Satya Nadella, CEO of Microsoft, explains it, "Leaders need a learning mindset to move from 'Know it all' to 'learn it all.' They have to challenge the current way their business operates and be open to new ways of implementing their strategies."

2.2 Encourage Failure

A crucial step in innovation is recognizing we have to fail before we can succeed. We have shifted from aiming to create a perfect product to a minimum viable product (MVP). Leaders are responsible for creating an environment that supports failure and encourages employees to raise their hands when they don't know something—and then experiment. Harvard

Business School professor Amy Edmondson calls this "psychological safety." It refers to the organization successfully creating an environment in which people know they will not be punished or humiliated for asking questions, experimenting, or failing.

The trend is for executives to move from controlling everything to empowering and encouraging employees to try new solutions.

2.3 Put Customer Obsession at the Heart of Everything

Over the last few years, we have moved from *customer service* to *customer experience* to *customer obsession*. The approach to digitalization provided an impetus as well as new tools to support this journey. Design-thinking, for example, leverages new approaches and technologies to create improved customer experiences. Employees are spending time identifying and fixing customer pain points and "the job to be done." As well, they are participating in hackathons to create new technology solutions that will improve the customer experience.

Leaders are encouraged to move their organizations from an "inside out" to an "outside in" approach. This means instead of looking internally, every decision starts and ends with what is best for their customers, based on what they need and want and the data that supports those decisions.

2.4 Leverage Data to Make Better Decisions

An organization needs to be driven by its data in order to make better decisions. In today's most successful organizations, data analysis has become as common as the air we breathe. For large organizations to become data driven can take up to three years as they clean up old data, transform the mindset of how employees work, and incorporate the use of data into day-to-day decisions.

Leaders have to ensure that their decisions are supported by the data. When they are not, leaders have been known to walk out of a meeting while stating the importance of data-driven decision-making.

2.5 Minimize Bureaucracy

Bureaucracy can sabotage the whole organization's transformation to competing in a digital world. Why? Because organizations need to operate faster in both decision-making and the way they operate. That means eliminating time-wasting meetings, reducing levels of bureaucracy, and speeding up decision-making.

2.6 Hold People Accountable

Holding people accountable for taking the right actions to implement the strategy is significantly underutilized in organizations. In the past, they depended on annual employee reviews, which are rapidly becoming obsolete. To support this acceleration, leaders have to check in with their employees more frequently. For example, managers would ask their subordinates how they are performing *every two weeks*.

This reflects a trend toward check-ins—that is, instead of looking at past performance during an annual performance review, check-ins support employees by praising them for work done recently. They also identify where employees need support and offer assistance removing roadblocks and challenges.

Although none of the six transformation steps required for leaders are rocket science, they do take discipline and adopting them takes discipline—and the disciple is often missing. As Warren Buffet said, "The chains of habits are too light to be felt until they are too heavy to be broken."

3. Leverage AI in Implementation

For some years, project management reports have said that Artificial Intelligence (AI) could disrupt the project management profession. A lot has been written about the threats and opportunities AI could bring for the profession and project results—and therefore for strategy implementation success.

According to Gartner Inc, by 2030, 80 percent of the work of today's project management discipline will be eliminated as AI takes on traditional PM functions such as data collection, tracking, and reporting.

AI will improve the outcomes of these tasks, including the ability to analyze data faster than humans and using those results to improve overall performance.

Taking a look at the current AI adoption in "The State of AI in 2020" report from McKinsey[1], half of the respondents to the survey said their organizations have adapted AI in at least one function. By industry, respondents in the high-tech and telecom sectors are the ones who report more AI adoption, followed by the automotive and the assembly sector. From a business functions perspective, they have taken the top spots of product or service development, service operations, and marketing and sales.

Regarding the use of AI in the projects, the use cases provided in a recent survey conducted were mainly related to the use of chatbots for getting information about project status and notifications sending.

Based on the data exposed above, we can identify two main areas where AI can make a bigger impact in the implementation. They are:

- Automation
- Prediction

Identifying in the automation area functions like:

- Reporting
- Tracking

- Reminders to the team
- Notifications

And in the prediction area, forecasts about:

- Risks
- Resources
- Timelines
- Budget

Let's review use cases currently available in some AI-based products:

Stratejos (https://stratejos.ai/): It provides assistance for teams using Slack with 85+ micro-jobs across Jira, Github, Trello, and more, with the goal of saving time. Stratejos:

- Gets context and actions in Slack when mentioning a JIRA issue
- Handles daily status updates and follow-ups
- Updates JIRA issues from Slack

Riter (https://riter.co/): Its main functions aim to automate sprints planning by distributing them in an optimal way with the data gathered.

Clickup (https://app.clickup.com/): A tool with easy-to-set automations to make jobs more pleasant and efficient, Clickup:

- Sends prompts and reminders to the team
- Does automatic budgeting
- Delivers pre-process schedules

Leaders need to be aware that AI that supports the implementation process is already a reality. The number of products and AI solutions available will increase dramatically in the coming years.

> *Based on their current and future business needs and the capabilities that AI will offer, leaders need to define their organization's strategy regarding AI adoption.*
>
> – Antonio Nieto Rodriguez and Robin Speculand

Based on "The State of AI and ML 2020" by Appen,[2] nearly three quarters of businesses consider AI critical to their success. However, nearly half of the respondents believe their organization is behind in their AI journey. This suggests a critical gap exists between the strategic need and the ability to execute.

To close this gap, it is suggested to use the Strategy Implementation Road Map (SIR) from the Strategy Implementation Institute. It addresses these seven components to be worked on so leaders succeed in strategy implementation:

1. Leadership Excellence
2. Financial Value
3. Business Model Redesign
4. Culture Evolving
5. Stakeholder Management
6. Employee Engagement
7. Track Performance

Adopting AI will save time, thanks to the automation of activities. It will also allow leaders to have better estimates and predictions about project needs and results. This means additional time is available for investing in key components such as Leadership Excellence, Business Model Redesign, Culture Evolving, and Stakeholder and Employee Engagement. These should help increase the success rate of strategy implementation, which is currently quite low.

4. Increasing Importance of Middle Managers in Strategy Implementation

The need for middle managers to be explicitly involved and accountable for strategy implementation is an ongoing trend with no end in sight. The future is already here!

Top-level organizational strategies that are developed and not aligned down through the organization, including multiple business lines and departments, are just that, a top-level organization strategy. Buy-in and support for the top-level strategy will not exist unless embedded at all levels. Middle managers provide the support, coaching, and facilitation of their direct reports by fostering the discipline to implement and execute the strategy. Once all organization levels take ownership for their share of the top-level strategy at their respective organization levels and assign accountability for strategy implementation, at that stage, the organization should be able to realize a fully aligned organization-wide strategy implementation.

> *Middle managers have a multi-faceted role to play.*

According to Clifton and Harter, today's managers are facilitators or coaches for their employees. The managers are coordinators or orchestrators, speak with authority while still being open to employees' input, and set transparent systems of accountability in a world where work time and space are flexible and blended work and life. Today, successful managers are more analytical decision-makers. They are decidedly more future-focused and systems-oriented, naturally intrigued by possibilities and new ideas, and more objective and empirically grounded problem solvers and consumers of data.[3]

Maister states that middle management listens, values input, is trusted, is a good coach, communicates well, practices what they preach, and treats other unit members equally. Also, Maister's research was among the top factors in predicting a business's profitability; a clear outcome of strategy implementation is trust and respect at the middle management level. Further research has shown that where trust and respect between management and employees are high, financial performance predictably goes up. That management success is less a property of firms (the business's systems as a whole) but is mainly about the individual manager's personality within the operating unit. Success is about personalities, not policies.[4]

Sull et al. propose that in large, complex organizations, execution lives and dies with a group we call "distributed leaders," including middle managers who run critical businesses and functions and technical and domain experts who occupy crucial spots in the informal networks that get things done. Distributed leaders, not senior executives, represent "management" to most employees, partners, and customers. Their day-to-day actions, mainly how they handle difficult decisions and what behaviors they tolerate, go a long way toward supporting or undermining the corporate culture depending on the leader's quality, ethics, and values.[5]

Organizations need to initiate a top-level strategy alignment process, thereby making strategy actionable to everyone by cascading the high-level enterprise strategy to business and support units and individual employees. In the alignment process, middle managers need training in strategy management fundamentals. This training will raise the manager's line of sight above the usual operational plan they typically work under each year.

Simultaneously, the top-level strategy and implementation need to become centralized into a Strategy Management Office (SMO). The SMO will support the entire organization by managing all aspects of the top-level strategic plan and incorporating monitoring and evaluation of the departmental middle manager's strategy and the top-level strategy. The middle manager's departmental, employee, and team strategies will soon realize that they are the front line of its top-level strategy. Their objectives are now explicitly linked to the top-level strategic objectives.

Middle Managers and the Future of Strategy Implementation

Middle managers and their effect on strategy implementation need to be guided by their leadership capabilities, work experiences, and the organization's needs from the manager and their respective teams. There are four attributes that middle managers need to implement for successful strategy implementation: staying tough, working smart, maintaining a united stance with the team and with other team leaders, and always acting in a disciplined manner when implementing the strategy.

Maintaining a tough professional approach can cover striving for the best work from everyone on the team, keeping schedules, managing the team members' expectations, and striving for the organization's best outcomes while collaborating with the SMO and other departments' middle managers.

A middle manager in a strategy implementation position must work hard but smart and understand that strategy always does not perform as designed. The COVID-19 pandemic implications are an excellent example of how middle managers had to adapt, improvise, and overcome conditions never before encountered in the past to continue the organization's strategy implementation.

The middle manager needs to maintain a united position for strategy implementation at all times. A united intra-departmental and inter-departmental position with other strategy implementation middle managers are required to carry out a strategy for the common good of the organization. Strategy implementation is not for some departments or units and not for others, and not just for some team members and not for others. Middle managers need to constantly communicate outcomes, propose team-developed interventions to fix problems, and give recognition where recognition is due.

Once the top-level strategy alignment completes down to departments, teams, and individuals, the middle manager must establish a disciplined approach to monitoring and evaluation. Monitoring entails taking accountability for a regular cadence of monitoring the strategy's strategic objectives' performance through key performance indicators, project milestone attainment, and if the project is on budget at those milestones. The middle manager evaluates the strategy's performance from two perspectives at least four times per calendar year: (1) Strategic Effectiveness and (2) System Effectiveness.

The strategy implementation middle managers' work never ends since the strategy implementation needs constant attention, so middle managers are essential.

5. Purpose-Driven Strategy Implementation

Consider the following: a leadership team comes together to formulate strategy including the organization's mission (purpose) and vision (desired future state). Then, armed with specific intentions, leadership directs units and teams to implement initiatives and programs they have chosen. All too often in these circumstances, middle managers and their teams do not understand the real value behind what they are being asked to do. When this occurs, momentum is lost, and failure is likely.

Does this sound familiar? If it does, that is because:

> *Strategy implementation often fails due to non-alignment and ineffective communication caused by a lack of common purpose from those involved in the effort.*
>
> – Antonio Nieto Rodriguez and Robin Speculand

Two significant steps are required to correct this. First, demonstrate how employing a purpose-driven strategy implementation program increases your organization's chances of a successful implementation effort and, second, explain what that entails. Successful strategy implementation in today's uncertain socioeconomic environment requires leaders to engage and align everyone in the business, at all levels, around a shared purpose. Focusing on profitability of the business alone in today's world is not enough.

According to Gary Harpst, founder of Six Disciplines, "A purpose-driven leader helps others discover the meaning that is inherent in the work they are doing today and reinforces the value of who they are and what they are contributing to the benefit of others."[6]

The importance of a purpose-driven strategy implementation is the focus of a 2019 *Harvard Business Review* article entitled "Put Purpose at the Core of Your Strategy" by Malnight, Buche, and Dhanaraj.[7] The most important point the authors make in the article is that the organization must include purpose in everything the organization does at every level, top-down and bottom-up.

The importance of purpose in strategy was also cited in a 2019 Oxford Said Business School study. The Oxford study reached a similar conclusion that, as the *Harvard Business Review* article, to move from "ambition to action" an effective purpose should be relevant to what the organization does AND encompass all the diverse roles and responsibilities in the business/organization.

Finally, the importance of purpose in strategy implementation was the focus on an April 5, 2021, McKinsey article entitled "Help Your Employees Find Purpose—or Watch Them Leave." Their findings point out, "People who live their purpose at work are more productive than people who do not. They are healthier, more resilient, and more likely to stay at the organization. Moreover, when employees feel their purpose is aligned with the organization's purpose, the benefits expand to include stronger employee engagement, heightened loyalty, and a greater willingness to recommend the organization to others."[8]

Meaning of Purpose

Purpose is like a North Star illuminating the fact that while the "means" may evolve, the "end" will remain constant. As Bob Patton, EY's Americas Vice Chair of Strategy, put it, "Purpose must resonate at every level, from the C-suite to business units to teams to the individual worker. When it's brought to life at the individual level—when each employee can find meaning in their work and see how it contributes to the organization's purpose—that's when you see purpose get real."[9]

To be successful in today's disruptive environment, organizations need to deliberately implement their organization's strategy, products, and services in ways that make someone's life better. In so doing, they give employees a heightened sense of purpose to their own lives. This is the essence of a purpose-driven organization and a purpose-driven strategy implementation.

Consider the case of the Finnish oil-refining organization Neste. Neste was facing setbacks—a sharp fall in oil prices, market overcapacity, falling margins, and new carbon-emission legislation across the EU. In response, the Neste board and leadership team embraced a new mission (i.e., purpose) centered on protecting the environment by moving toward renewable fuels.

To begin their strategic transformation journey, Neste examined its historical roots, current situation, and ambition to become a leader in sustainability. The new strategy was deployed by launching value creation programs to operationalize "purpose-driven" action plans. The programs would also actively promote culture change by encouraging new behaviors and ways of working, and by launching customer-focused projects.

At the heart of Neste's work was a focused effort to motivate its employees to get on board with renewable fuels. At the same time, it carefully observed the impact that this shift in corporate culture delivered. After examining what the changes had wrought, organization leaders addressed issues that needed to be tackled differently. The result? Over a span of three years, Neste's renewable fuels business went from a €163 million loss in 2011 to a €56 million loss in 2012, before shooting up to a €273 million profit in 2013. By 2017, profits were €561 million. Today, renewables account for more than 70 percent of Neste's profits.[10]

Ideas for Implementing a Purpose-Driven Strategy

To implement a purpose-driven strategy, leaders and organizations must:

- Define a compelling purpose that captures the hearts and minds of their employees and key stakeholders.
- Transform their leadership agenda to focus on implementation driven by purpose, team alignment, effective communication, and effective engagement, and by rewarding efforts that demonstrate purpose.
- Invest the resources required for their team to establish competencies and OKRs (Objectives and Key Results), when and where appropriate. These are based on goals and objectives aligned with the organization purpose. (This adds to other implementation activities such as cutting back on unnecessary work, carefully prioritizing initiatives, tracking performance, and maintaining agility.)

All leaders and managers are obligated to the organization and to each other to deliver positive results. Unfortunately, too often a gap between strategy and implementation occurs for those charged with implementing the approved strategy directives. In today's disrupted environment in which agility in implementation is vital, this "strategy implementation gap" can be a fatal error. It could lead to unwanted (and worse, unexpected) costs, increased risk, lost opportunities, and ultimately failure to execute.

When an implementation failure occurs, the losses are significant for the organization, its employees, and those who depend on them. Ultimately, the customer is affected, too. To mitigate this painful gap, organizations, small teams, and individuals are best served when they drive strategy implementation by focusing on their organization's purpose.

6. Culture of Flexibility

In 2013, PwC found that 51 percent out of more than 2,000 employees surveyed in 50 countries said that their workplace culture must evolve in the next five years for their organization to succeed, grow, and retain the best people. In a 2018 survey, the percentage rose to 80 percent.[11] Moreover, a clear misalignment between culture and strategies emerged.

The main trends responsible for this are:

> *Much shorter strategy life cycle and rapid changes required by the digital transformation, fast-changing competitive landscape, and changes resulting from the pandemic—remote and hybrid working affecting how individuals learn, perform, and interact with each other.*
>
> — Antonio Nieto Rodriguez and Robin Speculand

Research undertaken in 2020 by Gartner revealed that 74 percent of organizations plan to permanently shift office workers to remote working once the coronavirus pandemic is over.[12] Moreover, research by Future Forum in 2020 has found that hybrid working is the "office of the future." In this environment, organization headquarters are digital, not physical, and digital tools enable greater engagement and collaboration in comparison to traditional office work.[13] Therefore, if organizations do not adapt their culture to become flexible, they risk losing talent.

Consequently, all the processes are accelerating, implementation strategy included. The uncertainty on what to do and how to do it is also growing. Leaders must review their organization's culture to ensure it aligns with the current flexible working environment. Failure to do so may result in strategic drift or misalignment (Johnson et al., 2008).

Research on Organization Culture

Schein (1997) defines organization culture as composed of four main elements: values, beliefs, behaviors, and the paradigm (defined as taken-for-granted assumptions).

Johnson (et al., 2008) explains that the taken-for-granted nature of a culture is what makes it centrally important to strategy and implementation, to the extent that culture is an unintended driver of strategy.

Stacey (2007) suggests that organizations are complex. Individuals are constantly interacting with each other within communicative interactions where power relations emerge, with different people having different values, motives, ideas, and intentions. These communicative interactions form part of an organization's culture and help shape it.

De Wit and Meyer (2010) advocate that organizations align their culture with the structure, processes, business model, and members of the organization as well as being able to simultaneously respond to changes in the macro-environment. It is a paradox that needs careful planning and management.

Focus on the Cultural Side

Strategies are a complex matter (Stacey, 1996; Appelo, 2008) due to a lack, or redundancy, of information, opinions, possible scenarios, business approaches among decision-makers, and the overlapping of all these elements. While organization culture is mostly unspoken and unwritten, it refers to and is affected by assumptions, beliefs, habits, routines, symbols, the environment, and even the kind of product/service provided. Employees as well as leaders might operate with a scarce, if not absent, awareness about their interpretations of all these elements. If asked about them, they give answers that are uncertain, inconsistent, or even contradictory.

The main issue is that when strategy and culture are misaligned, usually the implementation is a struggle and strategic plans might fail. How do we address this problem? Instead of designing new strategies, we propose focusing on the cultural side—that is, to make the organization culture less chaotic, more agile, and consequently better equipped to support the strategy implementation.

We also need to define a new cultural paradigm. In it, cultural discrepancies, inconsistencies, and clashing approaches unconsciously born by employees are assessed as we work toward a conscious, transparent cultural realignment. In doing so, we nudge the idea that the main goal of the renewed culture is to support the strategy implementation within a new reality in which remote and flexible work is becoming the main priority.[14]

Example of a Flexible Culture

We have selected the Bain & Organization case[15] as a good example of an organization that has created a flexible culture. The organization's philosophy is centered around collaborating, having fun, working hard, and fully supporting its employees. For example, its slogan is "a Bain never lets another Bain fail."

Bain & Organization advocates the following five best practices to develop a flexible culture.[16]

1. Ensure flexibility is flexible.
2. Link flexibility to strategy and the customer.
3. Model flexibility.
4. Encourage and enable team flexibility.
5. Support individuals to work flexibly.

Actions for Leaders to Promote Flexibility

To make the organization culture more flexible and adopt a cultural paradigm to provide resources, support, and consistency to an organization's strategic planning and implementation, consider these suggestions.[17]

1. Involve the leadership in all phases of the cultural transformation and strategy implementation.[18]

2. Engage employees by their talents more than formal roles, to count on all the skills and knowledge available.[19]

3. Be aware that flexible and remote work will not suit everyone.

4. Embrace a non-blaming approach for those who highlight issues and provide value-adding incentives for those who adjust their behaviors.

5. Adopt a research-based approach to assess the "current" state of cultural chaos present at your organization by identifying subcultures and differences in values interpretation and behaviors.[20]

6. Ask people what they would like changed. This will help in mapping the "desired" organization culture.

7. Set a new clear organization's vision, or reinforce the current one around the importance of adopting a flexible culture able to support strategy implementation.[21]

8. Create flexible working policies that support the desired culture.[22]

9. Devote special attention to helping middle managers who might be particularly under pressure because of their need to support the front-line staff while learning how to navigate the new situation themselves.

10. Design an evaluation plan to tell you if and how your staff members are working on their cultural aspects while following the principles of the desired culture. It is important to constantly observe how well the strategy implementation is supported by the new cultural framework and if any adjustment is needed.[23]

Difficulties for Public Sector Organizations

In our view, private organizations may have the capability and freedom to transform their culture and support the strategy implementation. However, this may not be possible for some public sector organizations where strategy is "imposed" (Mintzburg et al., 2008) and culture might be chaotic—that is, policies are dictated, and they work within the confines of the central government.

From a complexity science perspective, this could be described as a "wicked" problem for public sector organizations. Immediate solutions are not available due to the complex and interconnected nature of the problem. For instance, there is limited control over those processes that could help transform the culture from chaotic to flexible (agile). There are also conflicting interpretations about the best ways to support the strategy implementation.

References

1. "Analytics Insights," McKinsey, accessed March 28, 2022, https://www.mckinsey.com/business-functions/mckinsey-analytics/our-insights/global-survey-the-state-of-ai-in-2020#

2. "The State of AI and Machine Learning," Appen Whitepaper, accessed March 28, 2022, https://resources.appen.com/wp-content/uploads/2020/06/Whitepaper-State-of-Ai-2020-Final.pdf

3. Clifton, Jim; Harter, Jim. (2019). It's the Manager: Gallup finds the quality of managers and team leaders is the single most significant factor in your organization's long-term success. Gallup Press.

4. Maister, David H. (2001). Practice What You Preach: What Managers Must Do To Create A High Achievement Culture.

5. Sull, Donald; Homkes, Rebecca; Sull, Charles. (March 2015). Why Strategy Execution Unravels - and What to Do About It. *Harvard Business Review*.

6. Why & How to Build a Purpose-Driven Organization, Gary Harpst, Six Disciplines. https://sixdisciplines.com/wp-content/uploads/2019/08/Six-Disciplines-for-Building-a-Purpose-driven-Organization.pdf

7. 2019 HBR article entitled "Put Purpose at the Core of Your Strategy" by Malnight, Buche and Dhanaraj https://hbr.org/2019/09/put-purpose-at-the-core-of-your-strategy

8. 2021 McKinsey article entitled "Help Your Employees Find Purpose or Watch Them Leave" by Dhingra, Samo, Schaninger and Schrimper https://www.mckinsey.com/business-functions/people-and-organizational-performance/our-insights/help-your-employees-find-purpose-or-watch-them-leave

9. "Ten Ways Leading Companies Turn Purpose into Strategy," Ernst & Young, September 19, 2019, www.ey.com/en_qa/purpose/ten-ways-leading-companies-turn-purpose-into-strategy

10. 2019 HBR article entitled "Put Purpose at the Core of Your Strategy" by Malnight, Buche and Dhanaraj

11. "Where Organizational Culture Is Headed," Strategy&, accessed March 28, 2022, www.strategyand.pwc.com/gx/en/insights/2018/global-culture-survey.html

12. www.gartner.com/en/newsroom/press-releases/2020-04-03-gartner-cfo-surey-reveals-74-percent-of-organizations-to-shift-some-employees-to-remote-work-permanently2

13. Brian Elliott, "The Hybrid Office of the Future," Future Forum, January 8, 2021, https://futureforum.com/2021/01/08/the-hybrid-office-of-the-future

14. www.weforum.org/agenda/2020/08/flexible-remote-working-post-covid19-company-predictions/ and www.pwc.com/us/en/industries/financial-services/library/balancing-remote-and-in-office-work.html

15. "What Makes Bain Different: An Inside Look at the 'Bainie' Culture," Casecoach, accessed March 28, 2022, https://casecoach.com/b/what-makes-bain-different-an-inside-look-at-the-bainie-culture

16. https://www.bain.com/insights/flex-for-success-five-practices-that-build-a-flexible-workforce

17. Working on culture needs time, and even if ready-to-go suggestions might be made, we prefer to share principles to follow while crafting your way throughout the cultural transformation you want for your organization.

18. More about leaders' role and actions here: William Craig, "10 Ways Leaders Influence Organizational Culture," Forbes, October 9, 2018, www.forbes.com/sites/williamcraig/2018/10/09/10-ways-leaders-influence-organizational-culture/?sh=5f07262456b4

19. Emma Stewart, "Why the Post-COVID Workplace Must Be Inclusive and Flexible," CBI, November 24, 2020, www.cbi.org.uk/articles/why-the-post-covid-workplace-must-be-inclusive-and-flexible

20. A way to do so is to use any tool that your organization is already familiar with, i.e., the PESTEL analysis (https://www.business-to-you.com/scanning-the-environment-pestel-analysis/), the McKinsey's 7-S framework (https://www.mckinsey.com/business-functions/strategy-and-corporate-finance/our-insights/

enduring-ideas-the-7-s-framework), or the SWOT analysis(https://www.business-to-you.com/swot-analysis/) and look for the different beliefs and interpretations of each key aspect of your business.

21. Matthew Corritore, Amir Goldberg, and Sameer B. Srivastava, "The New Analytics of Culture," HBR, January-February 2020, https://hbr.org/2020/01/the-new-analytics-of-culture#

22. For instance, the Bath People and Performance model (Purcell et al., 2003) advocate that performance outcomes can be increased if HR policies and management provide individuals with "ability, motivation and opportunity." Talking about hybrid work and organizational culture, individuals need the right skills (ability to adapt to the "new normal"), feel motivated and committed (motivation to actively participate in the cultural transformation), and utilize their skills to deliver organizational goals (opportunity).

23. Storytelling (www.convinceandconvert.com/digital-marketing/storytelling/), scorecards (https://hbr.org/1992/01/the-balanced-scorecard-measures-that-drive-performance-2) and cognitive maps (Spicer, 2011) can help.

Additional References

Appelo J., August 20, 2008, blogpost: Simple vs. Complicated vs. Complex vs. Chaotic, https://noop.nl/2008/08/simple-vs-complicated-vs-complex-vs-chaotic.html

Buchanan D. and Huczynski A., 2017, Organizational Behaviour. Ninth Edition, Pearson Education Limited: Harlow.

De Wit B. and Meyer R., 2010, Strategy: An International Perspective. Fourth Edition, Cengage Learning EMEA.

Johnson G., Scholes K. and Whittington R., 2008, Exploring Corporate Strategy: Text and Cases. Eighth Edition, Pearson Education Limited: Harlow.

Mintzburg H., Ahlstrand B. and Lampel. J., 2008, *Strategy Safari: The complete guide through the wilds of strategic management. Second Edition.* Pearson Education Limited: Harlow.

Mowles C., 2015, *Managing In Uncertainty: Complexity and the paradoxes of everyday organizational life,* Routledge: London.

Purcell, J., Kinnie, N., Hutchinson, S., Rayton, B. and Stuart, J., 2003, *Understanding the People and Performance Link: Unlocking the Black Box.* London: Chartered Institute of Personnel and Development.

Schein E., 1997, *Organisation Culture and Leadership. Second Edition,* Jossey-Bass.

Spicer D.P., 2011, Changing Culture: A Case Study of a Merger Using Cognitive Mapping, *Journal of Change Management,* 11:2, 245–264.

Stacey R., 1996, Management and the Science of Complexity: If Organizational Life Is Nonlinear, Can Business Strategies Prevail?, *Research technology management,* Vol.39 (3), p.8–10.

Stacey, R., 2007, *Strategic Management & Organizational Dynamics: The Challenge of Complexity.* Fifth Edition. Pearson Education Limited: Harlow.

DBS Bank Case Study

Only one in three digital transformations succeed. Various research[1] reveals that over 70% up digital transformations fail!

When did one of the top ten digital transformation successes of the last decade according to Harvard is DBS Bank.

Under the stewardship of Piyush Gupta, it has been recognized as the world's best bank for four consecutive years. It is also the first bank in the world to win the top three most prestigious banking awards simultaneously.

In 2014 the senior leaders of DBS met in Phuket, Thailand, to discuss their new strategy. The leaders reflected that at the time nobody woke up in the morning wanting to do banking. The question the leaders addressed was not "what does the bank want to do?" but "how do we make dealing with DBS easy, fun, convenient, and meaningful?" The leadership team migrated toward making banking the opposite of painful—that was, to "Making Banking Joyful." This became the internal name for the strategy.

Due to the emergence of numerous technologies, the means for Making Banking Joyful was rapidly evolving, and the bank's leaders recognized that, by leveraging these new technologies, they could make banking "invisible" to their customers. That would, in turn, create opportunities for customers to have enjoyable interactions when dealing with the bank and, ultimately, to experience a sense of happiness and peace of mind throughout their banking journey.

To implement Making Banking Joyful, the bank had three strategic principles:

1. Become Digital to the Core
2. Embed Ourselves in the Customer Journey
3. Culture by Design and Think Like a Start-Up

1. Become Digital to the Core

It is key to transform your technology approach to create the core platform for the digital transformation. Becoming "digital to the core" means that core platforms, legacy systems, networks, and data centers all need to be redesigned.

Its challenges included transforming from outsourcing to insourcing, becoming cloud native, and improving the cadence of development.

The bank visited leading tech companies such as Google and Amazon to identify how digital native organizations operated. To change the way the bank framed the digital transformation and to think like a tech company, the bank considered how Amazon CEO Jeff Bezos ran his company. This knowledge then led to adopting the question across the bank, "What would Jeff do?" It meant employees would shift from thinking like bankers—thus turning to banking approaches as solutions—to thinking like a tech company that creates digital-driven solutions, as Amazon does.

A catchphrase alone, however, is not enough. To support employees in adopting digitally driven solutions, the technology across the bank needed to create a rock-solid foundation of core systems. The bank also came up with an acronym that captured the technology transformation—GANDALF. GANDALF is the wizard in *The Hobbit* and *The Lord of the Rings* novels by J. R. R. Tolkien.

In this acronym:

> **G** is for Google—using open-source software like Google.
>
> **A** is for Amazon—running on Amazon's cloud platforms.
>
> **N** is for Netflix—using data and automation to scale and provide personalized recommendations as Netflix does.
>
> **A** is for Apple—designing systems as Apple does.
>
> **L** is for LinkedIn—pushing for continuous learning.
>
> **F** is for Facebook—becoming more community focused.

What about the **D**? The bank, DBS, would be the D in GANDALF—the digital and data bank of Singapore.

Success came from benchmarking against the world's best.

The bank also moved from designing for ops, to designing for no ops, to designing for AI ops.

2. Embed Ourselves in the Customer Journey

DBS focused on embedding itself in the customer's journey. The goal was no longer about the product or service but about being customer obsessed—to make banking invisible by leveraging technology and adopting customer journey thinking throughout the organization. This approach drove every employee toward becoming customer obsessed.

Its challenges included delivering a delightful, hassle-free customer experience, having the highest customer satisfaction scores in the banking world, and building ecosystems to enhance customer journeys.

DBS leaders became even more customer obsessed by constantly asking, "Is this change making banking joyful for our customers?" From that core question, they adopted design-thinking and solutions based on their *customers'* perspective.

This also drove the shift from cross selling to cross buying.

Design-thinking, called "4Ds" in DBS's terminology, guided employees to know what needed to be done. The bank designed solutions that improved the "jobs to be done." The *overall* job to be done in the Digital Wave was Making Banking Joyful, which involved stepping back from the day-to-day business to identify the customer journey and continuously improve upon it.

Today, the bank continues to enhance customer journeys by developing APIs as part of its ecosystem strategy while continuing to collaborate with ecosystem partners.

3. Culture by Design and Think Like a Start-Up

DBS Bank's key challenges are to continue to transform the culture, continually experiment, and innovate and create the happiest workforce in the industry.

A question DBS's leadership asked early in the bank's digital transformation was: "What is the biggest roadblock to adopting a start-up culture?" It turned out that it was the way meetings were conducted, a scourge common to many large, complex organizations. There were too many meetings, and too many of them were ineffective or had no stated purpose.

Enter "MOJO," short for Meeting Owner Joyful Observer, a campaign to do away with meetings that went nowhere. It had a simple rule: Meetings must start and finish on time and have a fixed agenda. MOJO produced serious benefits, saving the bank more than 500,000 employee hours.

In DBS, the bank wanted to imitate the culture of a start-up organization. To develop its culture, the leadership team critically defined five characteristics, captured under the acronym ABCDE, which have been thoroughly woven into their DNA. They are:

Agile—Teams in traditional organizations often move slowly, operate bureaucratically, lose sight of customer needs, and require too many meetings and layers of approvals. The agile methodology counters these challenges.

Be a learning organization—Building a growth mindset among its employees is critical so they could continuously learn, grow, and adapt. This belief translated into continual innovation, growth, and resilience across the organization while building individual career resilience.

Customer obsessed—Being customer obsessed is not simply a slogan at DBS bank; it's embedded into its DNA. Everyday operations and efforts to resolve challenges start by thinking about the "job to be done" for the customer and employs customer journeys to find new solutions.

Data driven—The bank identified how it could use data to scale in the digital experience and how to leverage data to improve the number and frequency of "wow" reactions from customers, the same way technology organizations do. The organization's overriding theme in transforming to a data-driven culture has been to maximize value using data for the customer, for determining risk (both credit and operational), and for revenue.

Experiment and take risks—In traditional banking, the idea is to mitigate risk. But as part of DBS's transformation and any digital transformation, its leaders wanted to encourage risk—to behave like a start-up and be open to experimentation. Employees who typically want to protect their jobs and their bonuses have learned to play safe—the opposite of what was required for DBS to transform to a digitally driven organization.

References

1. Michael Bucy, Adrian Finlayson, Greg Kelly, and Chris Moye, "The 'How' of Transformation," McKinsey, May 9, 2016, https://www.mckinsey.com/industries/retail/our-insights/the-how-of-transformation# and https://enterprisersproject.com/article/2019/8/why-digital-transformations-fail-3-reasons

External Papers

- The Five Essential Roles of Corporate Ecosystems, INSEAD
- The End of Strategy in Business Ecosystems? IMD
- How Covid 19 Has Pushed Companies over the Technology Tipping Point, McKinsey
- How to Make Big, Old Companies Act Fast, Strategy & Business
- Closing the Agile Achievement Gap, Strategy & Business

Video Links

- What Is Meant by Healthy Disengagement? by Rita McGrath

IMPLEMENTATION QUIZ QUESTIONS

1. The adoption of a new strategy means changing the way the organization operates. This is critical for an organization because?

   A   The strategic landscape is changing more rapidly than ever before

   B   New technologies are creating significant new opportunities

   C   Strategy implementation is happening more and more frequently

   D   All of the above

2. The "Strategic Inflection Point" is when an organization needs to fundamentally change. The best time to do this in the cycle is when?

   A   The organization is in Phase One, which is start-up mode

   B   The organization is in Phase Two, which is when all the indicators are positive

   C   The organization is in Phase Three, which is when all the indicators are negative

   D   The organization has a new CEO

3. Digital execution is showing to be more challenging than traditional strategy execution. A key reason for this is?

   A   Leaders were better equipped to manage traditional strategy execution

   B   Digital execution is predominantly about technology transformation

   C   Digital execution involves both emerging technologies and transforming the organization

   D   None of the above

4. To succeed in digital execution, leaders need to create an environment that allows employees to try, fail, and learn. Leaders need to recognize that?

   A   They need to maintain a tight control over employee actions

   B   Mistakes should be punished, as they can be costly

   C   To innovate you have to experiment, and to experiment you have to fail

   D   They need to maintain a tight control over the culture

5. In implementation, it's important to eliminate non-value-adding work to create space for employees to take the right actions. In a large organization, an estimated what percentage of work is non-value-adding?

   A   25%

   B   33%

   C   50%

   D   67%

6. Some digital executions struggle because they do not have a digital vision. Establishing a digital vision ensures within the organization that?

   A   There is alignment across all departments

   B   There is control from the top of the organization downward

   C   The transformation can be managed gradually and systematically

   D   None of the above

7. Some organizations establish project-driven business model. The main challenge of building a project-driven organization business model is?

   A   Struggling to shift away from the legacy and inertia of an existing model

   B   Difficulty in creating enough projects

   C   Shifting away from the legacy and inertia of the existing model of providing allocation in the annual budget

   D   None of the above

8. A goal of the renewed culture can be to support the strategy implementation within a new reality in which remote and flexible work is becoming the main priority. To develop a flexible culture, organizations should?

   A   Link flexibility to the customer requirements

   B   Reinforce hierarchical management

   C   Introduce more standard operating procedures

   D   All of the above

9. Projects are timeless and universal. A project canvas can be used to?

   A   Create visual images of the people involved

   B   View the different steps involved in the process

   C   Define a project and identify whether it is worth starting

   D   All of the above

10. Leaders need to reflect on their leadership style to implement strategy in the digital world. Part of this includes creating more?

   A   Procedures

   B   Meetings

   C   Policies

   D   Data

Answers to the quiz questions can be found on page 314 in the Appendix.

CHAPTER 5

Culture Evolution

STRATEGY
IMPLEMENTATION
INSTITUTE

Culture drives the way an organization implements its strategy. Two organizations can have the same strategy, but how they implement it will always be different, as every organization's culture is different.

Culture no longer always *eats strategy for breakfast* because of the speed at which we are working today. Strategy can now drive the culture in many organizations, which in turn drives the way they implement.

Figure 13.0: Strategy Implementation Road Map©

This section addresses:

- How culture drives strategy
- Ensuring culture is an implementation enabler
- How to develop a culture of accountability and why this is critical for implementation
- Understand why and how culture life cycles are changing

CRAFTING

Introduction

Culture is important in strategy because it drives the way an organization implements the strategy. Two organizations can have the same strategy, but how they implement it is driven by their culture. And as every organization's culture is different, it means every implementation is unique.

- Leaders' Role in Culture
- Understanding Your Organization's Culture
- Importance of Culture in Implementation

Leaders' Role in Culture	
Goal	An organization's culture needs to change to support the implementation. The responsibility for ensuring this lies with the leadership team.
Implementation Challenge	Every implementation is different, as culture drives the way an organization implements its strategy, and every organization's culture is different. However, leaders tend to adopt past approaches without adapting them to the new implementation and/or underestimate the role and importance of culture in implementation.
What Needs to Change	You need to ensure that the implementation and the organization's culture are aligned.

Identify Implementation Approach

Your first task is to identify an implementation approach that fits the culture of the organization. If the implementation of the strategy moves too fast for the culture, you'll end up overpromising and underdelivering—and the effort dissipates. If the implementation moves too slowly for the culture, then you'll lose momentum and key people, such as change agents who will lose interest over time. In both cases, the implementation fails.

Every organization's culture is different; therefore, every implementation is unique. That's why you need to identify how the culture drives the implementation and make it your own. Each leader's role is to ensure the culture enables the new strategy's implementation. If the current culture does not do so, you need to build a culture that reinforces implementation.

This involves recognizing that culture is not static—that is, cultural values need to be refined and strengthened over time.

Start by examining the day-to-day life of the organization to make sure it drives the new strategy's implementation. For example, one leadership team in the United States noted that their internal meetings took too long and slowed the implementation process. Employees were spending too much time talking in meetings and not enough time on the job, taking the right actions. To change this, all the chairs were taken out of the meeting rooms, making all meeting attendees stand! This helped dramatically shorten meetings from two hours to 20 minutes, which released time to take meaningful action.

Implementation Tool

How to Understand Your Current Company Culture

It is difficult for leaders to assess and understand their own culture. When you are at work every day, many manifestations of culture become almost invisible.

How to Observe Your Current Culture

As a leader, you can obtain a picture of your current culture in these ways:

- Become an impartial observer of your culture in action. Look at the employees and their interactions in your organization with the eye of an outsider. Ask questions such as: How do people interact with each other? If there are conflicts, how are they resolved? How do senior leaders interact with middle managers and employees? How do middle managers interact with the employees who report to them?

- Watch for how emotions are expressed, for these are indicators of values. People don't get excited or upset about things that are *not* important to them. Do people seem engaged, involved, excited, happy, friendly, morose, or withdrawn? Do they smile and interact with you as you walk by their desks? How do they show their emotions?

- Look at the objects that sit on people's desks and hang on their walls. Observe common areas and furniture arrangements. Are they inviting, or do they seem sterile?

- When you observe and interact with employees, watch for things that are *not* evident. If nobody mentions something you think is important (such as customers or expected sales growth), that is important information in helping you understand your organization's culture.

You can assess your current organizational culture with these three approaches:

a) Participate in a Culture Walk:

To observe the culture of your organization, take walks around the office and look at the physical signs of culture. Ask yourself:

- How is the space allocated? Where are the offices and the people located?

- What is posted on bulletin boards or displayed on walls?
- What is displayed on desks or in other areas of the building? In the work groups?
- How are common areas utilized?
- What do people write to one another in memos or emails? What is the tone of the messages (formal or informal, pleasant or hostile, and so on)? How often do people communicate with one another? Is all communication written, or do people prefer to communicate verbally?
- What interactions do you see between employees? What emotions are expressed during the interactions you observe, and how strong are they?

Make this process a frequent habit to observe organizational culture in action. Over time, you will reach a point where you can assess and feel subtle differences.

b) Conduct Culture Interviews:

Another way to understand the culture of your organization is to interview your employees in small groups. During these interviews, it's as important to observe the behaviors and patterns of interaction within the group as it is to hear what they say about the culture.

Here are examples of indirect questions you can ask during a culture interview:

- What would you tell a friend about your organization if he or she were about to start working here?
- What is the one thing you would most like to change about this organization?
- Who is a hero around here? Why?
- What is your favorite characteristic that's present in your company?
- What kinds of people fail in your organization?
- What is your favorite question to ask a candidate for a job in your company?

c) Culture Surveys:

Written surveys taken by people in the organization can also provide information about the organizational culture. Note: Be sure to create or select survey questions using the information collected during the Culture Walk and Culture Interviews.

The results from your organizational culture assessment will either confirm the efficacy of the culture you have or provide the encouragement you need to change your organizational culture.

> *You must create a culture of trust and commitment*
> *that motivates people to implement the*
> *strategy, not to the letter but to the spirit.*
>
> — W. Chan Kim and Renée Mauborgne, authors, *Blue Ocean Strategy*

> *We shape our environment, then*
> *our environment shapes us.*
>
> — Winston Churchill

Understanding Your Organization's Culture

If an organization's culture needs to change to support strategy implementation, it is a top-down responsibility. But leadership teams often don't address the culture challenge early enough into the journey.

The leadership team may not even agree on a definition of their own culture. The following questions can be useful to understand the culture changes that may need to happen.

Culture Questions

1. How do leaders define our organizational culture?
2. How do employees perceive your culture?
3. What is unique in the way we work that makes us useful?
4. What are the stories told about our organization?
5. Who are the heroes, and what stories are told about them?
6. What new actions do employees need to take to implement the strategy?
7. What aspects of the culture must change to support the implementation?
8. What supporting mechanism will encourage these actions?
9. How will the culture contribute to implementing the strategy effectively?
10. What actions should the leadership team be modeling?
11. Does the reward and recognition scheme encourage the action required to implement?

Importance of Culture in Implementation

You need to develop a shared understanding of your organization's culture and recognize its powerful influence and relationship with implementation.

Many organizations fail at implementation due to a lack of alignment between their culture and their strategic ambitions. According to Brightline research, the most frequently cited barrier to implementing strategy is culture.

When the implementation is not aligned to the culture, it causes mixed and confusing messages as well as disconnects between policies, processes, and systems. The relationship between culture and implementation is critical, and you need to be conscious of the culture you cultivate.

The initial challenge is often for the leaders of an organization to assess and understand its own culture.

What Is Organizational Culture?

Culture has many different meanings, depending on who you talk to in the organization. We define it as "the way that people do things."

Culture is sometimes referred to as the personality of the organization. It shapes actions and involves different components such as vision, mission, values, leadership style, operation structure, language, stories, reward, and recognition.

Organizational culture also includes an organization's expectations, experiences, philosophy, and the values that hold it together, and is expressed in its self-image, inner workings, interactions with the outside world, and future expectations. It is based on shared attitudes, beliefs, customs, and written and unwritten rules that have been developed over time and are considered valid.

Culture is reflected in:

1. The ways the organization conducts its business and how it treats its employees, customers, and the wider community
2. The extent to which freedom is allowed in decision-making, developing new ideas, and personal expression
3. How power and information flow through its hierarchy
4. How committed employees are toward collective objectives
5. The way employees dress or conduct meetings

> *Culture is critical in strategy implementation, as it*
> *impacts the way an organizations works.*
> *Culture is critical in strategy implementation, as*
> *it drives the way an organization implements.*
>
> — Antonio Nieto Rodriguez and Robin Speculand

Your Culture Drives Your Implementation

Research at Hack Future Lab, led by Terence Mauri, showed that an overwhelming 84% of leaders agree that culture is critical for business success and 60% agree that culture is more important than strategy.

Findings in Kearney's 2014 strategy study: More than 80 percent of global executives consider agility as important, or more important, than strategy when it comes to securing a company's future success.

Gallup's 2020 Q12 Meta-Analysis report , revealed business units in the top quartile in terms of employee engagement outperformed business units in the bottom quartile by 23 per cent in profitability.

External Papers

- Leaders Can Shape Company Culture Through Their Behaviors **by Jim Whitehurst**
- Creating a Culture of Digital Transformation **by Microsoft**
- Digital Transformation: 3 Steps to Build a Digital-Ready Culture **by The Enterprise Project**

Video Links

- What Is Corporate Culture?

EMBEDDING

Introduction

How can you embed the culture to support implementation?

- Changing an Organization's Culture
- Culture Drives the Way Leaders Implement
- Align Culture and Implementation
- Make It Your Own—Amazon Entering India
- Building a Culture to Encourage Experimentation in DBS Bank

Changing an Organization's Culture	
Goal	Recognizing that culture drives your implementation, leaders need to step back and assess the current culture to ensure it is enabling the implementation.
Implementation Challenge	Changing an organization's culture is the hardest transformation to do. Why? Because culture is the way you do everything, and therefore you are impacting the way every part of the organization operates.
What Needs to Change	You need to recognize the challenges if you need to change the culture.

Steps in Organizational Culture Change

There are three major steps involved in changing an organization's culture:

1. Understanding your current culture
2. Alignment to the new strategy
3. Ensuring employee commitment to decide to change their actions to create the new desired organizational culture. This can be the hardest step in culture change.

1. Understanding Your Current Culture

Your starting point is to ensure all the leaders have a consistent picture of the organization's desired future.

The leadership team needs to be able to answer the following questions:

- What does the organization want to create?
- What will it offer tomorrow?
- How will its customers and employees benefit?
- What are the core values?
- Are the mission, vision, and values clearly articulated and disseminated so that employees have a clear understanding of the organization's direction and where they fit within it?
- What cultural elements support the success of the organization?
- What stories are shared among employees?
- What elements of the current organizational culture need to change?

2. Align It to the New Strategy

Appreciating that culture drives your implementation, you need to ensure the culture is aligned to the new strategy and enabling the implementation. This may require tweaking or adjusting the culture. The two most important elements for creating organizational cultural change are executive support and training.

- Executive Support—executives need to support a cultural change in ways beyond simple verbal assent. You need to show support for the cultural change by visibly changing your own behavior.
- Provide Training—culture change depends on changing behavior and belief. Employees need to understand clearly what is expected of them, what new behaviors involve, and what actions are required. Training can be leveraged to communicate expectations and new behaviors. Mentoring also helps employees learn and change.

3. Ensuring Employee Commitment to Change Their Actions and Create the New Desired Organizational Culture

Employee involvement and their willingness to learn, adapt, and change their behaviors are key to sustaining changes in culture. To enable this, consider the following ideas:

- Creating value and belief statements: Ask employee focus groups to put the organization's mission, vision, and values into words that state the impact on each employee's job. For one job, the employee stated, "I live the value of quality patient care by listening attentively whenever a patient speaks." This exercise gives all employees a common understanding of the desired culture that reflects the actions they must commit to in their jobs.
- Practicing effective communication: Keeping all employees informed about the organizational culture change process ensures commitment and success. Telling employees what is expected of them is critical for effective organizational culture change.
- Reviewing organizational structure: you may be required to change the physical structure of the organization to align with the desired organizational culture.
- Moving employees and teams: You may need to create the sense of cohesion and camaraderie among groups that must work together to serve customers. To help accomplish this closeness, consider moving coworkers together in the same space.

- Redesigning the rewards and recognition: New behaviors and/or actions require reinforcement by the reward system. For example, if you want to encourage employees to work as cohesive teams, you need to reward them for their success as team players and not just on the basis of individual performance.

- Reviewing operational systems: Make sure operational systems such as employee promotions, pay practices, performance management, and employee selection align with the required culture.

Expert Advice

It is more difficult to change the culture of an existing organization than to create a culture in a brand-new organization or team. When an organizational culture is already established, people must unlearn the old values, assumptions, and behaviors before they can learn the new ones.

But with time, commitment, planning, and proper implementation, you can change your organizational culture to support the accomplishment of key business goals and needed outcomes.

Case Study

Microsoft's CEO Satya Nadella announced to employees in 2014 that Microsoft Windows' monopoly was under attack and the organization needed to function more effectively. Nadella's goal was to reduce the amount of time and energy needed to get things done in the engineering area. The cultural change required reduced the number of people involved in making decisions, thus making each individual more accountable. This shift has been changing Microsoft's culture.

Organizations need a nimble culture that embraces the accelerated pace of doing business and readily supports rapidly shifting strategies.

In the 2013 Katzenbach Center survey, 84 percent said that the organization's culture was critical to the success of change management, and 64 percent saw it as more critical than strategy or operating model.

Culture Drives the Way Leaders Implement	
Goal	To shape the organization's culture to serve as an enabler of successful implementation.
Implementation Challenge	As most aspects that compose culture are intangible, it is challenging to understand, define, and influence culture. Leaders and employees tend to ignore or undermine the important role that culture plays in implementing strategy. This can result in the culture being a hindrance rather than an enabler.
What Needs to Change	The understanding that culture drives the way an organization implements its strategy. People who argue that culture drives strategy say culture is extremely difficult to change, that it dominates more than strategy. This may have been true in the past, but it can no longer be a valid way to think about or conduct business due to the fast pace that business models are required to transform. When it's said businesses today must be *agile*, this largely refers to the agility of the organization's culture in response to the rapidly changing strategic landscape.

Aligning Implementation with Culture

Organizational culture includes the shared beliefs, norms, and values within an organization. For a strategy within an organization to develop and be implemented successfully, it must fully align with the organizational culture. Thus, initiatives and objectives need to be established within an organization to support and establish an organizational culture that embraces the organization's strategy over time. To do this, the culture needs:

- **Fluidity**

  A fluid culture, one that will systematically support strategy implementation, is one that fosters a culture of partnership, unity, teamwork, and cooperation among employees. This type of corporate culture will enhance commitment among employees and focus on productivity within the organization rather than resistance to rules and regulations or external factors that prohibit success.

- **Strategic Objective Unification**

  Flexible, strong, and unified cultures will approach strategy implementation and affect implementation in a positive manner by aligning strategic goals. Strategic objectives can come into alignment when the organizational culture works to focus on productivity and getting the organization's primary mission accomplished. This may include getting products delivered to customers on time, shipping out more products than the organization's chief competitor, or other similar goals. A unified culture will create a domino effect in the organization that ensures that all work performed by each individual in the company and work group focuses on performance and on the strategic importance of the company.

It allows culture to align with strategy implementation at the most basic level. For this level of unification to work, goal setting must align with and be supported by systems, policies, procedures, and processes within the organization, thereby helping to achieve strategy implementation and continuing the cultural integrity of the organization.

- **Cultural Alignment**

When culture aligns with strategy implementation, an organization is able to more efficiently operate in the global marketplace. Culture allows organizational leaders to work both individually and as teams to develop strategic initiatives within the organization. These may include building new partnerships and reestablishing old ones to continue delivering the best possible products and services to a global market.

Case Study

Oracle acquired more than 100 companies in five years. Its leaders don't talk of mergers and acquisitions (M&A) but only acquisitions. Whether it's Sun Microsystems or PeopleSoft or SelectMinds, Oracle has had to absorb dozens of other organizations into its culture. Oracle's culture is said to be autocratic, but then how can an organization successfully acquire so many others and also entertain everyone's opinions in the process?

Why Cultural Needs to be Nimble

Historically, big beat small. Scale was a sufficient advantage. Now, fast and adaptive beats slow and steadfast.

New technologies, evolving customer preferences, and changing employee expectations are fundamentally challenging established ways of working in more and more sectors. It's time to move beyond a rigid hierarchy, siloed business units, crippling bureaucracy, and an increasingly unwieldy matrix. A nimble culture combines the efficiencies of scale with the speed, flexibility, and resilience to compete and win in today's world.

Leaders are asking:

- *Why does our organization struggle to move quickly, and what can we do about it?*
- *How do we empower our people to take more accountability for performance and truly embed customer centricity?*
- *How do we organize for both sides of the productivity equation—cost and innovation-driven growth?*

Keeping the culture nimble requires constantly adjusting it to support the implementation of the strategy. The paradox is that organizations are built to be stable, yet they must keep transforming!

Engaging workers on an individual basis is important because organizational culture is the sum of all employee behaviors. That is, organizational culture is not created in a leadership off-site on strategic planning. Instead, organizational culture is made up of the mindsets, beliefs, and behaviors of employees throughout the organization who have to implement that strategy on a daily basis.

People adopt a new culture when it's clear the current strategy threatens the individual's future. Leaders must be able to demonstrate this. Here's an example.

Case Study

A leadership team from an organization in Malaysia supplying medical products noted that occasionally a leader would speak angrily to a staff member in front of others in the department. This had a negative effect on the staff member being spoken to and those nearby. Not only was it embarrassing for the target to be shouted at in public, but, in Asia, it was also a major loss of face. To stop this, the leadership team started a code blue policy. This meant that if, after all the leaders agreed to stop this detrimental behavior, one leader persisted with it, the rest would take action. They would immediately take the offending leader to the conference room, where the offender would have to explain the lapse in front of the team. Implementing this policy effectively stopped the negative behavior.

References

- Juan Carlos Perez, "CEO Nadella promises to shake-up Microsoft's culture: 'Nothing is off the table,'" PCWorld, July 10, 2014, http://www.pcworld.com/article/2452820/nadella-on-microsofts-culture-change-nothing-is-off-the-table.html

> *Companies that are great:*
> *Apply strategy and execution to tap the*
> *power of the ingrained thinking and behavior*
> *that already exists below the surface, using*
> *culture, no structure, to drive change.*
>
> – Paul Leinwand, Cesare Mainardi, Art Kleiner

> *Leadership is not about maintaining the status quo*
> *but maintaining the highest rate of change that the*
> *organization and the people within can stand.*
>
> – Sir John Harvey-Jones, English businessman

Align Culture and Implementation

To align implementation and culture, there are a few key steps leaders need to take.

First, you need to assess what will genuinely work in your organization and then, if adopting changes, you need to accurately identify everything that needs to be done and the implications of all of the changes (both intended and unintended).

Key areas you should assess include:

1. Change the Language

Part of aligning implementation into culture is the language used in the organization. A classic example is Disney renaming its engineers *imagineers* and adopting the terms guests, cast members, volunteers, and the show in its theme parks.

Recognizing the importance of language, Singapore Public Service created an approach to ensure customers never hear that dreaded excuse, "That's not our department." Its leaders started an initiative called *No Wrong Door.* Anytime someone calls a government department, the person answering will manage the call until he or she reaches the right department, even if it's from a completely different part of the government. The simple language they adopted helped drive the right actions of the implementation.

When you move from crafting to implementing the strategy, the language changes.

Language When Crafting Strategy	Language of Implementation
▪ Strategy creation	▪ Execution
▪ Analyzing and planning	▪ Implementation
▪ Thinking	▪ Doing
▪ Initiate	▪ Follow through
▪ Leadership	▪ Whole organization
▪ Goal setting	▪ Goal achieving

2. Leadership Styles

There is a direct correlation between your leadership style and your organization's culture.

How you respond to the challenges of the implementation and how you interact with employees plays a large part in culture versus implementation relationship. For example, when an employee makes an implementation mistake for the first time, are they punished or coached to do it right? Through your day-to-day actions, you frame and maintain your organization's culture.

Part of your influence over culture is through role modeling. If the strategy focuses on being customer centric, you can't afford to sit behind your desk. You must be visibly connecting with your customers.

3. Transparency

As former CEO of GE Jack Welch said, "Trust happens when leaders are transparent, candid, and keep their word."

Transparency builds trust, and trust is the cornerstone of accountability and results. Leaders at all levels understand how and why decisions are made, and it fosters open dialogue. When people trust and believe in leadership and understand what is expected, they are more committed to their work.

According to a study in Harvard Business Review, employees in high-trust workplaces are 76% more engaged and 29% more satisfied with their lives.

4. Physical Layout

The layout of the office is a strong indicator of an organization's culture. If the organization has a value around communication, then the physical layout of the organization needs to reflect this. If people are working in cubicles, sending emails to the person sitting beside them, then the physical layout is a hindrance, not an enabler.

5. Celebrate Successes and Heroes

A basic of change management recommends the power of celebration. Many organizations know about this, but few celebrate enough. The celebration needs to reinforce the right actions and involve the right people. Endeavor to make the celebration about the actions that delivered the outcomes. In addition, ensure you have rich content and that the story is inspirational and authentic.

According to the Society for Human Resource Management and Globoforce, values-based employee recognition significantly contributes to bottom-line organizational metrics and helps create a stronger culture and more human workplace.

It's about celebrating both small and large success. This means an organization needs to set and celebrate both small and large targets.

Make It Your Own—Amazon Entering India

Although you can examine principles and adopt tools that work in other organizations, the approach you adopt must fit your organization's unique culture. Working out how to make it your own is a constant challenge throughout the journey. When you attain it, you're well on the way to achieving Excellence in Execution.

The entry of Amazon.com (Amazon) into India provides a good example of making the execution your own. In the United States, most people have access to the internet, a home address, and an option of delivery organizations. That's not true in India.

Amazon entered the Indian market in 2013 by offering access to products that millions of people have never been able to buy or afford before—a shop window for making dreams come true. Goldman Sachs claims that the Indian e-commerce market will be worth over $300 billion by 2030, a 15-fold increase. Amazon adds a staggering 40,000 products a day as well as selling 30 million products across hundreds of categories, with more than one million products in stock.

To succeed in India, though, Amazon has to make the execution its own. Its leaders have demonstrated their commitment to the process, investing more than US$5 billion. Amazon is expanding its network of warehouses and data centers while strengthening its marketplace platform ecosystem for its service. Its unique challenges require Amazon to have a different execution plan in India than in other countries.

> *We're adapting to the local model.*
>
> — Jeff Bezos, CEO Amazon

The three elements of its plan include:

1. Internet access
2. Delivery and payment system
3. The competition

1. Internet Access

In India, around 45 percent of the population can access the internet either from a computer or on a smartphone. To overcome the limited internet access, Amazon placed computers in stores where owners assist people who are unfamiliar with the internet. To reach potential customers through advertising, Amazon used billboards and lucky draws.

2. Delivery and Payment System

Reaching customers with their orders and receiving payment are distinct execution challenges in India. To overcome them, Amazon had to redesign its business model. Some addresses in India are hard to find. So instead of delivering its distinctive brown boxes to customers' homes, they may be sent to a designated neighborhood store—not by FedEx or UPS but by an army of Amazon motorbike delivery people.

Because some people in India don't own credit cards, the owners of these designated stores collect COD (cash on delivery) on behalf of Amazon. They inform customers when their package arrives and receive a small commission for their efforts. They like the arrangement because as well as the commission, it drives business to their shops where people purchase other items.

3. The Competition

Amazon doesn't have a monopoly on the internet shopping market. It has to compete with local firms such as Flipkart (about 37% market share) and Snapdeal (about 14%) and a newer entrant, Tata, which is starting to see success. Six months after entering the market in India, Amazon had attracted half the amount of traffic Flipkart had built up in six years. According to comScore, within three years of entering the market, Amazon became the most visited e-commerce site in India and has about 24% market share. Its number of visits overtook Snapdeal in 2016.

> *The biggest surprise is how fast our size in India has grown. I never guessed we would become this size in just over two years.*
>
> – Diego Placentini, Senior VP for International Business, Amazon

CEO Jeff Bezos estimated that, in record time in India, Amazon would surpass US$1 billion in retail sales.

Flipkart (whose founders both worked at Amazon before leaving in 2007 to create their own start-ups) is going head-to-head with Amazon to win business, but each has its own implementation style.

Two organizations can be heading in the same direction with similar strategies. However, their execution will always be different because of their cultures and the language they use.

Building a Culture to Encourage Experimentation in DBS Bank

DBS Bank, Singapore, has been recognized for the fourth year in a row as the world's best bank. Under the stewardship of Piyush Gupta, the bank transformed from a traditional to a digitally driven organization, and it's been recognized by the most prestigious banking awards as well as one of the top ten digital transformations of the last decade by Harvard.

In 2014 the bank set the audacious goal of being recognized as the best bank in the world by 2020. After the global financial crisis in 2008, many people started distrusting banks and even called banking "painful."

The question the leaders addressed was not "what did the bank want to do?" but "how do we make dealing with DBS easy, fun, convenient, and meaningful?"

Then people would be able to see the kind of good the bank did for businesses and individuals as well as the value it added to society. The team migrated toward making banking the opposite of painful—that was, to Making Banking Joyful.

Due to the emergence of numerous technologies, the means for Making Banking Joyful was rapidly evolving. DBS leaders recognized that, by leveraging new technologies, they could make banking "invisible" to their customers. That would, in turn, create opportunities for customers to have enjoyable interactions when dealing with the bank and, ultimately, to experience a sense of happiness and peace of mind throughout their banking journey.

A key component of the "Making Banking Joyful" strategy was encouraging employees to experiment to find better ways of serving customers and themselves.

In other industries, this may not be a dramatic occurrence, but bankers have been traditionally taught to mitigate risk, and experimentation is about taking risks. Therefore, asking employees to experiment was counterintuitive to everything they had been taught. The challenge was to change the thinking in the bank.

As the bank set about understanding and improving what its customers wanted, it developed a culture of innovation, driven partly by a new openness to experiment. Rather than focus on creating products, employees experimented with various options so they could identify the best solutions for their customers.

To eliminate the fear of failure and create a safe environment to experiment in, the bank based its approach on the concept of psychological safety.

The concept of psychological safety has been developed by Amy Edmondson, Novartis Professor of Leadership and Management at Harvard Business School. To reinforce that employees were safe to experiment and fail, the bank created the Dare to Fail award.

Also, the leaders had to lead by example and set the right expectations. They started by not holding employees accountable for every last piece of success. This encouraged people to participate in changes at any level and be recognized for trying. It also unlocked their energy, creativity, and imagination. This proved particularly effective in areas such as customer journey and data transformation.

The leaders also recognized how fear of failure could impede innovation and realized that some experiments needed to fail before success could happen.

Thousands of experiments now take part across the bank every year, and employees have been spurred to pursue new ideas in a safe environment. Some of the examples of experiments are:

Branchless Bank

The bank adopted hackathons within the first 12 months prior to launching the digital transformation as one of the approaches to encourage experimentation and innovation. From the very first hackathon came the suggestion to create a branchless bank in India where a customer could open an account within 90 seconds. Digibank demonstrated what the bank could achieve. It changed employee mindsets, created digitalization success stories, and expanded the bank's capabilities.

SPARKS—Online Miniseries

By embracing the spirit of a start-up culture and a desire to experiment, the marketing team created a miniseries to convey relevant customer stories in a touching manner.

Sparks required a completely new way of thinking about marketing. The two seasons of Sparks have garnered 276,000 million views and 50 million engagements. It has also influenced close to 10 percent of the inquiries the bank has received online; for example, it generated 40 percent more visits to DBS's home page in 2020 over 2019. Because people think Sparks is cool, it's also helpful as a recruitment tool.

Virtual Reality at Branches

This experiment introduced virtual reality (VR) for customers. When they put on VR goggles, they were immersed into their desired lifestyle 20 years into the future so they could calculate how much money they needed to save for retirement. The experience guided them through four key expenditure lifestyle areas that included dining, transportation, travel, and household. They could then calculate the retirement funds they needed to achieve their desired quality of life and start working toward their goals.

Video Teller Machines (VTMs)

In 2019, the bank rolled out Singapore's first video teller machines (VTMs). These machines provided a private booth for customers to do transactions through the machine. Alternatively, they could receive face-to-face assistance from a bank teller located in a central operations area rather than at a bank branch. The 24/7 VTMs are able, for example, to replace bank cards and security tokens.

This article has been partly extracted from author Robin Speculand's new book World's Best Bank—A Strategic Guide to Digital Transformation.

External Papers

- Managing Across Cultures, **INSEAD**
- American Red Cross Cultural Transformation, **Brightline**

Video Links

- Managing Across Cultures, **INSEAD**
- Culture Drives the Way You Implement Strategy, **Robin Speculand**
- How Do You Create Psychological Safety at Work? **Interview with Amy Edmondson**

EXECUTING

Introduction

Culture is the hardest element within a change, as culture can be defined as "the way you do everything." Therefore, if you need to change the culture, you are changing the way you do everything.

- Developing a Culture of Accountability
- Strategy Can Now Eat Culture for Dinner!
- Six Steps for Creating a Culture of Accountability

Developing a Culture of Accountability	
Goal	To ensure everyone in the organization knows they are accountable for their implementation actions. Engage as many people as required in the implementation, and encourage them to take their own initiative when required.
Implementation Challenge	Accountability is possibly one of the most underutilized leadership practices even though it is relatively easy to incorporate. It does not require any capital investment, but it does require a focus and discipline that many leaders lack. After the launch of a new strategy, multiple activities start to happen. Exactly what happens and in which department depends on the enthusiasm of the leadership, and they are rarely aligned. In one organization, for example, two different departments hired two different training companies to provide the same training to their employees. In another organization, two different departments hired two different PR companies to support their internal marketing. Time and money were wasted in both cases because there was no alignment in the implementation actions.
What Needs to Change	Accountability requires holding one individual responsible, with the emphasis on "one." Leaders need to hold each employee accountable, with continual follow-through. Several experts agree that "holding people accountable for implementation is one of the most powerful actions you can take."

There is a difference between accountability and responsibility. You are responsible for things and accountable to people. That report is not going to hold you accountable but your co-worker will. Accountability is keeping your commitments to people. Those commitments may be spoken like "I will meet you at 11:00." Some commitments are unspoken like "I will value you as a person," or, as the leader, "I will make sure you are in a position to succeed." When we take the time to truly understand what our commitments are and then work to keep those commitments, we become accountable.

– Sam Silverstein, author of *Non-Negotiable*

Strategy Can Now Eat Culture for Dinner!

One of the late Peter Drucker's most famous quotes is "Culture eats strategy for breakfast." This is no longer always true and, in fact, it can more often be the other way around. Because of the accelerated pace of change in business today, strategy tends to eat culture.

The landscape has altered dramatically since Drucker's day. Today, with businesses moving faster than at any time in history, the pace has dramatically reshaped the relationship among the elements of strategy, culture, and execution.

In Drucker's era, a strategy for an organization could span 10 years and assumed a decade of stability and growth. Today, most are working in a medium or fast Strategy Cadence (cadence is their speed of implementation), which means the strategy has to change every three years or so. This fast pace of change also means the organizational culture is constantly in a state of flux and is more readily influenced by rapidly transforming strategic decisions.

In 2014, Constellation Research stated, "Since 2000, 52% of the companies in the Fortune 500 have either gone bankrupt, dropped out, been acquired or ceased to exist."[1] Former CEO John Chambers of Cisco claimed that 40% of companies will be gone in 10 years, adding that "either we disrupt or we get disrupted." The BBC reported that Professor Richard Foster from Yale University said that by 2020, more than three-quarters of the S&P 500 will be made up of companies unknown in 2016.[2]

The relationship affecting strategy, culture, and execution is shifting. To accentuate this shift, the question to consider is, "Does strategy drive culture or does culture drive strategy?" Strategy is about crafting the organization's future; it can't be constrained by the culture. To support the strategy, the culture may need to be adjusted. When crafting strategy, leaders have to keep an open mind and avoid limitations the culture may place on the vision.

Culture does not drive strategy. Rather, culture drives the way you execute.

People who argue that culture drives strategy say culture is extremely difficult to change, that it dominates more than strategy. This may have been true in the past, but it can no longer be a valid way to think about or conduct business due to the fast pace that business models are required to transform. When it's said businesses today must be "agile," this largely refers to the agility of the organization's culture in response to the rapidly changing strategic direction. See Figure 14.0.

Figure 14.0: Strategy Cadence

Keeping the culture nimble requires constantly adjusting it to support the execution of the strategy. The paradox is that organizations are built to be stable, yet they must keep transforming!

Six Steps for Creating a Culture of Accountability

Creating a culture of accountability in your organization requires knowing what is important to the organization and then instilling this principle in everything you do.

At Singapore Airlines, the employees are held accountable for demonstrating the airlines' core values: pursuit of excellence, safety, customer first, concern for staff, integrity, and teamwork. Due diligence is conducted on new hires to ensure they have integrity. Cabin crews are held responsible for owning customers' concerns onboard a flight. Onboard issues are captured in a Voyage Report, tracked for review, and followed up internally.

Some employees in organizations feel accountability has negative connotations. They assume it only happens when something goes wrong—that is, leaders hold people accountable only when there are mistakes or problems. If this belief prevails, then the organization will struggle to deliver results. Organizations who are good at implementation leverage accountability as a powerful and positive tool. They use it not for pinpointing faults but as an opportunity to drive the right actions and coach their employees.

To create a culture of accountability, people need to know they will be held accountable for their actions, and then this needs to happen.

Implementation Tool

Six Steps for Creating a Culture of Accountability

There are six steps for creating a culture of accountability in an organization. They are:

1. **Knowing the organization's core values**—The values act as your guiding principles of what is important and acceptable, and the accountability has to be aligned with values. For example, if the organization values innovation, then employees should be held accountable for new ideas.

2. **Clarifying expectations**—People need to know how they are expected to perform and what they're expected to deliver before they can be held accountable. For example, does accountability mean attending meetings on time and/or submitting reports on time and/or checking that the right actions have been taken?

3. **Adopting measures**—Putting in place the right measures allows you to track performance, show what is important, and measure accountability.

4. **Assigning only one person**—You can't have more than one person responsible because this confuses the accountability.

5. **Conducting reviews**—People need to know they will be asked how they did against the planned actions on a regular basis. They need feedback. Regular one-on-ones and team meetings create the opportunity to build a habit around accountability. Reviews should be held weekly or biweekly and need only take a few minutes with each employee.

6. **Linking actions to consequences**—People need to be recognized in a positive way when they take the right actions. There also needs to be negative consequences for inertia or the wrong actions, and the consequences need to align with the values.

Try the 5-Question Quiz: Does Your Company Have a Culture of Accountability?

https://blog.commandhound.
com/5-question-quiz-does-your-company-need-a-culture-of-accountability

Top Down and Bottom Up–Aligned and Driven Culture
Initiatives to Support the Implementation

A common expression in transformation is the dichotomy of *top down* and *bottom up*. From various research we know that for a major initiative to succeed, the leaders must not just support it but drive what needs to happen in the organization. Top down-driven transformation implies high-level decision-making, a more autocratic leadership style, and a command-and-control culture.

Top-down change is already a challenge for some organizations. What is an even larger challenge is to initiate the right bottom-up actions. This happens when employees understand what is transforming and why, have embraced the implementation, and are engaged and want to contribute.

Your employees' response depends largely on your influence. Leaders initiate the implementation in their own business, based on their enthusiasm, and they become a "state inducer." This is someone who induces their own thinking and actions onto others.

It is also essential in implementation to ensure there is transparency throughout the organization—specifically that actions are not replicated.

Some people perceive top down and bottom up as two opposing models. They are not.

An organization can embrace them both. Initially, strategy is top down, as leaders are ultimately responsible for crafting strategy. But implementation happens at ground level with employees taking the right actions and generating bottom-up momentum.

To encourage bottom-up and aligned initiatives to support the implementation, consider the "4Es of Bottom-Up Implementation":

1. Empower employees to make their own decisions (with clear parameters)
2. Encourage regular two-way conversations about the strategy and its implementation
3. Engage employees—understand what inspires employees to participate and lead them
4. Energy levels need to be increasing as employees see the implementation as an opportunity

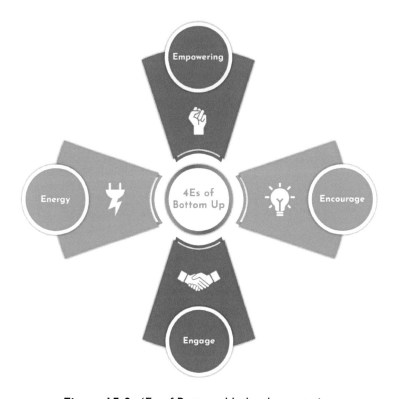

Figure 15.0: 4Es of Bottom-Up Implementation

> *Do every job you're in like you're going to do it for the rest of your life, and demonstrate that ownership of it.*
>
> — Mary Barra, CEO of General Motors

> *The single most important change in actions that needs to occur during a time of cultural transition is the shift to greater accountability.*
>
> — Roger Connors & Tom Smith, *The Oz Principle*

References

1. R. Ray Wang, "Research Report: Inside The 2015 Boardroom Priorities (Parts 1 & 2)," Constellation Research, December 16, 2014, https://www.constellationr.com/content/research-report-inside-2015-boardroom-priorities-parts-1-2

2. Kim Gittleson, "Can a Company Live Forever" BBC News, January 19, 2012, https://www.bbc.co.uk./news/business-16611040

Links

- How to Instill a Culture of Accountability at Work, James Brooks, PhD, https://www.youtube.com/watch?v=blgVdMAfEJQ

- 5 Leadership Tips for Building a Culture of Accountability, Robert Velasquez, https://www.youtube.com/watch?v=WSmAYCatlc4

- Creating a Culture of Accountability, https://www.youtube.com/watch?v=Qe323dmrJ0g

External Papers

- Does Your Company Have a Culture of Accountability? by Command Hound

- The Hard Side of Change Management, HBR

- How the Strategic Landscape Has Changed During COVID-19 by Nieto-Rodriguez & Speculand

Video Links

- Creating a Culture of Accountability, Culture Crossing

SUSTAINING

Introduction

Change life cycles are becoming shorter, and consequently you need to maintain an open mind to your own organization's culture. Counterintuitively, you need to sustain the culture while also maintaining fluidity to change it!

- Continuously Evolve the Culture
- Leaders Stuck in the Status Quo

Continuously Evolve the Culture

Goal	To understand that leaders need to drive the continuous evolution of the culture. With the business landscape changing rapidly around us and organizations' average life span dramatically shrinking, leaders need to be constantly aware and to reinforce the right desired culture to meet the evolving short- and long-term strategic objectives.
Implementation Challenge	Human nature tends to look for comfort, and so do employees and leaders. They like to keep the status quo; they continue to extend yesterday's way of doing things rather than inventing tomorrow. This is an inherent trait in people. For example, consider that 80% of New Year's resolutions fail by the second week of February. People set out to do things and then don't do them.
What Needs to Change	You need to accept that your organization's culture changes more frequently than ever before, and the change is likely to accelerate going forward. This therefore requires regularly questioning the strategy, its implementation, and the associated desired culture to support the implementation. It also requires you to establish an ongoing burning platform in order to keep the organization and employees vigilant and open to transformation.

We have seen throughout this chapter how culture has a significant impact on whether or not an organization achieves its implementation. Leaders may need to tweak the culture, or they may need to completely overhaul it.

You need to challenge the status quo frequently and to adjust the culture according to the new realities of your business and strategic landscape. When you fail to respond to the changing outside world or when you become complacent, you may find yourselves losing customers, revenue, top talent, and shareholder value because the culture is becoming a hindrance to performance.

Evolving Culture

Culture is like habit; it's hard to change. Changing your habit takes effort, time, and often requires a prime motivator. Culture change is no different, and you need to find and articulate whatever it is that will motivate people to change.

A new strategy requires changes to the current operating model—sometimes minor adjustments and at other times radical transformation. Sometimes the disruption is externally forced, while other times it's internally driven.

Changes to the evolving culture require:

- Clear expectation of what will change and why
- Reframing the narratives that are used to change beliefs
- Constantly communicating the what and why of the changes
- Reviewing the organizational structure
- Consistent leadership commitment and involvement
- Identifying new training for employees and leaders
- Reinforcing new actions

> *"Just because you are CEO, don't think you have landed. You must continually increase your learning, the way you think, and the way you approach the organization. I've never forgotten that."*
>
> – Indra Nooyi, former CEO of PepsiCo

> *A culture of execution requires constancy and discipline—you can't give up.*
>
> – Liz Mellon & Simon Carter

Leaders Stuck in the Status Quo

Leaders become stuck in the status quo, and many are too scared to challenge the way the business operates.

There are five reasons leaders remain stuck in the current status quo:

1. Unwilling to turn the spotlight of accountability on themselves
2. Afraid of risk
3. Don't know how to get started
4. Lack organizational readiness
5. Not evolved as leaders

1. Unwilling to Turn the Spotlight of Accountability on Themselves

Responsibility and accountability require hard work. But too often leaders run from one meeting to the next with no time to follow through. They don't take responsibility for holding themselves accountable for what is agreed from one meeting to the next.

2. Afraid of Risk

Who wants to put their reputation on the line when there is no actual support for taking a risk? But we must because leaders who want real change must embrace risk as the new normal. We live in uncertain times. We must learn to anticipate the unexpected and create high-performance environments in which people work well together under pressure and can readily adapt to a constant wave of change to stay ahead of the market and the competition.

3. Don't Know How to Get Started

When leaders lack an entrepreneurial mindset, they can't align expertise, break down silos, operationalize change, or figure out ways to evolve and incentivize their people to connect the dots in an environment that encourages outside-the-box thinking. Instead, everyone is just stuck.

4. Lack Organizational Readiness

Do the corporate values support the behaviors that encourage one to challenge the status quo? Are employees and leaders living them and consistently standing by them? If they aren't, then the core values are not rooted in the belief that success comes to those who are surrounded by people who want their success to continue and are inspired to do more—and employees are just doing what they are told.

5. Not Evolved as Leaders

Some leaders who have been in their jobs for a long time think they know everything because they have been there for a long time! But when they have not reinvented themselves as a leader to serve the changing workplace and marketplace, they lack the desire to evolve—and see and seize new opportunities.

External Papers

- Inside the 2015 Boardroom Priorities **by Constellation Research**

Video Links

- No Rules: Inside Look into Netflix's Culture, **Reed Hastings and Erin Meyer**

IMPLEMENTATION QUIZ QUESTIONS

I. An organization's culture often needs to change to support the implementation. Corporate culture can be described as?

   A   Defined by the CEO and leadership team

   B   Explained by employees and customers

   C   Explained by the way the organization conducts business and freedom of decision-making

   D   Explained by employees and CEO

2. The debate between the relationship of strategy and culture is still ongoing. One school of thought is that strategy now eats culture for dinner because?

   A   Culture has become less important in the last few years

   B   Strategy has been taught more in business schools

   C   Strategy is understood better

   D   None of the above

3. Changing an organization's culture is the hardest transformation to do. This is because?

   A   Culture, once established, should not be changed

   B   Culture impacts every part of the organization

   C   It receives the greatest resistance from employees

   D   None of the above

4. Leaders need to ensure the culture is aligned to the new strategy and enabling the implementation The three major steps involved in changing an organization's culture are?

   A   Gaining board support, gaining leadership support, and gaining employee support

   B   Customer focus group, employee focus group, and creating a committee

   C   Gaining board support, employee focus group, and aligning commitment

   D   None of the above

5. Leaders play an important contribution in defining an organization's culture. Two important leadership behaviors to support a culture change are?

   A   Mandating actions and driving behaviors

   B   Investing in training and customer research

   C   Changing their own behavior and providing required skills

   D   Sharing the strategy message at a town hall meeting and going around departments

6. To ensure employees are committed to changing their actions to support a new desired culture, leaders should:

    A   Create value and belief statements

    B   Practice effective communication

    C   Review organizational structure

    D   All of the above

7. An organization needs to constantly ensure alignment of its culture and implementation. To make this happen, leaders can?

    A   Change the language and adapt their style

    B   Change the language and environment layout

    C   Change the environment layout and celebrate success

    D   All of the above

8. One of the poorest performing behaviors but easiest to adopt is accountability in organizations. Adopting accountability into a culture involves?

    A   Knowing the organization's core values

    B   Clarifying expectations

    C   Adopting measures

    D   All of the above

9. Leaders can become stuck in the status quo. Key reasons leaders remain stuck in the current status quo include?

    A   Unwilling to turn the spotlight of accountability on themselves

    B   Afraid of risk

    C   Don't know how to get started

    D   All of the above

10. Leaders need to drive the continuous evolution of the culture. To frequently challenge the status quo, organizations need to?

    A   Create a committee to identify what needs to be done

    B   Reframe the narratives that are used to change beliefs

    C   Organize more meetings to discuss the topic

    D   None of the above

Answers to the quiz questions can be found on page 314 in the Appendix.

STRATEGY IMPLEMENTATION PLAYBOOK 2.0

A STEP-BY-STEP GUIDE

ROBIN SPECULAND & ANTONIO NIETO-RODRIGUEZ

STRATEGY
IMPLEMENTATION
INSTITUTE

STRATEGY
IMPLEMENTATION
INSTITUTE

Strategy Implementation Institute Pte Ltd
Second edition 2024, version 2.0
Published by Strategy Implementation Institute Pte Ltd
Copyright © 2024 Robin Speculand & Antonio Nieto-Rodriguez

FOR FURTHER INFORMATION, CONTACT:
info@si-institute.org

ISBN paperback 978-981-18-4597-0
ISBN ebook 978-981-18-4598-7

CHAPTER 6

Stakeholder Management

STRATEGY
IMPLEMENTATION
INSTITUTE

The initial challenge for any transformation is to introduce the new strategy to the whole organization. While this can be done effectively by initially *teasing* internal stakeholders prior to the launch, you need to recognize that the launch is only 15% of the overall implementation communication goals.

Figure 16.0: Strategy Implementation Road Map©

Too frequently in stakeholder management, communication around the implementation dissipates after the first six months. A heavy emphasis in this chapter is placed on nurturing communications throughout the whole implementation journey (Figure 16.0).

What you will learn in this module:

- Mistakes to avoid when communicating a new strategy
- A tool for mapping and prioritizing stakeholders
- Why and how to brand your strategy message
- Identifying key roles and responsibilities
- Ensure the communication is nurtured throughout the whole journey

CRAFTING

Introduction

Leaders are responsible for setting their employees up for success by starting to identify what new skills and information employees require. You need to identify the most effective way to prepare the different stakeholders and to communicate key messages.

- Teaser Campaign
- Planning the Strategy Launch
- Roles and Responsibilities
- Stakeholder Analysis Matrix
- Template for Questions for Developing the Communication Plan

Teaser Campaign

Teaser campaigns can be adopted by organizations to start to create awareness around the new strategy before it is launched, in the same way that a film studio launches a trailer of a new film before its release date to galvanize interest.

> *A strategy teaser campaign galvanizes interest by showing images that reflect a serious problem currently in the organization. It provokes and stimulates.*
>
> — Antonio Nieto Rodriguez and Robin Speculand

The teaser campaign is based on the principle that employees like to reach their own conclusion about what is happening. David Sibbet puts it this way, "People are more engaged by things that are suggestive than by things that are crystal clear."

The teaser campaign has two main objectives:

1. It reflects a serious problem in the organization.
2. It starts to make employees aware that something new is coming without telling them fully what it is.

Case Study

Teaser Campaign

When Steve Ballmer took over from Bill Gates as CEO of Microsoft, he identified a new approach was required and wanted to launch the strategy called "The Customer Partner Experience" (CPE) globally.

At the time, a serious problem for Microsoft was that while many of their businesses still looked good on paper, they were under threat from competition. For example, Microsoft had a 93% market share in computer operating systems, but this was under threat from Linux and Apple.

To prepare for the launch of the strategy in Asia Pacific, the leaders decided to conduct a teaser campaign. Three posters were designed to lay the groundwork for the strategy launch and were distributed with two weeks between them.

The three posters created an initial groundswell of curiosity, and two weeks after the publication of the third poster, the new strategy was launched with an image of a rowing team and the tagline, "Every little step you do right today, contributes to tomorrow's memorable Customer Partner Experience."

The outcome in Asia Pacific was that the new strategy was adopted quicker and easier by employees because they knew why it was important for Microsoft to transform and what the new strategy was.

> *No matter how much information you communicate to people, they still need assistance to interpret it correctly.*
>
> – Robin Speculand

> *Clearly, employees who do not understand the strategy cannot link their daily activities to its successful execution.*
>
> – Kaplan and Norton

> *If a picture is worth a thousand words, then a one-minute video is equivalent to 1.8 million words.*
>
> – Dr. James McQuivery, Forrester Research

Planning the Strategy Launch

Is it better to launch a new strategy:

1. When the organization is doing well?
2. When the organization is doing badly?

One of the best times to design and implement a new strategy is when an organization is doing well—it's easier to craft and execute a new strategy when all is going well. When it's doing badly, the organization is struggling, people are under pressure, working capital is less, and you could be losing key customers and employees.

However, when the organization is performing well, it appears illogical to many employees (and some leaders) to start changing it.

> *Leaders are challenged to explain that although the outlook may look good today, circumstances are changing and the organization needs to transform or be left behind.*

Reflect on how Steve Jobs eliminated the iPod when launching the smartphone. Why? Because Jobs recognized that the short-term loss of revenue would more than be offset by new revenue from the smartphone and that by doing so, Apple was also staying ahead of its competitors.

The Burning Platform

When the outlook for the organization looks bad, leaders need to explain the dramatic reasons for transforming. This is sometimes referred to as *the burning platform*.

A classic example is how Louis Gerstner stepped in as a technology outsider when IBM was losing $8 billion a year in the 1990s and 90% of IBM's profit came from sales from its mainframe computers. IBM had to change to survive, and Gerstner successfully transformed the organization from selling a product to selling solutions. For more, read *Who Says Elephants Can't Dance* by Louis. V. Gerstner.

> *Only 16% of supervisors say that they understand*
> *how strategic priorities fit together.*
>
> – Donald Sull, professor at MIT

Impactful Ways to Communicate the Launch

Effective communication is not simply an email or a town hall meeting; it requires a coherent internal branding strategy. Internal branding is a powerful way to explain both the logic and emotional reasons for the new strategy.

In business, leaders tend to overcomplicate communication, making it hard for people to understand important messages. The communication branding can be developed by the internal communication team in consultation with the leadership.

The objective in communicating a new strategy to all stakeholders is to:

- Explain *why* the organization is changing.
- Share the strategy objectives and timeline.
- Enable employees to understand *what* is changing inside the organization.
- Define what employees should do differently.
- Explain how employees will benefit.

What Is the Goal of Communicating Strategy?

There are four immediately apparent elements to strategy communication, but they don't, by any means, all carry the same weight.

Element	Weight	Significance
Explaining the right actions to take	25%	We've already emphasized that everyone involved needs to be clear what the strategy means for them (as well as the business), and this implies they need to understand how to act in response to it. It's a mistake to assume that what seems obvious to you can be easily translated into activity by those doing the work.
Communicating updates against the strategy objectives	50%	Depending on the scale and nature of your strategy, neither the exact destination nor the precise means of getting there may be apparent when you take your first steps. That means that you need to be continually listening for and sharing information on progress as well as any course corrections if you want to make sure that you end up where you need to be (as opposed to where you thought you needed to be when you first conceived the strategy).
Sharing the strategy	15%	Although sharing the strategy perhaps should only occupy 15% of your time, it is an important 15% that should not be neglected. In any organization, the number of people who know what the strategy is, is usually dwarfed by the number who don't. Staff changes or noise from operations or other programs can all drown out the message.
Inspiring people to take the right actions	10%	Inspiration and personal motivation are important sources of impetus and momentum for anyone required to change the way they see things or tackle new challenges. But the reality is that these rely more on the behavior and the actions of those in senior positions who can be far more effective champions as role models than as orators.

Avoid the mistake many organizations make of frontloading the communication. This is when leaders provide too much information too soon and then little or no follow-up communication.

Your aim is to nurture the communications about the implementation continually by *sharing* and *resharing*:

- Progress against the objectives
- What's not working
- Customer feedback
- Best practices
- Milestones achieved
- Lessons learned

Roles and Responsibilities

A lack of clarity in roles and responsibilities can dramatically impede the implementation, just when it needs to be building momentum. Symptoms of this may include:

- Inertia
- Employees not clear about their role in the implementation
- Confusion around who needs to do what
- Different teams pulling in different directions
- The passing of blame between each other
- Poor morale from concern over job security
- Confusion about who has to make the decisions

Roles are defined as the positions employees hold. Responsibilities are defined as the specific tasks employees are expected to complete.

Clearly, both showing employees how to participate in the new strategy and inviting them to work out how to do so is a critical success factor and is often missing.

When the launch doesn't include an explanation of how to participate, most employees hear the new strategy and continue working the same way they always have been. It's your responsibility to bridge the gap by explaining what to do and providing examples of how to do it. Because each employee's contribution is contextual to their particular capabilities, skills, and motivation, this is one task that is best communicated by an immediate line manager or team manager to his or her subordinates or team.

Defining Roles and Responsibilities

Defining key roles and responsibilities can be done by adopting and completing the following exercise at the department head level:

	Employees Position	Employees Position	Employees Position	Employees Position	Employees Position
Specific Tasks					

Figure 17.0: Defining Roles and Responsibilities

Stakeholder Analysis Matrix	
Goal	To make leaders aware of the different people involved in the implementation and their level of interest and influence.
Implementation Challenge	It's not uncommon for implementation to be sabotaged by the organization's own leaders! A nod of the head in the conference room does not translate to full-fledged commitment in the implementation.
What Needs to Change	You need to recognize who is involved and assess each key person's commitment to either the success or failure of the new strategy.

Stakeholders

Stakeholders are individuals and groups that are affected by, involved in, or have an interest in the outcome of the implementation. As a general rule of thumb, the more stakeholders, the more effort is required in terms of communication and implementation activities.

Most people need stability to feel at ease. Yet many implementations bring changes to the status quo. Therefore, resistance is natural, especially in strategy implementations that introduce significant shifts into the organization. The larger the number of people resisting the implementation, the more difficult the challenge ahead.

Resistance doesn't always equate to influence, and in any organization there will be a small number of key players who are in an immediate position to provide resilience or fatally undermine the strategy, so remember the simple aphorism: "There are always those who will be happy if the implementation fails. Find them and understand why."

Example

Berlin Brandenburg International Willy Brandt Airport continuously missed deadlines and took more than nine years to open. It has become a symbol of engineering catastrophe. Stakeholders included state of Brandenburg, the German federal government, the city mayor, the airlines, and others. Construction started in 2006 and it finally opened in 2020 just as the pandemic significantly reduced travel around the world, thus the airport has remained relatively empty. Its supervisory board had too many politicians who did not know how to implement.

The more stakeholders, the more complex the project and the more effort required in the areas of communication and change management. Projects that challenge the status quo often face resistance.

In this case, an up-front identification of the key stakeholders would have helped the project team understand the stakeholders' needs and interests in a particular project. In any project, if the resistance is too strong, the rationale for doing the project is likely not clear enough. To be compelling, it has to address the needs of the groups and people affected by the project. In certain instances, if there is not enough buy-in from key players, it is better to postpone or not start the project at all.

Berlin Brandenburg Airport is a good example of a project that should not have started until full engagement from key parties was secured.

Key Questions to Ask:

- How many stakeholders does the implementation have?
- Can you identify the major sources of resistance to the implementation?

Tool to Adopt

Stakeholder analysis matrix: This matrix (Figure 18.0) is commonly used for weighing and balancing the interests of those who are affected by or involved in the implementation.

The trick to stakeholders is to follow the deceptively simple rule whenever possible: address the needs of those stakeholders to meet the implementation objectives. Stakeholder analysis should be performed in a small group, as some of the discussions can be quite sensitive.

The initial assessment is usually performed during the preparation phase by a leadership team. After the major stakeholders have been identified, each one is categorized according to two dimensions. The first is the level of interest (positive or negative) in the implementation or its outcome. The second is the level of influence (positive or negative) that the stakeholder could have on the implementation. Usually, this dimension is linked to the power of the individual or group in the organization. The third dimension is represented using the color-coding red, amber, and green to indicate the stakeholder's current position toward the implementation.

This analysis can be done regularly to track the changes in stakeholders' attitudes over time. The matrix itself is an example of a stakeholder guide to identify and address the stakeholders affected by and involved in an implementation.

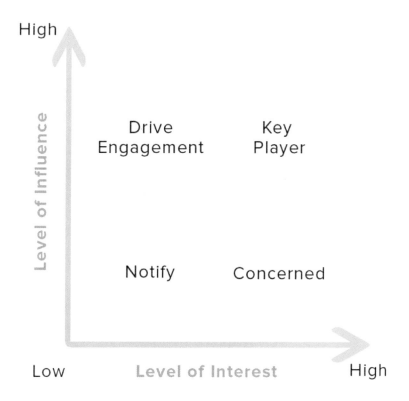

Figure 18.0: Stakeholder Analysis Matrix

Project Stakeholder Analysis Matrix

Stakeholder management is an area that rarely gets enough attention. Understanding the needs of the key stakeholders, identifying win-wins, and aligning stakeholders to actively support the implementation are key contributors for success. Still, accomplishing all that can be a daunting task.

Template for Questions for Developing the Communication Plan

Questions for Developing the Communication Plan

Goals	Achieved Yes/No	How Do You Know?	Guidelines
What is our overall goal of the communications?			The leadership team identifies the goal of communicating the strategy and translates it into a statement.
What are our objectives?			What does the communication need to achieve and by when?
Who is the target audience?			Who do you want and need to influence? How do you prioritize the audiences?
What is the environment we are dealing with?			What is the organization's culture? How does this culture influence the implementation? What has been done before that has worked/not worked? What are the Critical Success Factors (CSF)?
What are the key messages?			What messages do you need to apply to be consistent with the other parts of the organization? On what are the messages based? What are possible supporting facts? What is the WIIFM (what's in it for me)? What is the WEXFM (what's expected of me)? What are the different messages for each target audience?

Goals	Achieved Yes/No	How Do You Know?	Guidelines
How do we brand our communication strategy?			What core theme or big idea can we develop that ties the program together in a creative, easily understood, and memorable fashion?
What are the key tactics, activities, and budget?			What tactics and activities do we need to develop in a phased way to achieve the objectives across all target audiences? What budget has been allocated?
What are the right measures?			How will we know when we have achieved our communication objectives? What quantitative and qualitative measures do we need to show that we're achieving the desired outcomes?

(Row label, left margin: Questions for Developing the Communication Plan)

Guidelines to Questions for Developing the Communication Plan

- The eight goals in the template are noted in these short questions (first column), but each of them requires time for in-depth discussion.
- The answer to all eight goals should be "yes" (second column) but only after considerable thought has been given to the communication challenges involved.
- After answering "yes" to each, then state how you know it is "yes" (third column).

External Papers

- Create a Burning Platform by the Management Center

EMBEDDING

Introduction

Your responsibilities now shift to ensuring that different stakeholders have the right information, skills, and understanding to implement the strategy. Too many implementations fail at this stage because leaders don't invest the time to prepare their employees.

This section discusses communication:

- Communicate, Communicate, Communicate
- Cascade Key Strategy Messages and Expectations to Key Stakeholders
- Communicating Strategy Ideas
- Cascade Kit
- Case Studies on CEOs Communicating to Employees

Communicate, Communicate, Communicate

Goal	To ensure employees know the purpose of the new strategy.
Implementation Challenge	Initially, communication in implementation focuses predominantly on sharing why it's important for the organization to transform but does not explain to employees why it's important directly to their job and how they can participate.
What Needs to Change	Any sense you have, whether following a town hall meeting or reading an email from the CEO, that the whole organization is committed to the transformation.

Communication when implementing a strategy involves explaining why the organization is transforming—engaging everyone's heart and their mind, in other words their intellect and their emotions. Then, during the crafting stage, preparing what employees are expected to do differently after the launch of the strategy. For example, if you are launching a digital initiative, you may ask employees to participate in hackathons. Or if you are launching a productivity improvement initiative, you may ask employees to participate in cross-functional process redesign teams.

Various research has revealed that only 10% of people attending a town hall meeting understand the message, and even fewer start taking the right actions. Therefore, you need to remind employees and reinforce their understanding of how each of them can participate in the implementation. An engaging, clear, and applied set of messaging builds momentum right from the start by encouraging and enabling employees to take the right actions.

> ## *Everything should be made as simple as possible, but not simpler.*
> – Albert Einstein

> ## *Implementing strategy successfully means changing the conversations in the organization.*
> – Antonio Nieto Rodriguez and Robin Speculand

What's In It for Me—WIIFM

A common acronym used globally when communicating strategy is WIIFM (What's In It for Me), which articulates the benefits employees derive personally from participating in the new strategy. When they first hear about the strategy implementation, employees determine how they will be personally impacted: will they have less responsibility or more, will their boss change, might they lose their job, and so on?

When you see a photo of a party you attended, the first person you look for is yourself. It takes a determined and conscious effort to think of others before you think of yourself, and such altruism is seldom demonstrated; the first two things each person asks are "what might I lose?" followed (often as an afterthought) by "what might I gain?"

Appreciating and realizing this, you need to answer these questions before the launch by describing the strategy's impact to different segments, showing how it will benefit them to participate, and explaining how they will benefit after it succeeds. You also need to prepare to address every individual's concern because each one is key to making the implementation work. Doing so spurs on their motivation to get behind the strategy and take the right actions. Don't expect to have all the answers, and don't create the expectation among employees that you have all the answers or you will struggle to involve them in helping shape the emerging process.

What's Expected from Me—WEXFM

Employees are also likely to ask the WEXFM question. It's essential that you also clearly explain what employees need to do differently to participate in the implementation.

The WEXFM needs to clearly guide each and every employee touched by the implementation on the right actions to take.

When crafting the communication, identifying what is expected from employees shouldn't either be a major challenge and/or overcomplicated. From an individual's point of view, it might mean joining a team, meeting new customers, mapping a process, or tidying their work area.

Expert Advice

Employees require three things to make strategy implementation work:

- *Inspiration—why it is important*
- *Means—how it can be accomplished*
- *Opportunity—the chance to make it work, to do their best*

Expert Advice

7X7X

This is a shorthand way of saying, "Give people the message seven times in seven different ways." Employees need to hear the message numerous times in different ways, as they will notice different things every time they hear it.

Sending one email isn't enough. You must also hold a meeting, start a social media group, celebrate a hero, mention the topic at the start of every meeting for three months, create physical and online images of the key message, and so on.

> *Senior managers get lulled into believing that a well-conceived strategy communicated to the organization equals implementation.*
>
> — Professor Michael Beer

Cascade Key Strategy Messages and Expectations to Key Stakeholders

Goal	To nurture communications over the whole life of the implementation journey, ensuring targeted messages are received, understood, and acted on.
Implementation Challenge	After the initial launch of the strategy, communication typically starts to dissipate. Leaders start talking more about day-to-day business and less about the strategy and its implementation. When leaders stop communicating about it, so do employees, and when the implementation communication stops, so do the actions to implement it. The number one reason strategy implementation fails, according to various research, is poor communication. Leaders know what to do, but they just don't do it.
What Needs to Change	Leaders expecting that after attending a town hall meeting and reading an email from the CEO, that the whole organization is committed to the transformation.

What Leaders Need to Do Differently

You need to sustain communication across the whole life of the implementation journey.

A massive communication chasm exists between employees' awareness of a new strategy and employees actually knowing the right actions to take. Leaders bridge this chasm by sustaining the communication, explaining the right actions to employees, and driving and championing the implementation itself.

You should spend a minimum of three months from the launch consistently communicating the strategy across the whole organization, no matter how large or small. You need to communicate the message in as many different ways as possible and use every opportunity to be the medium personally. You need to be the *voice of the strategy*.

Consider how politicians communicate before an election. They make sure they are visible, reaching out to as many people as possible, sharing a consistent message over numerous mediums. You need to adopt a similar approach:

- Be visible across the organization.
- Connect with employees through one-on-one chats, small meetings, and town hall meetings.
- Ensure all your colleagues are sharing the same strategy message.
- Adopt numerous different communication approaches.

In many organizations, after the initial fanfare, the communication about the strategy dissipates, becoming unstructured and ad hoc (Figure 19.0). As a result, employees rarely know what is happening, start to lose interest, and generally stop participating.

Communication

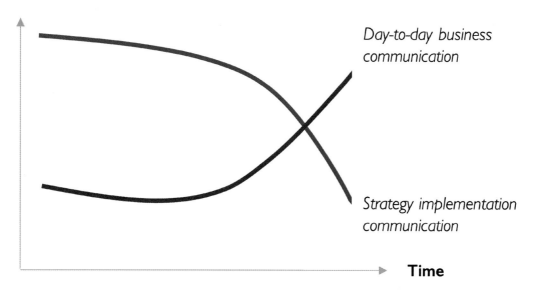

Figure 19.0: Time Versus Communication Graph

A consistent, coherent, and structured communication is required.

> ### You need to continue to nurture your communications.

Build on the initial excitement, and work to fan the implementation flames continually. Structured communication involves targeting different stakeholders with selected messages, typically designed to accomplish the following:

- Regularly update employees on the progress of the implementation.
- Share success stories.
- Share lessons learned from failures.
- Provide updates of upcoming activities, changes, and developments.
- Share news of the strategy's impact on the business and customer.
- Ensure employees remain engaged in the implementation and take the right actions.

While overseeing the messages being broadcast, you should also ensure consistency. This means providing regular updates based on the objectives we've just highlighted. Consistent communications keeps the implementation at the forefront of the minds of employees, as well as keeping them informed.

While overseeing the messages being sent out and nurturing the communication, you should work hard to make the communication concise and transparent. Keep in mind that the Gettysburg Address is only 272 words and takes four minutes to say. A standard memo to boost organizational productivity typically contains 2,000 words! Keeping communication concise and transparent builds understanding and confidence in the implementation. Remember, video and audio are likely to be a more engaging medium than written memos or even presentations.

The agenda for leadership meetings needs to include implementation messages. For example, weekly team meetings can now start with the leader asking, "What has been achieved this week in implementing the strategy?" or sharing updates on progress being made.

Expert Advice

Most middle managers don't know their own organization's top priorities. This causes numerous problems with middle managers themselves then communicating or sharing the wrong messages, taking the wrong actions, and possibly even opposing the strategy. Ensure everyone knows what the strategy is and what to do.

Only 15% of people in an organization can identify their organization's most important goals and priorities, according to Franklin Covey's research.

Expert Advice

There is no way you can identify all the actions your organization needs to take to implement a strategy. You need to assist and coach employees to identify the right actions to take and then support them.

Communication is a process, not a one-time event.

Email Is a Poor Tool for Communicating Important Messages.

Expert Advice

3X3 Rule

The human brain has a cognitive bias, which means humans are more likely to believe a familiar statement than a brand-new one, even if the familiar statement is wrong! The more people hear it, the more they believe it's true. You can use this effect to your advantage by identifying three different ways of phrasing the key message into your speeches about the new strategy.

Make the same argument three times (3X). Note, it's not about repeating the same words; it's about phrasing it in three different ways, thus "3X3." As the basis of learning, repetition strengthens the connections between neurons that convey information. It's why children who are learning constantly repeat their words.

> *If you have an important point to make, don't try to be subtle or clever. Use a pile driver. Hit the point once. Then come back and hit it again, then hit it a third time with a tremendous whack.*
>
> – Sir Winston Churchill

> *The greatest problem with communication is the illusion that it has been accomplished.*
>
> – George Bernard Shaw

Communicating Strategy Ideas

Communicating strategy that will galvanize employees in your organization takes patience and imagination. The following ideas may help:

- Invite the CEO to record a short voice message (90 seconds) and share it via social media tools each Monday morning so that everyone receives a message from the CEO reinforcing the importance of the strategy.
- Create controversial statements to grab people's attention.
- Storyboard a collection of pictures that tell a story.

- Make use of dedicated web pages on the intranet, mixing messages from the top with stories of employee experience.

- Produce a three-minute animated video of the key strategy message.

- Place messages on everyone's desk.

- Place key strategy message signs in the elevator.

- Translate strategy messages into posters and postcards.

- Make T-shirts with the strategy message on them.

- Have a blank wall where employees are invited to put up suggestions for improvement, then set up a team to work on them.

- Ask senior managers to act as coaches and give them each a whistle, hat, and stopwatch. Keep a logbook of actions staff have taken to further the strategy, and publish significant ones online.

- Create a strategy implementation tool kit addressing what employees need to know about the strategy. It might include a strategy guide book, cards with key questions to ask, Strategy Map, templates to use, videos, and an aspirin in case it becomes too much!

- Develop a video montage of how different departments/countries are participating in the implementation. Provide each team with video cameras or just invite them to use their smart phones, and challenge them to create a montage of employees going the extra mile.

- Offer an advice column: Dear Agony Aunt and Unbelievable Uncle, which can offer written responses to staff problems or even tackle them with a regular "Ask the CEO" hotseat session on the intranet.

- Give employees a take-home icon—something that resembles what you are aiming to achieve.

- Design a strategy that is passed around each department each week to be worn by the person whose actions are deemed to have particularly supported the strategy.

- Employees act as customers.

- Create an Implementation Council of elected individuals who meet once a month or quarter to provide feedback on how employees perceive the initiative.

- Set up lunch meetings to discuss progress with the C-suite.

- Plan a half-day employee retreat to review the current state of play and solicit ideas.

- Establish a repeated activity every month, e.g., on the last Friday of the month, where everyone wears the strategy T-shirt and does a strategy activity.

- Visit companies who have completed a successful implementation.

- Set up a series of debates on what is working and what's not.

- Use ticker-tape messaging on the website to carry strategy implementation updates.

Cascade Kit

The cascade kit is built on the principle that the person to whom employees listen to most is their immediate supervisor.

Using this principle, organizations can create a communication package to assist you to brief your immediate reports. They in turn brief their immediate reports and so on, until the message has been cascaded throughout the whole organization and everyone has received a consistent message.

Cascade Kit Contents

- Electronic presentation
- Speakers' notes and video
- Strategy explanation video
- FAQs
- Cascade feedback survey

Slide Deck Presentation

- A 45-minute slide deck explaining the strategy and how it's going to be implemented.
- The presenter shares the objectives and challenges of the strategy to their direct reports. This is delivered to between five and 12 people (groups of this size foster an environment that encourages people to participate).

Speakers' Notes and Video

Speaker notes guide the presentation to ensure consistency in the message. They also indicate:

- Where the presenter can ad-lib
- Customized examples
- The video is a recorded briefing that shows supervisors what is expected of them and offers as many examples of different ways to deliver the message efficiently and effectively.

Strategy Explanation Video

- A three- to five-minute summary of the key messages. This is another visual medium that can repeat and reinforce the standard message.
- A popular approach in some organizations is to use an animated video. A good example is Dan Pink's "The Surprising Truth About What Motivates Us" or Bridges's video on the "Strategy Implementation Challenge."

FAQs

- Frequently Asked Questions is an additional tool to make it easier for the presenter to respond consistently to questions raised during the group discussion, ensuring a uniform understanding of the strategy across the organization. You'll need to regularly refresh the questions and answers to reflect what people are asking.

Cascade Feedback Survey

- After completing the cascade, use Mentimeter or a similar tool to solicit feedback from frontline employees. The aim is to ensure that everyone has been briefed personally by his/her immediate supervisor and to identify what employees know and don't know about the strategy.

Case Studies on CEOs Communicating to Employees

Continental Airlines

Jeff Smisek, former CEO of Continental United, shared lessons he learned from the merger of the airlines that saved Continental in the mid-1990s.

Referring to the company's business plan called the Go Forward Plan (a short statement of the company objectives on marketing, finance, operations, and people), he said, "It's a simple plan, easy to understand no matter where you work in the company. It's one piece of paper that focuses everyone."

> *If you're doing something and can't track it back to the Go Forward Plan, stop what you're doing and do something else.*
>
> – Jeff Smisek

IBM

Former IBM CEO Lou Gerstner told the story that during the IBM transformation of the late 1990s, he constantly referred to the metaphor of Tarzan. He encouraged his leaders to think of leading change as swinging through a jungle and letting go of the old vine to grab the new vine, representing an aspect of the new business they were creating—all with the threat of hungry lions below and the horizon of success indistinct through the trees.

Singapore Post

Faced with declining postal volumes and a rapidly changing consumer landscape, the Singapore postal service aimed to become the leading e-commerce logistics and communications provider in Asia Pacific. Wolfgang Baier, Group CEO at SingPost, used a soccer metaphor to translate his strategy of transforming the organization to both mail and e-commerce.

This worked well because many of his employees were soccer fans. They related to the SingPost transformation as if the organization were a soccer team striving to win.

Video Links

- The Biggest Mistake I See: Strategy First, Urgency Second, **Kotter**
- Effective Strategy Communication, **Shaji Bhaskaran**
- Stamford Essentials of Strategic Communication, **Stanford Graduate School of Business**

EXECUTING

Introduction

Executing stakeholder management focuses on sustaining communication while ensuring transparency and employee engagement

- Over Communicate to Stakeholders While Providing Transparency

Overcommunicate to Stakeholders as Transparently as Possible

The Challenge

It is a mistaken belief that the effectiveness and impact of communication cannot be measured. In implementing strategy, anything of importance is worth monitoring, and that includes the communication. What you will need are pragmatic metrics that are appropriate to communication.

The Aim

- Measure how effectively employees understand the strategy objectives.
- Identify how many employees have been briefed about the new strategy by their immediate boss.
- Ensure the communication is enabling employees to contribute to the strategy and the implementation.

Companies with effective communication strategies have 47% higher returns to shareholders, more engaged employees, and less employee turnover, according to the Holmes Report, 2011.

The Methodology

- Measures of communication effectiveness are typically poorly executed in many organizations, if conducted at all. This is as much an art as a science, and your objective is both to gather hard data and feel the pulse of what's going on, hence the different approaches.

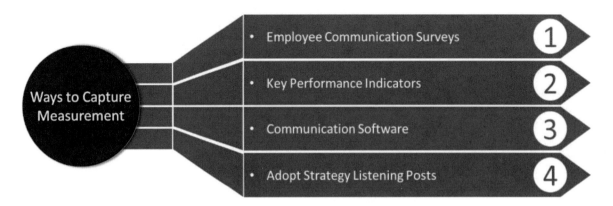

Figure 20.0: Ways to Capture Measurement

Employee Communication Surveys

- Conducting an employee communication survey allows the leaders to place a measure against how well the messages have been cascaded and what actions they are driving.

- Following the launch of the strategy, employees are questioned on their understanding of what's been shared. This can be done via focus groups, online questionnaires, or other means.

Suggested questions include:

1. What is our new strategy?
2. Why does the organization need to transform?
3. What does the new strategy mean to you?
4. What will you do differently to implement the strategy?
5. What support do you need to be successful?

Key Performance Indicators

As part of implementing a new strategy, new measures need to be introduced. The new key performance indicators enable you to track not only the success of the implementation but also the impact of your communication. Indicators that indirectly and directly reflect these include:

- Employee satisfaction
- Number of new initiatives initiated to implement the strategy

Strategy Listening Posts

Leaders need to know what employees think about the implementation, what they are doing and not doing, what they are saying, and challenges they are facing. This can be captured effectively by creating various strategy listening posts to take the pulse of employees (Figure 21.0).

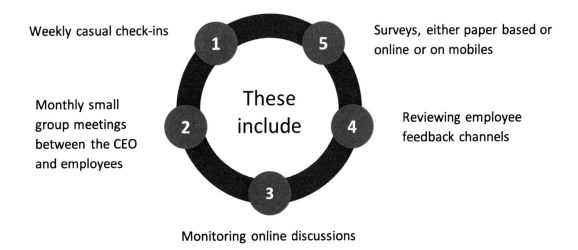

Weekly casual check-ins

Surveys, either paper based or online or on mobiles

Monthly small group meetings between the CEO and employees

Reviewing employee feedback channels

Monitoring online discussions

Figure 21.0: Adopt Strategy Listening Posts

Transparency

It is essential to be transparent in everything you do during the implementation. This will:

- Keep everyone on the same page and aware of changes.
- Align initiatives across the organization.
- Contribute to improving employee engagement.

Transparency is a principle of excellence. Forget *need to know*; everyone should know.

Research by Slack shows that over 80% of workers want a better understanding of how decisions are made, and 87% of job seekers say they look for transparency in a future workplace.

The HP Way

When Meg Whitman took over as CEO of Hewlett Packard, she wanted to encourage a return to the HP Way. One thing she noticed was how the executive leadership was fenced off from the organization.

This was sending the wrong message to the employees. In her April 2013 online post "The Power of Transparent Communication," she commented, "Nothing symbolized this disconnect more than our executive offices and what I called the *commando fence*—a large fence outfitted in barbed wire surrounding our executive parking lot. The walled offices and military-style fence represented just how far HP had departed from the culture of the company's founders.

"One of the first things I did was tear down the fence and move all of our executives into cubicles. We now walk in the same door as the rest of our employees. This was symbolic of the kind of culture that we wanted to build. And in organizations as large as ours, symbolism actually matters. What you communicate by your actions—the things that are visible to

320,000 people—make a real difference." Whitman ensured that the organization's actions reinforced its communication.

Don't Give Up

Measuring communication and providing transparency is not easy, particularly if it is unfamiliar to your organization, your senior leaders, and your employees.

But it is a critical component of successful implementation, as leaders need to track how much people know about the new strategy and the different actions they are taking.

External Papers

- The Irrational Side of Change Management by McKinsey
- Evaluating Your Communications by Westminster City Council

Video Links

- 7 Strategies for Overcoming Resistance to Change, Primeast US

SUSTAINING

Introduction

By this stage, nurturing the communication should be instinctive for the organization. What is required now is to start subtly changing the message to prepare employees for what's coming next.

External Papers

- 12 Corporate Communication Metrics You Should Be Tracking, **Papirfly**

IMPLEMENTATION QUIZ QUESTIONS

1. To introduce a new strategy in an organization, many leaders leverage town hall meetings to initiate the launch. What percentage of people attending a town hall understand the message being delivered?

   A 10%
   B 30%
   C 66%
   D 90%

2. Employees need to understand what the new strategy is before they can start to adopt it. In communicating strategy, what percentage addresses the launch?

   A 80%
   B 55%
   C 15%
   D 5%

3. A key contributing factor to strategy implementation failing is poor communication. When employees do not know their own organization strategy, the impact is?

   A They cannot link their daily activities to its successful implementation
   B They arrive late to work
   C They will spend more time in meetings
   D They take more holiday time

4. Teaser campaigns are an effective means to build awareness of what a new strategy means to an organization, partly as employees like to reach their own conclusions about what is happening. The best time to launch the new strategy is when?

   A The organization's key performance indicators have never looked better
   B The organization's key performance indicators are just beginning to show signs of improvement
   C The organization's key performance indicators have never looked worse
   D None of the above

5. Effective communication for implementing strategy requires a coherent internal branding as a powerful way to explain both the logical and emotional reasons for the new strategy. The objective in communicating a new strategy to stakeholders is?

   A Explain why the organization is changing and the objectives
   B Explain the objectives and their timeline
   C Explain what is changing and what employees need to do differently
   D All of the above

6. The Stakeholder Analysis Matrix is a useful tool to identify who is affected and involved in the implementation. The key reasons for this are?

    A   It creates greater attention on stakeholder management

    B   It enables clear understanding of what different stakeholders need

    C   It aligns stakeholders' activity in supporting the implementation

    D   All of the above

7. In communicating strategy, it's important to include the "WIIFM" (What's In It for Me). It is just as important to include the WEXFM (What's Expected from Me). This is because?

    A   Employees will only engage in the implementation if it matches their own interests

    B   It explains to employees what they need to do differently

    C   Leaders need to dictate exactly what needs to be done differently

    D   None of the above

8. Leaders need to ensure they are constantly communicating about the strategy implementation by constantly nurturing the communication. They can achieve this by?

    A   Targeting different stakeholders with selected messages

    B   Providing regular updates

    C   Sharing what works and what is not working

    D   All of the above

9. Only 5% of employees understand their own organization's strategy. What happens when the launch of a new strategy doesn't state how employees need to participate?

    A   Employees' absenteeism increases

    B   Employees keep working the current way

    C   Employees keep asking what they need to do until they find the answer

    D   None of the above

10. "Strategy Listening Posts" are a useful tool to measure the success of an organization's implementation communication. Effective Strategy Listening Posts include?

    A   Weekly casual check-ins

    B   Monthly senior leaders meetings

    C   Review of employee feedback channels

    D   All of the above

Answers to the quiz questions can be found on page 314 in the Appendix.

CHAPTER 7

Employee Engagement

STRATEGY
IMPLEMENTATION
INSTITUTE

The level of employees who are disengaged in their work is surprisingly high in many countries and industries. Asking employees to adopt a new strategy translates to asking them to do "more work," which makes transformation a particular challenge. Not least because initially they must keep working the old way while adopting the new way.

The challenge is for you to inspire, engage, and excite your people in the implementation. When employees are committed to the implementation, they will start to take the right actions, which then gains momentum and early success. We need lots of people taking small actions to create implementation.

It's also important to prepare employees with the right implementation attitude, knowledge, and skills.

Figure 22.0: Strategy Implementation Road Map©

This chapter addresses:

- How to identify new skills requirements
- The value of highly engaged employees
- The four different ways employees respond to implementation, as not everyone resists change
- Middle managers' role as lynchpin
- How to align and track resources
- How to sustain engagement and resources

CRAFTING

Introduction

Only 5% of employees (Bridges research) can tell you their own organization strategy. One of the first challenges is to make sure everyone in the organization knows why it is changing, understand what the new strategy is about, and identify the impact on themselves.

- Employee Engagement
- Identify Skills & Engage Talent

Employee Engagement	
Goal	The more engaged employees are, the more productive they are at implementing the strategy.
Implementation Challenge	The engagement levels of some employees in some organizations are deeply concerning. Gallup reports that employee engagement is steadily declining. There is a direct correlation between higher employee engagement and successful implementation. When people don't understand how to participate in the implementation, it lowers engagement, delays the rollout, and causes confusion.
What Needs to Change	You need to focus on developing an increased number of engaged employees. Why? Implementation requires employees to go the extra mile, and they will only do this if they are engaged. Well-publicized benefits of having engaged employees also include higher retention, greater inspiration, better performance, and more innovation. This is because engaged employees develop a deep connection and level of commitment with the organization. This in turn makes them willing and active participants in the implementation.

Only 23% of employees worldwide fall in the category of engaged employees according to Gallup.

Gallup estimated that actively disengaged employees cost U.S. businesses between $450 billion to $550 billion each year in lost productivity. "They are more likely to steal from their companies, negatively influence their co-workers, miss workdays, and drive customers away."

KPMG stated in "The Real Value of Engaged Employees" that "the level of engagement will positively or negatively influence their willingness to go the extra mile at work, innovate and assist a company in reaching the corporate or unit strategy."

An interesting claim by the Institute of Employment Studies is that "engagement levels decline as employees get older—until they reach the oldest group (60 plus), where levels suddenly rise and show this oldest group to be the most engaged of all." It also showed that "engagement levels decline as length of service increases."

The financial benefit of engaged employees has been recorded in these ways:

- New Century Financial Corporation identified that account executives in the wholesale division who were actively disengaged produced 28% less revenue than their colleagues who were engaged. Furthermore, those not engaged generated 23% less revenue than their engaged counterparts.

- As the Gallup study found, companies that increase their number of talented managers and double the rate of engaged employees achieve, on average, 147% higher earnings per share than their competitors.

- A frequently quoted 2006 Gallup survey involving almost 24,000 organizations compared financial performance with engagement scores. The results were:

  - Engagement scores in the top quartile averaged 12% higher customer advocacy, 18% higher productivity, and 12% higher profitability than in the bottom quartile.

  - Engagement scores in the bottom quartile averaged 31% to 51% more employee turnover, 51% more inventory shrinkage, and 62% more accidents than in the top quartile.

  - Gallup who has been measuring employee engagement for decades have identified:

    - The percentage of engaged employees increased to 36% in 2020, but it has been dropping since.

    - Gallup 2022 report states that "32% of full- and part-time employees working for organizations are now engaged, while 17% are actively disengaged, an increase of one percentage point from last year.

- The Department of Business and Innovation Skills in the UK revealed that organizations with a highly engaged workforce experience a 19.2% growth in operating income over a 12-month period.

- Standard Chartered Bank found that branches with a statistically significant increase in levels of employee engagement had a 16% higher profit margin growth than branches with decreased levels of employee engagement.

Implementing a new strategy provides leaders with an opportunity to focus on top-performing employees and to trim away poor-performing employees. This is important, as organizations need to be highly efficient and can no longer afford to carry low-performing and nonengaged employees.

The first part of engaging employees in strategy implementation is to appreciate that not all employees resist change and that they respond in four different ways.

> *Transformation requires that companies earn the intellectual and emotional commitment of their employees.*
>
> – Professor W. Chan Kim

Most managers believe that people will resist most of the time, but various research reveals otherwise. For years, leaders have worked with the notion that when their organization is making large changes, most people resist. This assumed resistance, they figured, could be from a fear of losing responsibility or stepping into the unknown, or of trying new things, and they have crafted strategy implementation and people policies based on these assumptions.

But most people do not resist strategy implementation when it's presented and communicated correctly. People don't resist change. As Peter Senge, the author and lecturer at the MIT Sloan School of Management, says, "They resist being changed."

People respond in one of four ways when being invited to participate in the implementation.

1. Indifference
2. Resistance
3. Doubt
4. Support

1. Indifference

The majority of employees—60% of them—sit on the fence. They neither support the implementation nor oppose it. Easygoing by nature, they see their job as just a job. They don't seek the spotlight or vie for promotions.

Typically, these fence-sitters arrive at 9:00 am and depart at 5:00 pm. In between, they do their work. They don't volunteer for additional work, but they don't actively resist transformation, either. They like the safety they find in numbers.

2. Resistance

Within an organization, 18% of people actively resist transformation. These resisters tend to complain about anything and everything. They badmouth the implementation behind leaders' backs. They try to convince others this strategy is just another management fad. They even see the new strategy as a threat. Based on these characteristics, they're called Saboteurs.

If their views win out, the whole implementation fails. These individuals can make choices or take actions that could damage the organization's new strategy. To deal with them, you either move them over to your view or move them out.

Today, organizations are transforming more often than at any other time in history. As a result, people are also being asked to implement more frequently. Some are willing and others struggle, depending on what's being asked. Organizations can no longer afford to carry people who don't engage in the new strategy, and leaders need to take corrective action. As Steve Jobs said, "It's painful when you have some people who are not the best people in the world and you have to get rid of them; but I have found that my job has been exactly that—to get rid of some people who didn't measure up, and I've always tried to do it in a humane way. But nonetheless it has to be done and it's never fun."

3. Doubt

Approximately 2% of employees are not easy to spot because they are hidden among the Saboteurs. They have seen attempts to transform before and think, "Most of them fail, so why engage?" However, they are very important. Although they initially resist, they can become the best supporters over time. Based on these characteristics, they're called Double Agents.

Double Agents start out acting like Saboteurs, but once they're convinced this implementation will succeed, they come on board and transform into your top supporters, driving the implementation with full engagement.

> *During a time of organization transition, we frequently see people at every level playing not to lose rather than playing to win.*
>
> – Roger Connors and Tom Smith, *Change the Culture, Change the Game*

4. Support

The remaining 20% are those who welcome the transformation, embrace it, and willingly support it. These early adopters drive the implementation as top talents who are enthusiastic and optimistic about the transformation. Excellence in Implementation lives or dies with those who support it.

Create the time to sit down and talk with people, especially the main supporters of the transformation.

Of the four groups, those resisting make the most noise and can lead others to wrongly conclude that most people resist transformation, while those indifferent keep quiet because they don't want to draw attention to themselves. Your supporters get on with the work at hand. As Tsun-yan Hsieh and Sara Yaks from McKinsey claim in their 2005 article "Leadership as the Starting Point of Strategy," "only 3% to 5% of employees throughout the whole organization can deliver breakthroughs in performance."

In implementation, if you target engagement of your people based on the belief that most people resist transformation, you risk developing the wrong approach. Instead, you need to support the people actively who support the implementation.

And yet many leaders focus on resisters, not supporters!

Leaders are responsible for creating the right conditions in the organization for supporters to thrive. You can do that by bringing like-minded people together. The resulting network creates easy communication between them and sets up an ecosystem that encourages engagement.

Implementation requires inputs from employees and especially the supporters. You can kick this process off by bringing like-minded people together on social media. The resulting network creates easy communication between them and sets up an ecosystem that encourages them to contribute.

To create a supporters' network in an organization, consider doing these seven things:

1. Create a social media group that people can join only when they receive an invitation from the CEO.
2. Provide training in the skills needed to implement.
3. Once a quarter, bring supporters together on conference calls to discuss challenges, best practices, stories, 90-day achievements, and lessons learned.
4. Once a year, hold a supporters' conference where they come together, discuss progress, and meet other supporters.
5. Demonstrate how being a supporter increases their opportunity for promotion.
6. Create the "Best of the Best Supporters" award.
7. Integrate supporters' performances into the annual bonus plan.

Expert Advice

Create a Line of Sight

Employee engagement also comes from people clearly being able to see how their daily actions contribute to the long-term strategic objectives. A way of making this happen is adopting a Strategy Map—created by Kaplan and Norton as part of the Balanced Scorecard.

A Strategy Map is a one-page summary of the strategy broken into objectives for the whole organization. When it's in place, leaders can explain how different activities across the organization are connected and drive the strategy. Middle managers and supervisors can use it as a tool to show individuals how they contribute to the strategy. This is very powerful for engaging employees in implementation. Consider also that millennials are five times more likely to stay in an organization if they feel a sense of purpose and part of it.

Expert Advice

Too many choices in implementation can be as demotivating as not having any choice at all.

> *By mastering the essentials of employee engagement, you can transform your team into a powerhouse.*
>
> – Dorrie Clark, Author and Professor

> *Connect the dots between individual roles and the goals of the organization. When people see that connection, they get a lot of energy out of work. They feel the importance, dignity, and meaning in their job.*
>
> – Ken Blanchard and Scott Blanchard

> *When people are financially invested, they want a return. When people are emotionally invested, they want to contribute.*
>
> — Simon Sinek, author

> *TURNED ON people figure out how to beat the competition; TURNED OFF people only complain about being beaten by the competition.*
>
> — Ben Simonton, author

Identify Skills & Engage Talent

What new skills do employees need to implement the new strategy?

How can you develop new skills that are necessary for employees to implement the strategy?

Skills Training for Implementation

Leaders, when preparing to implement the strategy, need to identify any new training requirements. For example, if you are adopting a digital strategy, do employees need to be trained in a digital mindset or, perhaps, how to participate in hackathons?

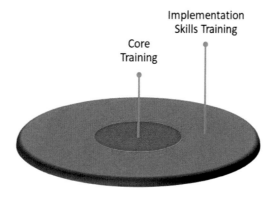

Figure 23.0: Skills Training for Implementation

Identifying the new skills is relatively straightforward but one too often missed by leaders.

The HR director should oversee the needs analysis while working in conjunction with the chief strategy officer or leadership team. Once the training has been successfully incorporated, it can become part of career path development and employees encouraged to be lifelong learners. Your organization might support this by providing, for example:

- A digital library
- Online courses
- Workshops
- On-the-job training

Students are studying for a job that does not yet exist, will be using a technology that has not yet been created, and will need to solve problems we have not yet created!

> *If everyone in the organization continues to think and act in the same manner as they do today, can you expect to achieve the results you need to achieve?*
>
> – Roger Connors & Tom Smith, authors

> *I'd rather have a first-rate execution and second-rate strategy anytime than a brilliant idea and mediocre management.*
>
> – Jamie Dimon, CEO of JPMorgan Chase

Engage Talent

According to *Harvard Business Review*, "The best companies get a 29% boost in productivity from their talent."

The HBR research also states that energetic employees who were also considered inspired were twice as productive as employees who were just satisfied.

Top talent are typically the most engaged and productive. They are critical to engage at the start of the implementation because they:

- Help build initial momentum
- Drive the right actions
- Create early wins
- Influence others
- Improve performance

> *Talent is the multiplier. The more energy and attention you invest in it, the greater the yield.*
>
> — Marcus Buckingham, author

> *Don't leave employees to figure out implementation; provide them the skills, systems, structure, and security to succeed.*
>
> — Robin Speculand

Video Links

- Hiring the Right People, **Mark Zuckerberg**
- Stop Trying to Motivate Your Employees, **Kerry Goyette**

EMBEDDING

Introduction

Your challenge is to identify the new skills employees require to implement the strategy and to ensure they are engaged.

- Allocating Resources to Support Employees
- Develop and Engage Key Employees
- The Middle Managers' Role as Lynchpin
- Tactics for Inspiring Employees to Take the Right Actions
- More Inspirational Tactics

Allocating Resources to Support Employees

To demonstrate the importance of the new strategy, leaders need to identify and allocate the resources required to support the right actions.

Organizations successful in implementation focus first on freeing up essential resources such as technology, people, time, and financial assets.

In some organizations, leaders set the budget before they plan the strategy, making resource management difficult. This is why it is best to craft the strategy and then set the budget.

Kaplan and Norton state that 60% of organizations don't link budgets to strategy. It's a leader's job to proactively manage essential capabilities such as budget and resources. They drive the organization's performance and ensure desired outcomes are delivered.

> *Companies tend to be timid capital reallocators. On average, they put 90% or more of their resources toward the same activities year after year, even though shifting resources as the business environment and company strategies change tends to deliver better, less volatile returns—particularly during down times.*
>
> — Jean-Hugues Monier, Ankur Agrawal, and Emma Gibbs commented in a 2016 HBR post

A McKinsey & Company survey noted that firms who actively reallocate capital expenditure across business units achieve an average shareholder return that's 30% higher than the average return of organizations that were slow to shift funds.

Implementation often fails because of a lack of resource availability.

> *Companies that are great at both strategy and implementation marshal their resources strategically, doubling down on the few capabilities that matter most and pruning back everything else.*
>
> – Paul Leinwand, Cesare Mainardi, Art Kleiner

A significant shift in strategy requires a significant change in resource allocation across the organization.

To leverage resources effectively requires reducing the number of ongoing initiatives so everyone is focused on the highest priorities with the right support.

Develop and Engage Key Employees

To gain initial momentum, target and train the employees who see the new strategy as an opportunity and show enthusiasm for the implementation.

Don't try and train everyone at once, as that can take too long and you will lose momentum at a critical time. Yet many leaders fail to recognize this fundamental fact: selecting champions or change agents works.

With the implementation failure rate being so high, you need to recognize that the odds of succeeding are against you even before you start the strategy rollout.

There are some powerful best practices that you can adopt to succeed. One of these is identifying and focusing on key employees. We call them your *supporters*. Others call them *change agents* or *champions*. The name is secondary to ensuring they are given every opportunity and the requisite resources to support the implementation.

Target and train the most influential people first.

Identify Supporters

There is a simple way to identify your supporters:

- If you were told to axe 80% of your employees, who are the 20% you would keep?

Every opportunity should then be given to ensure your supporters are set up for success. This includes:

- Training them in new required skills
- Allocating required resources
- Empowering them
- Recognizing their contribution
- Establishing them as role models
- Including them in senior leader meetings
- Making them team/project leaders

According to Paul Leinwand, Cesare Mainardi, and Art Kleiner, high-performing teams:

- Spend nearly 20% more time (compared to low-performing teams) defining strategy (i.e., translating a high-level vision into clear actionable goals).
- They spend 12% more time aligning the organization around that strategy through frequent internal communications and driving a consistent message downward into the organization.

> *If you want to build a company that has excellent discipline of execution, you have to select the doer. I'm not knocking education or looking for dumb people. But if you have to choose between someone with a staggering IQ and an elite education who's gliding along, and someone with a lower IQ but who is absolutely determined to succeed, you'll always do better with the second person.*
>
> – Larry Bossidy, author and former CEO of Honeywell

The Middle Managers' Role as Lynchpin

During the strategy implementation, the role of the middle managers becomes more and more critical in engaging, directing, and enabling employees.

Employees turn to their immediate boss for guidance in making everyday decisions. They also listen to their immediate boss more than anyone in the organization (including the CEO).

Your middle managers therefore require coaching and guidance when wrong decisions are made, and they need encouragement for taking the right actions.

Not enough attention, in many organizations, is paid to the middle managers' role as lynchpin in managing employees through the implementation. All the enthusiasm and energy from the leadership can vanish into the middle manager black hole to be lost forever. Consider that according to HBR, only 16% of supervisors say that they understand how strategic priorities fit together.

- Leaders design strategy.
- Middle managers redesign strategy!
- Frontline staff take the implementation actions.

What's critical is alignment across all three levels.

If an employee attends a speech by the CEO on the new strategy and then returns to their workplace where their immediate boss belittles the strategy and tells the employee to carry on doing what they were doing, then what will happen? Employees will listen and follow their immediate boss's instructions, and if this happens across the whole organization, then the implementation fails.

A common question and frustration among middle managers is, "Can I create change at my level?"

The answer is "yes."

The next question is "How?"

It happens by creating success within their area of influence.

Many middle managers initially feel they lack influence, as they are only a middle manager. Jennifer Overbeck, a social psychologist and associate professor of management who works in this area, recommends two steps:

1. Start by changing employee attitudes.
2. This in turn drives their actions.

This success then makes it easier to convince others to change, which involves persuading the manager's own people to do things differently. Jennifer Overbeck published an excellent article titled "You Don't Have to Be the Boss to Change How Your Company Works."

227

Success sells; theory promises.

Middle managers bridge the communication chasm by:

- Being more effective in their communication.
- Understanding the strategic priorities of the implementation.
- Ensuring the right actions are being taken.
- Providing corrective feedback throughout the implementation journey.

A McKinsey & Company study found that supervisors and managers who oversee the work of frontline employees spend more than half their time in administrative tasks, meetings, filing reports, and travel—all things that compete with coaching and mentoring their people.

In the worst cases, these tasks consume 90% of a manager's time.

Once traction is gained, middle managers coach their people along the journey by sharing best practices, learning from mistakes, removing roadblocks, and providing feedback. The coaching provides positive feedback and creates the conditions that encourage participation in the implementation.

> *Paying attention to the role of middle managers does not guarantee implementation. Ignoring their role, however, makes the challenge extremely harder.*
>
> – Antonio Nieto Rodriguez and Robin Speculand

Persuading Employees to Participate

To persuade employees to participate requires small steps to bring them along. Small actions by many people creates big change.

Consider also:

- **Translating strategy into actions:** Managers need to clarify individual responsibilities and expected outcomes to their employees.
- **Role modeling the implementation:** Employees are inspired to take the right actions when they see their immediate boss participating.
- **Reinforcing right actions:** Positive reinforcement drives employees to keep doing the right actions (negative reinforcement is used to stop the wrong actions).

- **Engaging employees in decisions:** This is more effective than dictating the changes and can become a listening post for issues and grievances so that people feel heard.
- **Coaching and mentoring:** Throughout the implementation, employees regularly find themselves at a crossroads and often need guidance to choose the right path. Middle managers need to be visible and supporting employees to make the right decision and take the right action.
- **Allocating resources:** Supporting people to succeed involves setting the strategy and then the budget. This ensures people have the funding and resources to implement and is a powerful symbolism of the strategy's importance.

Tactics for Inspiring Employees to Take the Right Actions

Goal	Implementation actions are taken by the employees while doing their everyday work. But they need to know what the new strategy is, the right actions to take, and how to be inspired to take the right actions.
Implementation Challenge	Only 5% of employees know their own organization's strategy, according to Bridges research. If employees don't know the strategy, they can't take the right actions. Remember, too, just because employees know what they should do does not mean they will do it. Consider that we know eating well and living healthily is good for us, but many people choose to eat fast food and to avoid exercise. The challenge is to create the right implementation discipline inside the organization.
What Needs to Change	Your challenge is to ensure employees know the strategy.

Everyday people are busy, but are the actions they take the right actions for implementing the strategy?

With so much to do each day, it becomes ever harder to make decisions and direct the actions to keep the vision of the long-term strategy front and center. Just because people know what to do does not mean they are doing it. Knowing what to do and actually doing it are two very different things. CEB research[1] indicates that more than half of employees are less focused on the right activities and do not feel aligned with corporate priorities.

To ensure the right actions are being taken

> *to implement, an organization needs to instill discipline—something that is often lacking.*

> *You can either choose the pain of discipline or the pain of regret.*
>
> — Jim Rohn

As you drive and champion implementation, think about how you might instill the required discipline. Below are four powerful best practices:

1. Giving People a Choice

People are more committed to outcomes they set themselves by a ratio of almost five to one, as noted by Carolyn Aiken and Scott Keller from McKinsey & Company in their paper "The Irrational Side of Change Management."[2]

The authors cite a famous behavioral experiment in which half the participants are randomly assigned a lottery ticket number while the others are asked to write down any number they would like on a blank ticket. Just before drawing the winning number, the researchers offer to buy back the tickets from their holders. The result: no matter what geography or demographic environment the experiment has taken place in, researchers have found they have to pay at least five times more to those who came up with their own number. Why? Because we are more dedicated to outcomes we set ourselves.

Leaders need to plan to allow their people to choose how they participate in the implementation to secure greater commitment. In practical terms, that means offering people two or three choices. For example, Infocomm (part of the Ministry of Communications) in Singapore terminated its contract with a single IT vendor in favor of allowing each business unit to choose from three different vendors, rather than being forced to use one vendor.

Beware, however, of giving people too many choices.

Focusing on between three and five options is motivating. Asking your people to focus on more than that is overwhelming. A focused set of options sends a clear and compelling message about what needs to be done most urgently. It also sets the tone for a high-performing culture, enables allocation of resources, and develops the discipline to prioritize.

When organizations try to execute more than 10 objectives, less gets done, and in some cases, none of the objectives are completed. People working on them are so overwhelmed, they do a little on everything, and nothing is finished.

2. Accountability

Accountability is a powerful leadership implementation tactic that is far too often underutilized.

Employees identify the action they need to take and then need to be held accountable. Creating accountability in your culture can make the difference between success and failure.

Adopting accountability is essential when implementing. It requires holding someone responsible, with the emphasis on "one." Leaders hold each person accountable with constant follow-through. Several experts agree that "holding people accountable for execution is one of the most powerful actions you can take."[3]

Sam Silverstein, author of *Non-Negotiable*, put it this way, "There is a difference between accountability and responsibility. You are responsible for things and accountable to people. That report is not going to hold you accountable but your co-worker will. Accountability is keeping your commitments to people. Those commitments may be spoken like 'I will meet you at 11:00.' Some commitments are unspoken like 'I will value you as a person,' or, as the leader, 'I will make sure you are in a position to succeed.' When we take the time to truly understand what our commitments are and then work to keep those commitments, we become accountable."

Creating a culture of accountability in an organization requires knowing what is important to the organization and inculcating it.

Six Steps for Creating a Culture of Accountability

1. **Know the organization's core values.** The values act as your guiding principles of what is important and acceptable.
2. **Clarify expectations.** People need to know how they are expected to perform and what they're expected to deliver based on the values before they can be held accountable. For example, does accountability mean attending meetings on time and/or submitting reports on time and/or checking that the right actions have been taken?
3. **Adopt measures.** Putting in place the right measures allows you to track performance, show what is important, and hold people accountable.
4. **Assign one person.** You can't have more than one person responsible because that eradicates the accountability.
5. **Conduct reviews.** People need to know they will be asked how they did against the planned actions on a regular basis.
6. **Link actions to consequences.** People have to be recognized in a positive way when they take the right actions. There also needs to be negative consequences for inertia or the wrong actions, and the consequences have to be aligned with the values.

3. 90-Day Chunks

Plan to take action over a 90-day period.

This is a powerful principle for successful implementation. Why? There's something magic about setting actions to be completed in 90-day chunks within business. If a task is not completed within that time frame, then:

- It might not have been important enough to demand your attention, or
- It was too complicated, or
- It requires more than 90 days and should have been broken down into smaller actions.

By consciously ensuring the actions can be completed within 90-day chunks, leaders make the actions manageable, and they start to gain traction. Theory promises and success sells. In this situation, the strategy is the theory, and the implementation is where success occurs by completing the action in 90 days.

People identify their action by asking this question: "What can I do in the next 90 days to implement the strategy?"

Some people struggle with this question because they don't see how their work contributes to the strategy or because they don't believe they should do anything differently. It's important, therefore, for them to report to their immediate supervisor—the person they listen to most—and discuss what actions to take toward implementing the strategy.

Their supervisors can assist them in identifying the right actions. During the 90 days, they constantly check in to see how they are progressing while offering support and guidance and holding people accountable. The agreed-upon actions are captured by supervisors so they can hold people accountable. Also, not all the actions will be the right ones or create the expected outcomes. This is why supervisors need to constantly review what is happening.

The aim of insisting on (at least) one action every 90 days is to have as many people as possible participating in the implementation.

> *Mindless habitual behavior is the enemy of innovation. The best way to stay in the game is to change it, and the best way to change it is to measure it. What gets measured gets managed.*
>
> – Rosabeth Moss Kanter, professor at Harvard Business School

4. Follow Up

The number one best practice of top-performing leaders is . . . follow up. If you want to become fit, you have to train. If you want a degree, you have to study. If you want to be promoted, you have to excel. All these require one constant: the right actions. To implement, you must believe in it, commit to it, and act on it.

These three components are consistently required when implementing. But just as important is that employees must know their immediate boss will check on their performance by following up to hold them accountable.

In the follow-up, leaders constantly check and make sure what was agreed on was acted on, the right outcomes were achieved, and people were recognized for their contribution.

They know if they don't frequently reinforce employees' contributions, the actions won't be sustained and people won't feel inspired to keep participating. They will likely slip back into doing what they were doing before the launch of the strategy.

When you transform the way people work, it won't always have the expected outcome. In fact, a new way of working can create the *wrong* actions, as this example from Jakarta, Indonesia, demonstrates.

Jakarta introduced the "3 in 1 Policy" to reduce traffic in its city center. Drivers had to travel with two passengers in the car or take longer routes around the perimeter of the city center, or they faced being fined. The expected outcome was to reduce the traffic in the city.

Instead of reducing traffic, however, the "3 in 1 Policy" created a whole new action. Leaving the freeway before entering the city, drivers would pull over to pick up a passenger or two from a group of people waiting. Each passenger would be paid the equivalent of US$1.50 to accompany the driver through the city center. Clearly, the "3 in 1 Policy" wasn't driving the right actions. Instead of encouraging drivers to travel with friends into the city, it succeeded in spawning a new service.

The following questions can be asked to follow up:

- Is the implementation progressing as planned?
- What is working well?
- What is hindering us?
- How are we reinforcing the right actions?
- How do we create the right implementation conditions?
- How do we sustain everyone throughout the implementation journey?
- How often should we review the implementation?

References

1. "Lead Your HR Function to Success," Gartner, accessed April 6, 2022, https://www.cebglobal.com/exbd/workforce-surveys-analytics/business-priorities/index.page

2. Carolyn Dewar and Scott Keller, "The Irrational Side of Change Management," McKinsey, April 1, 2009, https://www.mckinsey.com/business-functions/organization/our-insights/the-irrational-side-of-change-management

More Inspirational Tactics

You need to clarify individual responsibilities and expected outcomes to key people in the organization. In this rapidly changing world of people being self-directed, the old model of *control* is being replaced by *inspire*.

Example: American Cancer Society

Dr Robert Cialdini asked two slightly different question to identify what would drive people to donate (take a specific action) to the American Cancer Society.

A: Would you be willing to help by giving a donation?

B: Would you be willing to help by giving a donation? Every penny will help.

Which gave the most and why?

Almost twice as many people donated to B. By adding the minimum parameter of "even a penny," the request for action becomes more achievable and doable.

Inspire Employees

Employees have to be inspired to make the right decisions and take the right actions. This is because the right actions taken every day deliver the long-term strategic objectives.

After strategy launch, leaders are often guilty of not following through to ensure employees understand how the strategy impacts their job and that they are taking the right actions.

Leaders must convey relevant content and translate the strategy into an understandable language that will inspire people to participate.

Instead of motivation, look for inspiration.
Inspiration comes from the same word as spirit.
When you are inspired, the spirit moves you.

– Deepak Chopra, author

Employees who attend a strategy presentation may be motivated at the end of it but not necessarily inspired. The word *inspiration* means to be in spirit, to breathe life into something. When people are tuned in to their spirits, they are drawn to perform their best.

> *It would take two and a quarter satisfied employees to generate the same output as one inspired employee. Additional research revealed that inspired people are more creative, robust, and targeted in their work.*
>
> – Eric Garton and Michael C. Mankins, researchers

It's important to note that leaders can't dictate to the organization what to do, for two key reasons. First, by dictating to employees, those employees are less inspired to participate. Second, employees need to individually identify what are the right actions to take.

Employees are five times more inspired to take an action when they choose what to do, rather than being told.

> *It's important to offer people choices as they're more committed to outcomes they set themselves by a ratio of almost five to one.*
>
> – Carolyn Aiken and Scott Keller, "The Irrational Side of Change Management," McKinsey & Company

In this rapidly changing world of people being self-directed, the old model of *control* is being replaced by *inspire*. That means when implementing, first identify which factors inspire employees and then address those factors.

Leadership Example: DBS

One factor is people feeling the new strategy is personal to them. Piyush Gupta, the CEO of DBS Bank in Singapore, believed that to engage his people, he needed to shake hands with almost every one of the 17,000 people (at that time) in his organization. As he did, he personally invited each of them to participate in the implementation.

Leadership Example: Starbucks

Starbucks CEO Howard Schultz has inspired his people by treating them with dignity and respect.

Leadership Example: Virgin

Sir Richard Branson has expressed passion for team members by giving them all of the tools they need to elevate customer service within the numerous companies he owns.

The following extract from Bob Proctor's book, *It's Not About the Money*, demonstrates how to ensure employees take the right actions.

- Those who made the statement, "That's a good idea," only had a 10% chance of making a change.
- Those who committed and said, "I'll do it," had a 25% chance of making a change.
- Those who said when they would do it had a 40% chance of making a change.
- Those who set a specific plan of how to do it had a 50% chance of making a change.
- Those who committed to someone else that they would do it had a 60% chance of making a change.
- Those who set a specific time to share their progress with someone else had a 95% chance of making a change.

> *The single most important change in actions that needs to occur during a time of cultural transition is the shift to greater accountability.*
>
> – Roger Connors and Tom Smith, *The Oz Principle*

Video Links

- This is what makes employees happy at work—The Way We Work, a TED series
- Start With Why—How Great Leaders Inspire Action, **Simon Sinek**

EXECUTING

Introduction

As momentum builds among employees across the organization, leaders focus now to set everyone up for success with the resources and recognition that reinforce the right actions.

- Train the Rest of the Organization
- Continually Reward and Recognize
- Align and Track Resources
- Stop Doing What Doesn't Work

Train the Rest of the Organization

New technologies not only allow organizations to work more effectively and efficiently but create increased opportunities for employees to learn.

There has been a consensus to move away from classroom training that's managed by the HR department toward self-directed, employee-centric, continuous learning.

Employees must be trained in both the skills for their job and the new skills required to implement the strategy, as by default, a new strategy means asking employees to work differently.

Supporters or champions of the change are trained first to give the implementation momentum and traction. Once you've done that, the rest of the organization can be trained in the new skills you have identified.

How do your employees learn best?

From 100%, allocate the mix for:

a) On-the-job training
b) Learning from others
c) Classroom training

Would you put equal weight on each of these elements? Or would you favor one approach over another?

Classroom training is required, but now that employees are self-directed, its significance has been reduced. Stand-alone classroom training is pretty much dead. Any classroom training needs to be supported with coaching and on-the-job application to facilitate the adoption of new techniques and new behaviors.

If you send your employees for classroom training and then fail to provide any further support, you may inadvertently be contributing to the failure of your implementation.

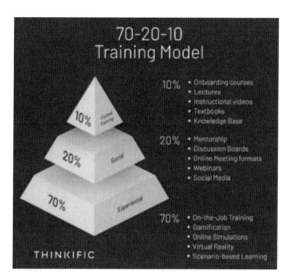

Figure 24.0: Learning Pie Chart

Even the simple follow-up questions such as, "What did you learn?" and "How does it apply to your job?" can make a big difference to how much of the learning is assimilated. And remember what we said about measuring progress. These questions provide your supervisors with an opportunity to gauge how the training is being received.

These days a 70%, 20%, 10% model has become popular. In this approach, classroom training represents just 10% of the learning, leaving you and the managers throughout the business responsible for providing the resources, time, and context for the 20% and 70%. This approach was pioneered way back in the 1980s and has stood the test of time.

- 70%—On-the-job happens during daily application, challenges, and practice.
- 20%—Coaching and support will occur only when you put in place the right structure and opportunities.
- 10%—Classroom learning is training courses and programs.

> ***Employees are no longer dependent***
> ***on organizations to train them.***

The advent of internet knowledge repositories, YouTube, and the explosion in 2020 of free webinars and online workshops now provide a rich platform for employees to develop themselves. That doesn't release you from the responsibility for making sure that it happens. Coaching, reviews, and reflection are all fundamental to every employee and can help guide them to resources, motivate them to make use of them, and enable them to apply what they have learned.

Self-Directed Employees

According to Sheila Heen, co-author of *Thanks for the Feedback,* employees require three types of feedback: appreciation, coaching, and evaluation.

1. Appreciation

Appreciation is a form of encouragement that shows employees their contribution is recognized. It can be as straightforward as a simple "thank you." Receiving the right kind of appreciation at the right time inspires people. Employees pay attention to what gets reinforced more than what is said. They also share with each other when they receive recognition, which is a useful way of amplifying the effect.

2. Coaching

As a coach, your role is to create meaningful goals, guide people to achieve those goals, assist when obstacles need to be overcome, and celebrate successes.

Coaching to improve performance can be informal on-the-job coaching or involve a more structured, scheduled session with a professional business coach.

3. Evaluation

You need to regularly evaluate each person's performance in a fair way. Each evaluation should clarify decisions and aim to manage expectations.

Appreciation can inspire us, coaching can assist us to improve, and evaluation can tell us how we are doing.

Competency Mapping

To ensure employees have the ability to implement, leaders need to identify any new required competencies and incorporate these throughout the various HR processes. A competency is defined as a behavior (i.e., communication, leadership) rather than a skill or ability.

> *Hiring the right people is the most important part of building a strong team, especially when it comes to hiring your first few employees. They set the tone for everyone else you hire.*
>
> – Sheryl Sandberg, COO of Facebook

> *The only way you're going to get the best*
> *out of your team is if you have people from*
> *different backgrounds, experiences, and cultures.*
> *Hiring the right people doesn't just mean*
> *skills and experience, it means diversity.*
>
> – Indra Nooyi, former CEO of PepsiCo

Continually Reward and Recognize

Goal	Reinforce the right behaviors across the whole organization.
Implementation Challenge	When organizations don't transform their rewards and recognition, they create a disconnect between what leaders say and what employees are recognized for. This leads to confusion, the wrong actions being taken, and potentially negative feelings toward the implementation.
What Needs to Change	You need to ensure that employees receive the right recognition for their contribution to the implementation.

Continuously reinforce the actions you want to encourage.

You can reinforce the right behaviors with a certificate, gift tokens, or simply a pat on the back. Whatever your approach, always keep reinforcing the actions you want to emphasize so as to encourage people to keep implementing. Otherwise they will stop!

The heart of the organization is its people. They are your differentiating factor, as they can't be reverse-engineered or simply copied. And yet in many organizations the leaders assume their employees will simply adapt their behavior and adopt new skills in response to the implementation, which, when you stop for a moment and consider it, makes no sense at all.

When you fail to change the rewards and recognition to drive the right behaviors, you are asking one thing but driving something else. This causes confusion at a time when clarity is needed and leads to employees taking the actions that *are* rewarded and recognized—which are guaranteed to deliver outcomes very different from those that you actually need, if not directly adverse to the changes you are looking for!

In some organizations, there is reinforcement of behaviors during the period of the launch but rather, as with communication, this often dissipates over the next few months.

> **The challenge for leaders is to re-create rewards and recognition that becomes permanent.**

> ## Expert Advice
>
> *Double your investment in your people; the rewards will exceed that investment.*
>
> ### Employees must associate benefits to participating in the implementation.
>
> *A guideline from behavioral psychology is that positive reinforcement encourages a behavior, and negative reinforcement stops a behavior.*

For employees to commit to a change, they must see more pleasure than pain in that change.

Rewards and Recognition

Once employees have shown their commitment to implement the changes and start taking the right actions, it is vital they are continually recognized for their efforts, especially when they demonstrate the right behaviors. Some surveys reveal that over 60 percent of US workers say they received no meaningful rewards or recognition for their efforts. Over 70 percent of workers consider themselves disengaged or clock-watchers who can't wait to go home.

Cognitive Dissonance

In 1957, Stanford social psychologist Leon Festinger published his theory of cognitive dissonance. Cognitive dissonance is the distressing mental state that arises when people find their beliefs are inconsistent with their actions or the actions of those around them (for example, if you believe that success with your supply chain depends on the strengths of the relationships you have with your suppliers, but your procurement team simply approaches contracting as a transactional exercise). Through his research, Festinger observed a need to eliminate cognitive dissonance by changing either actions or beliefs.

For an organization, this finding implies that if people believe in the organization's overall purpose, they would be happy to change their individual behavior to serve that purpose. Therefore, to feel comfortable with change and to carry it out with enthusiasm, they must understand the role of their actions in the implementation. Understanding is not simply an intellectual exercise but in this context also implies a belief in what they are doing personally.

You can publish inspirational statements and say all the right things, but if you recognize and promote people who take the wrong actions, cynicism will derail all your implementation efforts.

Positive Reinforcement

Expert Advice

Review your current recognition program and ensure it aligns with your implementation and encourages the right behaviors.

Is Money a Good Motivator?

During the implementation, it can be tempting to throw money at those people who you see as supporting the implementation as a means of recognition. Money, however, is not considered a good form of recognition.

"In motivation to work, pay is not a positive but a negative" is a famous quote from Frederick Herzberg. When people work hard and they feel their pay does not reflect their contribution, they will be demotivated. But the reverse is not true. Money does not motivate behaviors. This contradicts what many people think, so we will explain in detail.

Feelings of self-improvement, achievement, and the desire for the acceptance of greater responsibility are more important than money for persuading people to increase their performance. Take a moment to reflect on this:

If your boss gives you an additional $1,000 a month, would your work performance consistently improve?

The next day after your raise, you may work a little harder (but even then, maybe not). Six months later, it is almost certain you will work at the same pace as you did before receiving the additional $1,000.

AON, a business consultancy focused on risk, insurance, and people, contends that, at best, monetary compensation can only be a "non-negative." That means if you pay too little, you will fail to gain engagement and not attract the right people. If you overpay, the effect is not the opposite. You get neither overwork nor engagement because other factors drive employee motivation.

The Benefits of Awards over Cash

When recognizing employees, giving them awards has intrinsic and significant benefits because awards can provide an internal feel-good effect that money cannot. A certificate at the end of a course, for example, can be significant to someone who feels they have achieved a new milestone.

A study conducted at Massachusetts Institute of Technology and funded by the U.S. Federal Reserve Bank revealed a number of surprising findings. It demonstrated that, for straightforward tasks without much cognitive application, money motivated the worker. However, as soon as cognitive application was required, paying people more actually had a startling effect on their performance. A larger reward led to poorer performance!

Other research published reinforces the message that nonfinancial rewards are far more valuable than money:

- *Forbes* magazine: In the 2010 article "Money Is Not The Best Motivator" by Jon R. Katzenbach and Zia Khan, the authors argue that people are inspired by working autonomously, but more money doesn't often equal greater perceived autonomy.

- A 2010 Harvard study by Teresa M. Amabile and Steven J. Kramer examined the day-to-day activities, emotions, and motivation levels of hundreds of knowledge workers in a wide variety of settings. They concluded that the number one motivator for people at work was progress—that is, feeling they were moving forward and achieving a greater goal. "When workers sense they're making headway, their drive to succeed is at its peak," the article stated.

- McKinsey Quarterly: In a 2009 article "Motivating People: Getting Beyond Money" by Martin Dewhurst, Matthew Guthridge, and Elizabeth Mohr, the authors argued that three noncash motivators—praise from immediate managers, leadership attention, and a chance to lead projects or task forces—are no less effective motivators (or even more) than the three highest-rated financial incentives: cash bonuses, increased base pay, and stock or stock options.

- Research at Randstad claims that 36% of employees would give up $5,000 a year in salary to be happier at work.

Expert Advice

Money is the most expensive way to motivate people, so identify other options you can use.

A strong sense of purpose is the number one motivator of people at work in most jobs.

Yet in many organizations, the reinforcement program remains structured primarily around money as a motivator—a flawed design in most situations. These programs should be about inspiring and engaging your people by providing purposeful work.

Other reasons that awards can be perceived to be better than cash are:

- Symbolic awards are discussed among peers and often aspired to.
- Awards associated with a specific implementation behavior can elevate the importance of the action in the eyes of employees.
- Cash disappears through paying bills, taxi fares, and so on, thus leaving no lasting benefit.
- Awards are not interpreted as a taxable benefit; money is taxable.
- Awards can be personalized to the individual; cash is impersonal.
- The value of a noncash award is increased by what it represents—that is, awards can have a lower Value Creation than a cash payment yet provide the same or greater prestige and motivation.

Are you convinced yet?

Case Study

Citigroup Quality Dividends

Citigroup used the concepts discussed in this article to develop a quality recognition program across the Asia Pacific operations of its corporate banking group. The program was designed to encourage behaviors that leaders wanted to see in the bank's individuals and teams and to embed them into Citigroup culture. They branded the program "Quality Dividends," building on the concept that everyone owns a share of quality. They adopted this theme throughout the recognition program. Quality Dividends aimed to promote behaviors that:

- *Go beyond the scope of work expected*
- *Satisfy an internal or external customer beyond expectations*
- *Motivate, encourage, or enhance teamwork*
- *Create additional value for Citigroup shareholders*

Citigroup also expected to see outcomes such as financial benefits for the bank. The program was tremendously successful, later being rolled out in the organization across 60 countries and into its private banking operations.

Quality Dividends encouraged quality behaviors that ultimately improved customer satisfaction. It built on existing quality initiatives to unite them under a common branding and recognition process. The program had three categories:

1. *The Instant Returns Award—singled out actions and behaviors that went beyond the normal scope of work and were given by staff to staff.*
2. *The Idea Investment Award—encouraged and recognized staff for ideas that demonstrated the potential to lead to business improvements.*
3. *The Blue-Chip Award—recognized the completion of projects that led to business improvements.*

Dividends was launched through the Citigroup Quality IPO. Employees received a Quality Dividends prospectus, and an initial number of quality shares were the currency of recognition. Quality Dividends analysts' reports were produced throughout the program. To make the recognition program flexible and responsive to individual tastes, participating employees could choose to redeem their quality shares for awards from four categories:

- *Travel*
- *Personal/professional*
- *Development, entertainment, and relaxation*
- *Charity donations*

The flexibility to choose your own recognition whenever you wanted to redeem it was a large factor in the program's success. Employees selected their own form of recognition, which ensured it was seen as positive. They redeemed it whenever they wanted it, and they were certain they were going to get it.

> ## What motivates people is a sense of purpose.
>
> – Professor W. Bennis

Align and Track Resources

Reward and Recognize Key Players' Efforts to Encourage Right Behaviors

Goal	Ensure that resources are applied to the right priorities.
Implementation Challenge	In order to have accurate information on how resources are working.
What Needs to Change	Resource tracking is a process to identify how well the organization is using its resources and whether employees' activities are aligned with the priorities set by leaders during the strategic planning process.

While resource tracking needs some time to become really effective, once you have gathered a substantial amount of data, it will enable you to improve a range of aspects within the implementation that will help increase the strategy success rate.

1. Evaluating Team and Individual Performance

Team evaluation is an important indicator for leaders to take corrective actions. Understanding the performance patterns of different people can be useful to reward well-performing teams and employees and to increase engagement.

Similarly, knowing why the work of any one team is suffering or why a team takes more time to complete tasks than is needed may highlight the causes of some kind of a problem.

2. Increasing Planning Effectiveness

Some implementation activities and projects require a short amount of time to complete, but some of them can go on for years. By figuring out the exact time, budget, and number of people needed for certain activities, you can plan the resources ahead, while ensuring that any one activity doesn't (negatively) affect any other activities.

3. Increasing Capacity

Knowing how much time is needed for activities and projects helps leaders eliminate estimation errors and critically release resources for essential activities that support and accelerate the implementation.

4. Improve Communication

When you know how much time your team needs to complete a certain number of activities, you can be more precise in your communication. For example, instead of saying that a project would take three months to deliver, you could say that the project will be ready in two months and 20 days. This kind of communication increases your image as a good leader, but also reduces room for less potential errors.

Expert Advice

The more leaders know about anything at all, the more ways they can find to exploit that knowledge to the organization's advantage. Resource tracking is one of those techniques that, when mastered, can help leaders extract more benefits from the same source or, in other words, get more done using the same resources.

> **You don't build a business, you build people, then people build the business.**
>
> – Zig Ziglar

Stop Doing What Doesn't Work

To achieve business implementation success, Peter Drucker coined the term "purposeful abandonment."

> *If you want to grow your business, before you decide where and how to grow—the first thing you need to do is stop doing what's not working and get rid of the outgrown, the obsolete, and the unproductive.*
>
> – Peter Drucker

Take time to ensure the work being done is adding value to the new strategy.

"To-Stop" List

Because implementation happens at ground level, people need to be empowered to take the right actions to improve their work. This includes being able to eliminate non-value-adding work. We all have "to-do" lists, but employees also need "to-stop" lists of actions that don't contribute to the new strategy.

When you provide the opportunity, empowerment, and methodology for people to eliminate unnecessary tasks, they will stop doing non-value-adding work, improve what they are doing, and rise to the occasion. Examples of non-value-adding work include sending out reports people don't need, redoing work, being on a conference call unnecessarily, or checking work that's already been checked. Some will be excited because leaders are finally providing the opportunity to change activities they believe impede progress.

Example: VP

A vice president at one global company found that members of his management team were spending up to three quarters of their time in meetings.

He therefore decided to:

- Forbid morning meetings altogether, freeing time for value-adding activities

- For remaining meetings that were truly necessary, he imposed a one-hour time limit and required that all meeting hosts send an agenda and clear objectives in advance
- As the role model, he made a point of leaving meetings after 55 minutes, and whenever an agenda and objectives had not been sent by a meeting's starting time, he would ask that the meeting be rescheduled.

In a large organization, it's estimated that up to 33% of people's work can be non-value-adding. When people eliminate non-value-adding work, they critically create space and free up resources to take the right actions.

External Papers

- A Behavior Model for Persuasive Design **by BJ Fogg**
- You Don't Have to Be the Boss to Change How Your Company Works, **HBR**
- Eight Benefits to Measure Employee Engagement in Real Time **by Celpax**
- Being Digital: Engaging the Organization to Accelerate Digital Transformation, **Capgemini Consulting**

Video Links

- Where Do You Have to Start Culture Change? **Simon Sinek**
- Can the Purpose Be Kept in a Metric? **Simon Sinek**

SUSTAINING

Introduction

Strategy continuously needs to evolve, and leaders need to ensure employees do so as well by continuously adopting new skills and capabilities.

- Identifying Shifts in Resource Requirements and Ensuring Adequate Bench Strength
- Ensuring Continuous Engagement across the Organization
- Self-Directed Employees

> ### Identifying Shifts in Resource Requirements and Ensuring Adequate Bench Strength

You need to ensure that the new resource requirements are understood and taken into account in the subsequent year's strategic planning exercise. Resource requirements and planning is often seen as a numbers exercise—how many full-time employees (FTEs) do we have?—at the risk of ignoring the competencies and skills needed by the organization to implement your strategy successfully.

An organization that's well-versed and experienced in resource planning can make itself much more productive and cost-efficient. It can also make a real difference in the employees' morale if they know that decisions affecting their careers are being made in accordance with thoughtful, proactive analysis instead of last-minute reactive actions.

Tips for Managing Human Resources

1. Minimizing Wasted Dollars on Excess Personnel

A small organization that can manage with nine people but has 10 wastes nearly 10% of personnel costs that could be used elsewhere. While this may only be $30,000 to a small organization, the costs, following the 10% model, may waste millions of dollars for larger organizations.

Conversely, having too many tasks for too few personnel can cause stress to build up to a critical level as people struggle to get the job done. Matching the number of employees needed to complete the tasks is critical.

2. Forecasting Future Needs and Expenses

Situations change and so do human resource needs. Long-term forecasting allows an organization to make tactical plans to meet those needs. For instance, an expansion of the organization in three years might provide a need for 300 additional employees. If the community doesn't have the needed demographics, though, those new employees may have to be brought in from elsewhere, which raises the cost and takes much longer to accomplish.

For seasonal businesses, every six months may make a significant difference in the numbers of personnel needed. This may become a recurring problem if the HR department isn't proactive in planning.

3. Scheduling Implementation Requirements

Some organizations schedule multiple work shifts, though staffing levels may differ between each. This type of planning particularly requires the strategy and HR teams to work together. Implementation requirements may be apparent to those involved with the strategy but not necessarily to HR.

4. Leveraging AI in Hiring

Interviewing and selecting new hires is, at best, an inexact science. You can never know until weeks and perhaps months have gone by whether someone will work out. AI does not replace hiring but complements human intuition. It also eliminates routine tasks such as reading resumes, which allows for more value-adding activities from people.

The better the HR department has planned and leveraged AI for the organization's needs, the better it works out.

5. Training for Current and Future Skills

HR may be heavily involved in the training process for the employees. Effective implementation training can't be done without a plan that details what knowledge needs to be communicated, who will provide the training, and how the training will be done.

The HR department that ensures employees are thoroughly trained and competent in the current and new skills makes the difference between success and failure.

Ensuring Continuous Engagement across the Organization

The title of this section is "Ensuring Continuous Engagement across the Organization" because it's about ensuring leaders, as well as employees, stay engaged throughout the implementation.

As soon as leaders become disengaged,
so will their employees.

Leaders have a nasty habit of allowing their focus on the strategy and its implementation to wane over time. In many organizations, by this stage of the process, implementation is no longer on the agenda in meetings or even on the leader's radar. As soon as that happens, momentum stops dead. If leaders are no longer paying attention to it, then why should the employees?

Leaders' Engagement

It's slightly baffling that this paragraph is even needed. The strategy is the future of the organization, and leaders are responsible for directing the organization forward. However, as we know, leaders are only human, and as with the rest of us, can lack the discipline to follow through.

> *The greatest of strategies will fail if not executed well,*
> *and execution is a discipline that can be learnt.*
>
> – Piyush Gupta, Group CEO, DBS Bank

For you to live a healthy lifestyle, for example, discipline has to become part of your DNA. Along the way, you'll have many distractions. It requires focus, commitment, and passion to overcome them and succeed where many fail. This is also true for strategy implementation.

The Discipline

Everyday people are busy, but are the actions they take the right actions that are adding value to the strategy? With so much to do each day, it becomes increasingly difficult to make decisions and direct the actions to keep the long-term strategy view in place. You are responsible for maintaining the focus and discipline.

Also, just because people know what to do does not mean they are doing it. Knowing what to do and actually doing it are two very different things. Did you know, for example, that research reveals that 44% of doctors smoke!

CEB research indicates that more than half of employees are less focused on the right activities and do not feel aligned with corporate priorities.

Leaders are responsible not only for themselves but also for their employees' discipline in regard to implementation.

Discipline is the bridge between goals and accomplishment.

Discipline Tactics for Leaders

The following are tips that may help you stay focused and disciplined:

- Make the effort to stay involved in the implementation.
- Set up a process to continually review implementation progress and stick to it.
- Take every opportunity you get to coach employees.
- Listen to and nurture the communications.
- Manage the employees' moments of truth.
- Check regularly to ensure implementation remains on meeting agendas.
- Reward and recognize the right conditions and behaviors.
- Listen and respond to the measures you have established to manage the business.
- Synergize employees' work to the implementation requirements.

Self-Directed Employees

A recurring theme is the appetite employees have for self-direction in today's organizations, and as many organizations strive to be agile, this creates the opportunity for a fresh approach. In some organizations it's estimated that only 20% of employees have fixed positions, and the remaining 80% move from one project to the next. Their work is evaluated at the end of each project. Like actors working on a movie, they throw all their energy and talent into the current project. As soon as it's complete, they transfer that energy and talent to their next big role.

This represents a dramatic change to the management approach of the second half of the 20th century, which was heavily influenced by World War II. In that era, managers gave orders and employees carried out those orders—command and control.

In the 21st century, the transition from managers to leaders underlines how people respond more to guidance and coaching than to command and control.

1. Increasingly, employees no longer depend on the organization for training and development because they leverage what's available outside of the workplace.
2. Employees are empowered to make changes as organizations become more agile, and the ecosystem is built to support this.
3. Everyone is working cross-functionally in teams and across borders.
4. Most of us now have more than one boss.

To check on what team members are doing, team leaders need to meet regularly with them, either in person or on conference calls—to share feedback, learn about progress being made, and determine where they may need support.

To encourage employees to be self-directed, consider taking the following actions:

- **Show appreciation**—inspire your people by showing you recognize their contribution.

- **Set up a coaching structure**—and establish the processes and structures that assist people to improve.

- **Offer brief but frequent feedback**—plan team or departmental sessions to last 30 minutes or less.

- **Structure a minimum** of four company-wide feedback sessions a year, and allow for ad hoc meetings as required.

- **Be sincere and authentic**—Employees will abandon the process if they even sense insincerity. If you are too busy, then postpone a meeting rather than rushing through it. Don't say your door is always open if you never come out of your office. Sincerity and transparency (about both the opportunities and the challenges) will build trust and quality relationships.

- **Make sure people are appropriately remunerated**—should never be an issue in performing their work.

Sustaining Employee Engagement

Leaders have a bad habit of allowing their focus on the strategy and its implementation to waver over time. In many organizations, by this stage implementation is no longer on the agenda in meetings or even on the leaders' radar. As soon as that happens, momentum severely stops. If leaders are no longer paying attention to it, then why should the employees?

Each of the eight areas in the model are *moments of truth* (a popular term in business that actually comes from bullfighting!).

You need to ensure that contribution to the strategy is woven through every moment of truth.

For example:

- Are the people who contribute most to the implementation offered the fastest career development?

- Does the organization culture echo the contribution from the implementation? In other words, is your culture changing as the business changes?

- Do employee pay and benefits reflect their contribution to the implementation?

The End of Annual Appraisals

> ### *Think about new ways to emphasize employee recognition because annual appraisals are, finally, dying.*

In at least 15% of Fortune 500 organizations, annual appraisals have been abandoned. Why? Leaders can no longer wait 12 months before sitting down with employees to discuss their performance.

Annual appraisals are also expensive and, sadly, in many cases ineffective. Adopting a different approach to performance management can create a tremendous opportunity not only to sustain the execution but to generate better results, too.

Annual reviews have been replaced by quarterly *check-ins* to:

- Shift conversation from the past to the future
- Replace employee management with encouraging higher performance
- Increase engagement through feedback

Examples of how companies have weighed in on this approach:

- Microsoft abandoned appraisals in 2014 because leaders believed they restricted collaboration and creativity.
- Accenture abandoned its annual appraisals in 2015 for its 330,000 employees because leaders observed the appraisals were demotivating.

Video Links

- Managing People as Carefully as Money, HBR

IMPLEMENTATION QUIZ QUESTIONS

1. There is a direct correlation between higher employee engagement and successful strategy implementation. Employee engagement is critical because?

   A   Implementation requires employees to go the extra mile

   B   Lower employee engagement can cause confusion and delays

   C   Leads to higher employee commitment

   D   All of the above

2. Implementing a new strategy provides leaders with an opportunity to focus on top-performing employees and to trim away poor-performing employees. This is important because?"

   A   Organizations need to maximize efficiency

   B   Organizations can no longer afford to carry low-performing employees

   C   Non-engaged employees can be detrimental to the business

   D   All of the above

3. When launching a new strategy within an organization, employees will react differently. The most common reaction is?

   A   Most employees immediately engage

   B   Some employees immediately engage

   C   Most employees resist

   D   None of the above

4. Implementation often fails because of a lack of resource availability. To effectively leverage resources, leaders should?

   A   Increase the number of ongoing activities

   B   Spread resources across the whole organization so as to cover all eventualities

   C   Invest resources in the same activities year after year

   D   Double down on a few capabilities

5. The chances of succeeding in strategy implementation are against you even before you start. To support employees to improve the organization's chances, leaders should?

   A   Focus from the beginning on the people who are most engaged and supportive

   B   Immediately focus on overcoming those who resist the most

   C   Treat all employees as equally engaged toward the implementation

   D   None of the above

6. In implementation, not enough attention is paid to the role of middle managers. To rectify this, organizations need to?

    A   Recognize that middle managers translate the big-picture strategy into every-day actions

    B   Appreciate that middle managers act as coaches to employees

    C   Recognize that employees listen to their immediate boss the most

    D   All of the above

7. Employees cannot take the right actions if they do not know the strategy. To overcome this leaders need to?

    A   Tell employees exactly what needs to be done

    B   Check in once a year on performance

    C   Set targets for 12 months

    D   None of the above

8. By default, a new strategy means asking employees to work differently. Employees learn best from?

    A   Being left to their own devices

    B   On-the-job training

    C   Learning from others

    D   Classroom training

9. To encourage employees when they take the right actions, they need positive reinforcement. The best form of reinforcement is?

    A   Giving employees more money

    B   Giving employees more vacation time

    C   Giving employees more responsibility

    D   None of the above

10. As soon as leaders become disengaged in the implementation, so do employees. To sustain leaders' engagement, organizations should?

    A   Allow leaders to set their own approach within their area of responsibility

    B   Reinforce a command and control–style culture

    C   Conduct regular reviews with the leaders to ensure they have adopted the right discipline

    D   Focus only on operational performance during meetings

Answers to the quiz questions can be found on page 314 in the Appendix.

CHAPTER 8

Track Performance

STRATEGY
IMPLEMENTATION
INSTITUTE

Taking corrective action along the way is critical for the success of any implementation. How do you know where you are and what action to take if you are not diligently tracking your performance throughout the whole journey? Too many leaders start off with the right intentions, but somewhere between thought and actions they lose focus and commitment.

Tracking performance is an essential discipline, and this chapter focuses on ensuring your organization has the right measures in place to manage the implementation and the discipline to continually review the organization's performance.

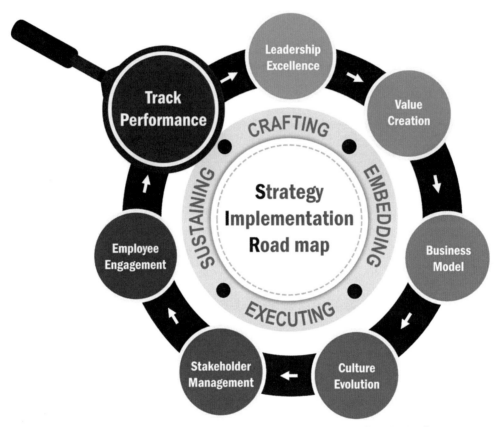

Figure 25.0: Strategy Implementation Road Map©

This section addresses:

- The importance of conducting frequent reviews to keep the implementation on track
- Why tracking performance is critical
- How to identify the right measures to track the implementation
- How to use measures to review and manage the business, based on the Balanced Scorecard
- How measures drive the right actions
- How to structure a review
- Tips for hosting effective reviews

CRAFTING

Introduction

By the time you start to implement your strategy, it's essential you have the right measures to track progress already in place and are instilling the discipline of continual performance review.

- Identify Strategy Objectives

Identify Strategy Objectives	
Goal	To start to translate the strategy into objectives so as to break the implementation down into small, deliverable components and identify specific measures to track the progress of each.
Implementation Challenge	Many organizations still persist in drafting a new strategy but ignore the requirement to establish the corresponding performance indicators. If this is your business, you will struggle to know how it is performing against the strategy. If you can't track your performance, then you won't know where to take corrective action or how you are progressing.
What Needs to Change	In early 1990s Robert Kaplan and David Norton introduced the concept of Balanced Scorecard (BSC). This has proved to be a breakthrough for management performance, as it provides greater structure and support and, consequently, it has been quickly adopted by leaders around the world.

First, break the strategy down into the smaller components that are your strategic objectives.

Breaking the strategy down into strategic objectives makes it easier for everyone to understand. It can also make it easier to track the cause and effect of how different elements impact the business which, in turn, allows for more meaningful progress and performance measures.

The methodology advocated by Kaplan and Norton creates what they have called a *Strategy Map*. This is a one-page visual summary of the strategy and its objectives that enables you to describe and communicate your strategies to employees, to show the relationship between strategy objectives, and to identify appropriate measures.

Before the introduction of the Balanced Scorecard, organizations relied largely on financial measures for tracking their performance. The problem, Kaplan and Norton argued, was that financial measures are lagging indicators of performance, which means they only provide the result once the business has been concluded. By that time, it's too late to influence or change what's happening.

Instead, Kaplan and Norton focused on creating indicators that gave a balanced perspective of the organizational performance against the strategy.

The areas Kaplan and Norton's research identified that a business needs to measure:

1. Financial Measures

These are normally the easiest to understand, as they are generally standardized and globally accepted. Financial measures, however, tell you the story after the events have happened. They tell you how well the organization *has performed* in serving its customers or selling its products or services. Because this is historical data, there's nothing you can do by the time you have analyzed it to change the outcomes in a given period (usually a year). Therefore, financial results alone aren't enough to track an organization's performance.

An organization must look beyond financial indicators as a stand-alone performance measurement.

2. Customer Measures

There is a direct relationship between customers and revenue. For example, the more satisfied customers are, the more likely they are to return and buy from you again and thus generate an increase in revenue. The BSC asks organizations to determine what the organization's value proposition is for its customers; that is, why should customers buy from you rather than your competition? Knowing the value proposition enables the organization to put measures in place to track your performance against the stated objectives.

In today's business environment it's concerning to find organizations that don't know if they are actually satisfying their customers, which customers represent which segments of their market, or even when they are in danger of losing their customers. The BSC puts in place a discipline to identify how customers perceive your product or service and to manage the customer relationship against the strategy objectives.

3. Internal Processes

Part of the process of implementation requires you to ask where your organization needs to excel to deliver the strategy—for example, improved productivity or better design. As your organization improves its internal processes, customers should feel the impact, and the customer indicators improve (and this is a good indicator of the significance of the processes you have selected).

The focus on identifying Internal Process measures will drive you to identify where the organization needs to excel internally to deliver the strategy. No organization can be good at everything, and you need to know where your competitive advantage lies.

4. Learning and Growth

Learning and growth is the element that describes the competencies employees require to implement the strategy. Introducing a new strategy means the organization is doing things differently, and you are responsible for training employees in any new skills that are required. For example, if the strategy is about becoming digitally driven, then your employees need to become data literate.

Generally speaking, competent employees are satisfied employees, which in turn creates the environment for improvements in productivity and then, eventually, improvements in customer and financial measures. (Customer and financial measures don't improve immediately because they depend on the increase in capability generated by competent and motivated employees, which enables better processes, better products, and better services.)

> *Adapting the organization's measurement system*
> *to the change agenda is critical for success.*
>
> – Kaplan & Norton

Case Study

Xerox

The following story exemplifies the danger of an organization relying on financial measures alone and ignoring others.

In the 1970s, Xerox had a virtual monopoly on plain paper copiers. It leased rather than sold the copier machines to customers and earned additional revenue from every copy made. Xerox also generated revenue from supporting items such as toner and servicing machines when required.

From a financial perspective, everything looked good and the leaders at the time were only using the financial measures to track performance. However, things were not quite as good as they appeared. The copiers kept breaking down because internal quality was poor, and many customers were unhappy. But these issues were not clearly visible to the leaders because they were not tracking them.

Eventually Xerox leadership heard their customers, but rather than improving quality to make the machines more reliable, they saw a revenue opportunity. They changed their model to allow customers to buy the machines instead of leasing them and established an extensive service center. The service center was not a cost center but was positioned as a new revenue opportunity by the leaders to repair broken machines at the customer's location and to charge for the service.

Given the demand for its services, the division grew into a substantial contributor to Xerox's profit growth. And, as no output could come from a broken machine, customers bought back-up machines, further increasing sales revenue. Thus, all the financial measures, such as sales, profit growth, and ROI, were signaling a highly successful strategy. The leaders were happy but their customers were not; they wanted reliable, cost-effective machines.

When a Japanese organization introduced a more reliable copier at a more competitive price and much smaller size, customers left Xerox in droves. Xerox, one of the USA's most successful companies at the time, almost failed. Only by hiring a new CEO, one with a focus on people, quality, and customers, did the organization survive.

Focusing only on financial indicators can be catastrophic for the organization, and the BSC aims to provide the organization a balanced perspective.

Strategy Maps

Strategy Maps offer a one-page visual summary of the strategy and its objectives that allows your organization to describe and communicate your strategies to employees, show the relationship between different strategy objectives, and identify appropriate performance measures. Considering only a small minority of employees actually know their own organization's strategy, this is an extremely valuable piece of paper that offers a powerful approach to overcoming some of the largest implementation obstacles.

The Balanced Scorecard first translates the strategy into objectives in the four areas on the basis of how you answer a series of key questions. This creates the basis for the Strategy Map, which was not part of Kaplan and Norton's original work and evolved a few years later.

Every strategy objective must have at least one measure identified to track its performance. There will frequently be more than one measure, but the golden rule is that there must be at least one to track the implementation of the objective. The measures then help drive the actions across the organization that deliver the results.

Your leadership team typically will need to meet, initially offsite, to translate the strategy into the objectives that create the first draft of the Strategy Map.

Start by revisiting your corporate vision and the strategy to ensure everyone has the same perspective and understanding for both. The strategy is the means for delivering the vision, which is why it is important to include it in the initial discussion. This is an important initial step because it will avoid issues appearing later in the process from leadership misunderstanding.

Once you have done that, discuss each of the four areas and create the strategic objectives by answering four broad questions:

1. What is the financial perspective of the organization that we need to project to our shareholders? For example, is the organization investing in new research or in expansion, or are we investing in new technology to become more digital savvy or perhaps looking to harvest results from new products and services?

2. What is the customer value proposition? Why should customers choose to purchase our products and services? Why purchase from us and not our competitors?

3. Where does the organization need to excel? What does the organization need to do better than the competition in terms of our internal processes and performance? What new technology can threaten our business and what can complement it?

4. What new competencies do employees need? A new strategy means doing things differently, and employees require training in new skills.

As you and your colleagues answer these questions, your aim is to break the strategy down into strategy objectives which provide the content for the first draft of the Strategy Map. During the rest of the offsite, these objectives are refined. You're likely to need up to two days to discuss and reflect on the objectives selected.

There is no right number of objectives. Too many objectives will strain the organization's resources and capabilities and potentially dilute the strategy focus. Typically, you may end up with around 20 to 25 objectives, but this is only a guideline. Nor does there need to be an equal number in each area.

Once you have identified the strategy objectives, spend some time exploring the relationship between them. Your aim is to show dependencies and cause and effect. This is central to Kaplan and Norton's approach.

For example, training employees typically improves their satisfaction and their productivity. When employee satisfaction and productivity improve, over time, customers will become more satisfied and spend more with the organization.

The logic of your assumptions also assist employees to see how their efforts contribute to the strategy by creating a clear line of sight between the actions and the objectives.

The four headings can be changed as and when required. For example, a nonprofit organization might have Mission on top of the map rather than Financials. A hospital places Patients on top. You may also add other headings. For example, one refinery included HSE (Health, Safety, and Environmental) as a key element in their map.

Once you have drawn the Strategy Map, it makes sense for you to take a couple of weeks' break before generating the measures for the strategy objectives. This will allow everyone time to absorb the new Strategy Map and ensure your leadership team is fresh to complete the Balanced Scorecard. When you are ready, invite the team to meet again for a second offsite (again, typically two or three days) to identify:

- at least one measure per strategic objective
- the targets and baseline data
- the actions and create the communication plan

Expert Advice

It is good to break the creation of a Strategy Map and generation of the measures into two separate leadership sessions. Both require considerable mental concentration, and you want the team to be at its best for both parts of the process.

Measurement is the first step that leads to control and eventually to improvement. If you can't measure something, you can't understand it. If you can't understand it, you can't control it. If you can't control it, you can't improve it.

– H. James Harrington

External Papers

- What is the Balanced Scorecard? **by Balanced Scorecard Institute**
- How Do You Develop A Data Strategy? Here're 6 Simple Steps That Will Help, **Bernard Marr**
- Use Data to Accelerate Your Business Strategy **by John Ladley and Thomas C. Redman**

Video Links

- What Is a Strategy Map, **Abu Dhabi Retirement and Benefits Fund**
- Introduction to the Balanced Scorecard, **IntrafocusUK**
- Hans Rosling's 200 Countries, 200 Years, **The Joy of Stats - BBC Four**

EMBEDDING

Introduction

Embedding is ensuring your organization has the discipline to track the implementation and take corrective action as required, while cascading the strategy.

- Developing the Discipline of Using Reviews to Run the Business
- Identifying the Right Measures and Prioritizing Actions
- Tips for Adopting the Balanced Scorecard

Developing the Discipline of Using Reviews to Run the Business	
Goal	Leaders frequently review the implementation and make appropriate adjustments to ensure the strategy stays on target. This also provides feedback on the progress to the whole organization and holds people accountable.
Implementation Challenge	The odds of successfully implementing a strategy that isn't regularly reviewed are slim to none. As you implement, you move from the *big think* to the *doing*. It becomes clear during the implementation that what sounded good in theory does not always work in practice. As a result, the implementation must be reviewed to ensure you are achieving the desired strategic outcomes. Implementation without proper review is like the man falling from a 30-story building. At each floor, someone asks him how he's doing, and he replies, "So far, looking good!" A Bridges survey revealed that leaders in almost 50% of organizations review their strategy implementation fewer than three times a year, while only one in five reviews it once a month.
What Needs to Change	Implementation is all about taking the right actions. Leaders throughout the organization are responsible for ensuring employees are doing this.

When you meet for reviews, you may well ask your team to prepare information. This initiates a cascading effect, as the team pays attention to the same things as their bosses and learns to recognize what's important to them. Any follow-up actions from the reviews have a similar impact.

Keeping the Strategy on Your Radar

You would think this message should be redundant. If leaders are responsible for strategy and its implementation, then it seems logical it's where they will spend most of their time. But as we all know, this is not necessarily the case. Leaders are distracted by both internal and external issues: product launches, staff turnover, emails, conference calls, new products from the competition, market movement, stock price, and others. These items succeed in distracting leaders. Regular reviews correct this and keep the implementation on their radar.

Some leaders say they only have so much time for implementation-review meetings. However, strategy implementation reviews are not just another meeting; they make up part of processing the future of the organization.

A good question to ask is:

"Can you afford not to meet on a regular basis, if you want to know how the organization's future is progressing?"

Focusing on Solving the Strategic Problems

By holding business meetings every two weeks and C-suite reviews every quarter, you focus your attention on solving the big picture. It helps you avoid being distracted by operational issues.

Your attention can easily be diverted by operational issues because you know you can assist with them, and it feels good to be in control. But that's not what you are being paid for. When you get together at the two-week meetings, leaders must report on the progress made. This will help keep you focused on the big picture and reinforces the need to delegate operational issues.

Members of the Red Arrows, the famous UK flying display team, believe that after every flight together, they should discuss their performance using the following guidelines:

- Be honest.
- Create an atmosphere in which people are comfortable enough to admit mistakes.
- Video everything to analyze everything.
- The leader critiques himself first.

In another example, the core of the Weight Watchers approach is its weekly meeting that promotes weight loss through education and group support, in conjunction with a flexible, healthy diet. Each week, 1.5 million people attend approximately 50,000 Weight Watchers meetings led by 15,000 classroom leaders around the world. In the Weight Watchers business model, the counselors talk to you, weigh you, and educate you through group involvement about food and exercise.

Procter & Gamble holds *bare knuckle* meetings. This expression is an old boxing term from getting into an encounter when the gloves come off. In these meetings, people are free to present controversial or challenging ideas; their discussions are hard-hitting and to the point. In this environment, the whole organization is held accountable for the actions agreed on.

The Number One Best Practice of Successful Leaders

In their seminal *Fortune* article "Why CEOs Fail," Ram Charan and Geoff Colvin indicated that one best practice of leading CEOs occurs at the start of every meeting. Successful CEOs follow up from the preceding meeting and make sure the right actions have been taken.

Here are six tips for holding effective reviews:

- **Ask for openness**—Emphasize the importance of being open and honest in your assessment. Make sure that people aren't in any way punished for being open.

- **Be objective**—Describe what has happened in objective terms, and then focus on improvements.

- **Document success**—Document practices and procedures that led to project successes and make recommendations for applying them to similar future implementations.

- **Look with hindsight**—Pay attention to the "unknowns" that may have increased implementation risks. Develop a way of looking out for them.

- **Be future focused**—Remember, the purpose is to focus on the future, not to assign blame for what happened in the past. This is not the time to focus on any one person or team.

- **Look at both positives and negatives as you identify positive as well as negative lessons.**

> *Those who cannot remember the past*
> *are condemned to repeat it.*
>
> – George Santayana, philosopher

The Alignment Exercise

The Alignment Exercise provides an opportunity to review what is currently keeping people busy and to make sure the work adds value to the new strategy. It also allows leaders to glance at current initiatives, check their alignment to the new strategy objectives, reduce the number of ongoing projects, and eliminate the non-value-adding activities. This exercise involves the following steps:

1. Hang up a flip-chart paper that has swim lanes. (To create swim lanes, fold a piece of flip-chart paper in half, then half again, then half again, and open it up.)

2. On the horizontal plane, list the new strategy objectives for the whole organization in separate lanes. (This can also be conducted at the departmental level.)

3. Identify and agree on the major initiatives currently underway. (A major initiative is one that affects the old or new strategy and is visible at the C-suite level. If you question whether an initiative should be included, err on the side of caution and include it.)

4. On the vertical plane, list all the major initiatives in the lanes.

5. Review the initiative against the new strategy objectives and place a tick in the lane that adds value to the objectives of the new strategy.

6. Review any initiative that does not have any ticks, and decide if it should continue or be stopped.

7. Review the boxes with ticks and prioritize them against the new strategy objectives.

By doing this exercise, you find you can eliminate the initiatives that no longer add value to the business. This also frees up time and resources to take the right actions that *do* add value.

The activities listed support you in integrating the discipline of constantly reviewing the implementation.

Identifying the Right Measures and Prioritizing Actions

Goal	To identify the right measures that track the performance of the implementation and work as a management methodology rather than just a measurement tool.
Implementation Challenge	When organizations don't have the right measures in place to track their progress, they don't know where they are in the implementation or where to make adjustments. Without the right measures: ▪ Employees become confused if they're told one thing but are measured against something else. ▪ Employees can take the wrong actions as they are aiming to complete the old measures, not the new ones. ▪ Organizations can't accurately track the progress being made or how the implementation is performing.

What Needs to Change

The Balanced Scorecard (BSC) is specifically explained by Kaplan and Norton as a management methodology, not a measurement tool. Consequently, it is not just a tool for measuring strategy but also enables you to manage the implementation of your strategy, align the business needs, and review the overall performance. For some leadership teams, adopting the BSC results constitutes a complete change in the way the organization is managed. For example, an organization might be seeking to transform from a process of financial reporting and subjective analysis of the results to a balanced perspective with a more objective and factual analysis.

The BSC is an exceptional tool and, like many other key management techniques, using it needs to become part of the DNA of the organization. With practice it can serve to:

- Enhance your understanding of the strategy across different business lines through the discussions generated.
- Provide greater clarity about the strategy—what's important and what isn't.
- Enable you to speak with greater consistency in your messaging by providing the strategy story.
- Demonstrate both the importance and commitment to the new strategy.
- Create a single-page document for sharing the strategy.
- Establish new measures that drive the right actions.
- View the progress of the implementation at all times.
- Make the necessary adjustments along the way.
- Know if the right outcomes are being delivered.
- Communicate facts, figures, and success stories about the implementation's progress.
- Reward and recognize people for their correct performances.

To illustrate how the BSC affects an organization's leadership style, consider a sales manager who seeks to explain poor sales figures by stating that they believe customers are becoming dissatisfied with a particular company product. To support their argument, they share a couple of emotional stories about recent meetings in which customers expressed their frustration. However, a shift has occurred since the organization started using the Balanced Scorecard. Facts and data reporting has been added to storytelling. The sales manager now reports not just the financial figures but also data on declining customer satisfaction, higher defects in production, and reasons for the problems. This allows the team to make more qualified decisions and more accurately manage the business.

Having created the Strategy Map, the next step is to identify the right measures. You need to identify at least one measure per objective. This is because without a measure against each strategic objective, you can't track its performance. More than one measure may be allocated to a strategic objective where appropriate. Once the measures are agreed on, the baseline and target can then be established.

The next stage is to identify the actions that will move the measure toward the target. This then allows you to use the BSC to manage the business toward delivering the strategy.

Once you have completed the offsite brainstorming for the Scorecard measures, you are in a position to start adopting the BSC, and you'll need to observe the implementation closely to ensure the right measures have been selected and that they are driving the right actions. Employees may then be held accountable against the actions.

> *The only way you know a strategy is good or bad*
> *is by implementing it, testing it, and reviewing it.*
>
> – Robin Speculand

Identifying Measures

Identifying the performance measures associated with the Scorecard requires its own discrete offsite session, once you have created the Strategy Map. Start by first reviewing the Strategy Map, with a fresh perspective, for any inputs and adjustments. Once everyone agrees on the Strategy Map, the team can move onto identifying the right measures to track each strategic objective.

The model in Figure 26.0 explains the thread from vision to organizational performance.

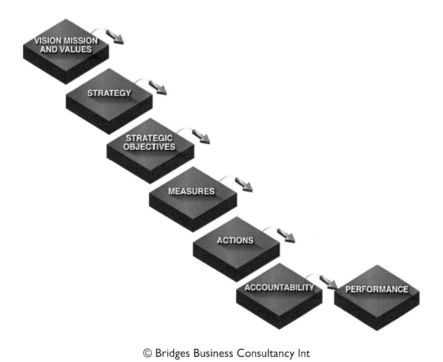

© Bridges Business Consultancy Int

Figure 26.0: Performance Model

The vision is the future state of the organization. The mission is the core purpose. The values are the guiding principles. The strategy is the detailed plan for how you differentiate yourself from your competitors and how you will achieve the vision. Identifying strategy objectives enables you to translate the strategy in practice. Every strategy objective must have at least one measure. Every measure has its own baseline and target that drives the right actions for how the organization will achieve the targets. Individuals may then be held accountable for the actions they own. These actions are constantly reviewed to ensure the organization is on the right path toward the vision and delivering the performance.

When crafting the BSC, leaders commonly ask, "How many measures should a Scorecard have?" There is no right number, just like the right number of strategic objectives. Since you need to have at least one measure for every strategy objective, the number depends on the complexity of the organization's strategy and business.

When you are designing the measures, don't ask, "What should we measure?" Unfortunately, this question can generate the wrong measures, which will drive the wrong actions. The right questions to ask are:

1. "What are the strategic objectives?"
2. "How will we know if we are successful in implementing each strategic objective?"

The process of creating the measures is not complicated, but selecting the right measures and implementing them can be challenging. Leaders need to pay specific attention to the selection of the measures as they drive the employees' actions.

This involves reviewing the measures as they are created and asking:

What actions do we expect to see from employees when we implement the measures?

You should then actively follow up during the implementation of the BSC to ensure the right outcomes are being achieved.

Remember, this is not an exact science but a process of trial and error. Measures do not always drive the actions that you anticipate, and you'll need to adapt or change your measures in response to feedback, customer behavior, or changes in context, as the following two case examples illustrate.

Case Study

National Library Board

In Singapore, the National Library Board has become a global benchmark for how to run an efficient library, and it frequently entertains visitors to share their success. In the 1990s, the leadership recognized a disconnect between their mission of getting as many people as possible to read in Singapore and the measures they were using. The team revisited its measurement system so as to encourage the right actions.

To encourage the public, they started to measure the number of books borrowed per member and the turnover rate for books. In addition, the librarians responded by adopting a number of measures aimed at encouraging more people to read and borrow books.

In the next step, the leadership reviewed the processes that supported the measures and changed them again to build further support for their mission. For example, they allowed customers to borrow books from one library and return them to another, as well as setting up stations at post offices and supermarkets for book returns. They also created an online service to allow readers to borrow in advance and pick up books once available at a library of their choice.

Case Study

Airline Call Center

A call center for an airline segments its customers and has a separate call line for its most important ones. When on a call, the line automatically disconnects after 59 minutes! Why? Because the manager of the call center gets penalized for calls lasting longer than 60 minutes. To make it worse, key customers who had been kept waiting for almost an hour were understandably angry if or when their calls were finally answered.

Knowing this, the Customer Service Officers started to avoid taking calls on the key customer hotline. Both the measure and penalty were selected by management to ensure key customers received responsive service from the call center. In practice, however, the opposite happened. When selecting the right measures, these managers should have first identified what's important to customers who call and then asked how they could ensure that the calls were answered well. The resulting measure is then based on customers' expectations rather than how long it takes to answer a call.

The right metrics drive the implementation; the wrong ones can derail it.

> *What we anticipate seldom occurs; what we least expect generally occurs.*
>
> – Benjamin Disraeli

The measure drove the right behavior for Johns Hopkins University when they impressively reduced its hospital infection rate from 4% to nil by adopting a five-step checklist in its intensive care unit. This checklist reminded doctors to take the key actions.

When starting to identify the measures, start with Learning & Growth.

Once you have completed your L&G measures, move onto Internal Processes, followed by Customers and finally Financials. The reason for this order is simple. Leaders typically find identifying Learning & Growth the hardest and Financial measures the easiest (as most indicators are already established).

Once you have identified the measures, the next step is to set the baseline and target for each. The right measures can then drive the right actions.

For each measure, invite the team to identify the baseline and set the performance target. They can then start to identify the actions required to achieve the targets. See the diagram below:

Figure 27.0: Actions to Attain Target

In a separate discussion, the team should also identify the actions to enable the organization to adopt the BSC. These may include, for example, sourcing some BSC software and communicating the Strategy Map.

The challenge in adopting the BSC is a hurdle that many organizations fail to cross, largely because they underestimate the effort required. They then fail to use the BSC to drive leadership discussions, assist in making decisions, or as part of meeting agendas.

> *50% of organizations who claim to be using the Balanced Scorecard are doing it wrong—for example, no executive ownership, scorecard not linked to strategy or management process.*
>
> – Kaplan & Norton

One CEO who adopted the BSC immediately changed the way she ran her senior leadership meetings. She started every meeting with a review of the Strategy Map and then a discussion on the measures and actions. This shifted the conversation from being predominantly about operations to the strategy implementation instead and reinforced the importance of adopting the new strategy to the rest of the organization—all of which had the desired effect of shifting the conversation among her direct reports to become more strategic. In addition, the impact also cascaded down to middle managers, who started to adopt the new strategy measures and language.

It takes a singular focus and staying power that must be led by the senior leadership to implement the Balanced Scorecard.

The Complexity of Measures

In addition to considering which actions your measures drive, remember to consider the complexity of the measure. When identifying measures, you may be tempted to be very imaginative, but there may be a high cost in adopting some measures. If they are too complex, alternative measures need to be identified that are simpler to implement and easier to understand. For example, a fashion retailer wanted to determine the conversion ratio in its stores (the percentage of shoppers who bought something). Various complex schemes were proposed, involving the use of radio frequency identification tags and various types of sensors. In the end, the organization decided on the simple solution of hiring students to sit outside their stores and count the numbers of people who went into the store and the number who then came out carrying shopping bags. The more inexpensive and convenient it is to calculate a metric, the better. You must also consider the frequency with which it needs to be calculated.

Complex scorecards can cause more confusion than clarity.

The discussion on a measure's complexity should happen when leaders are initially selecting the measure for the BSC. If they subsequently observe that adopting a measure is more troublesome than it is worth, then they must step in and consider adopting an alternative measure or dropping the point completely. Identifying the right measures is not easy, and no measure is almost always better than a poor one, which can drive inappropriate behavior, being difficult or costly to implement or undermining other, sounder measures. You need to take sufficient time to reflect on the long-term impact of any measure before implementing it.

Tangible versus Intangible Measures

Most organizations track a disproportionate number of tangible versus intangible measures. Historically, many measurement systems evolved from the pieceworking of early production processes and have not been updated to reflect modern times. In particular, they underrepresent the importance of intangible measures such as brand value or employer branding on today's business. But we are starting to make improvements.

The investment firm Ocean Tomo estimated that, in 1975, more than 80% of the value noted in the S&P consisted of tangible assets. In 2010, approximately 80% of the S&P market value was attributed to intangible assets.[1] This indicates how the practice of tracking intangible assets has made a massive leap.

Baruch Lev of the Brookings Institution showed that in 1982, 62% of the market value (measured by market capitalization) of organizations could be attributed to tangible assets and only 38% to intangibles.[2] Ten years later, the Brookings analysis of S&P 500 organizations showed that the relationship had been reversed: In 1992, it was 32% tangible to 68% intangible.

Infosys in India is a rare organization that since 2008 has marked its people as assets on the balance sheet. It adopted the Lev Schwartz human resources accounting model to calculate its people's collective worth. (The model is based on human capital theory that recognizes human capital as one of several forms of holding wealth for a business enterprise, such as money, securities, and physical capital. In this model of accounting, human capital is treated like other forms of earning assets and thus is an important factor explaining and predicting the future economic growth of the organization.)

Even though identifying the right measures is critical, linking the measures to action is what makes the biggest difference and drives the implementation.

> *Measure what is measurable and make measurable what is not so.*
>
> – Galileo

References

1. "Ocean Tomo 300® Patent Index," Ocean Tomo, accessed April 6, 2022, http://www.oceantomo.com/ocean-tomo-300/

2. Margaret Blair. (1995) *Ownership and Control: Rethinking Corporate Governance for the Twenty-First Century.* Washington, DC: The Brookings Institution, chapter 6.

Tips for Adopting the Balanced Scorecard

Tip #1: Build Awareness

One of the most significant roles of the BSC is as a tool to share the strategy and align the organization. This will only work if the whole organization is involved in the BSC creation and implementation. Your role as leader is to ensure everyone is engaged and appreciates the sense of urgency around the need for transformation.

To ensure a consistent message is being shared, some organizations conduct a communication workshop once the BSC is complete. Typically, half a day is sufficient for the leaders to practice sharing the strategy story and what needs to be done to adopt the BSC.

How B Braun Built Awareness of Its Strategy

B Braun in Asia used a sports metaphor to explain why the organization was adopting the BSC and how to use it. Using the strapline *Strategy into Action*, provocative posters asked such things as, "Are we singular in our focus, to ensure success?" and "Will the alignment to the mission see us overcoming challenges?" All the posters and internal marketing material carried the line, "From out of the many business demands of today, we must be clear and concise in our communication by adopting a balance scorecard to convert our strategy into actions."

Key players responsible for adopting the BSC received a fun sports bag containing a game plan for implementation, postcards of the posters, FAQ cards, wobblers for their desk, a whistle, a branded foam finger, a clipboard for reviewing performance, and a slide deck. The BSC is a serious subject, but for this organization the sports theme and especially the sports kit created a lighter side to its adoption that worked in gaining early engagement.

Following the leaders' communication workshop, a workshop can be conducted for key employees in how and why they should use the BSC.

Tip #2: Gain Commitment

The most effective way of securing commitment requires you to lead by example. Despite the overwhelming evidence of the power of modeling behavior, some leaders are guilty of persisting with an approach of "Do as I say and not as I do."

The BSC is an initiative that must be driven from the top down, as it transforms the way the business is managed. Employees need the reassurance of their bosses practicing the new way of managing the business before they will recognize the need to change themselves. They need to see you holding everyone accountable against their actions, reviewing the impact of the measures you have established, and communicating the strategy story repeatedly using multiple media and platforms.

Another critical way of securing commitment is by ensuring the organization's reward and recognition system is properly aligned to the BSC. Employees need to know they are recognized for their contribution and that the rewards and recognition system supports the right actions being taken across the whole organization.

Tip #3: Link Strategy and Annual Budgets

A common issue highlighted by Kaplan and Norton is that organizations set the budget first and then the strategy second. When this happens, you may inadvertently starve your implementation of the necessary funding.

Kaplan and Norton recommend identifying the new required operations and capabilities to implement the strategy that arise from the BSC discussions and then setting the budget on that basis.

The aim is to put strategy at the center of everything the organization does. This includes using the BSC to evaluate potential investments and initiatives.

Each business vertical also identifies first what it needs to do to implement the strategy and then sets its budgets. This creates synergy and alignment across verticals.

Tip #4: Adopt a Visual Dashboard

Airline pilots use a bank of indicators to help them fly the plane. Businesses, which are infinitely more complex, rely on a far wider, changing set of conditions to thrive, so a good dashboard is essential for you to make any sense of what is going on. The dashboard visually displays the strategic objective and the baseline and target. But more importantly, it shows the progress (or lack of it) toward the implementation across the organization. A well-designed visual dashboard can be used in meetings, off sites, and one-on-one discussions and is available online to employees, recalibrated to reflect their particular role and information requirements.

How: Procter & Gamble Adopted a Visual Dashboard

Spreadsheets have proved remarkably resilient, but they are now in decline as more organizations adopt visual data. With data becoming readily and instantly available to leaders, there has been a dramatic improvement in its presentation, making decisions easier and faster.

Procter & Gamble (P&G), for example, has Business Sphere and Decision Cockpits displayed on 50,000 employee computers. Business Spheres allow the leaders to see a global map of markets either growing or shrinking and to examine the countries and categories ranging from laundry detergent and shampoo to potato chips and diapers. The Business Spheres also assist employees to see and understand a variety of data and compress the time needed for making decisions. The cockpits track the consumer pulse of the brand. Instead of reading spreadsheets and trying to decipher the information, P&G uses data visualization that helps users analyze exceptions and trends.

Tip #5: Greater Accountability

Accountability is a powerful way to ensure employees take the right actions to implement the strategy by using the BSC. Several experts, including us, agree that holding people accountable for implementation is one of the most powerful actions you can take.

Nevertheless, for some, accountability has negative connotations. They assume it only happens when something goes wrong—that is, leaders hold people accountable only when there are mistakes or problems. If this belief prevails, then the organization will struggle to deliver results. By leveraging accountability as a powerful tool, organizations create a culture of accountability that demonstrably holds people responsible for taking the right actions.

To create a culture of accountability, ensure people know they will be held accountable and their achievements recognized, based on the organization's values. Then they will start to commit.

Tip #6: Review Performance

In some organizations, reviews are carried out only once or twice a year. By that time, minor problems have likely ballooned into large ones—some large enough to derail the whole implementation and miss the target. Therefore, regular reviews are required. The review also allows leaders to acquire feedback to learn about and improve the strategy and the implementation.

If the prospect of reading the Kaplan and Norton suite of books feels a little too daunting, you may find it easier to start with their articles published in *Harvard Business Review*.

External Papers

- Cascading Your Strategy **by Intrafocus**

Video Links

- How Data Science Helps Small Businesses

EXECUTING

Introduction

Executing is making sure the implementation is reviewed as required, and challenging the original strategy assumptions.

- Regularly Reviewing Performance to Manage the Business
- Best Practices for Using Measures to Manage the Business
- Lessons for Using the BSC
- Eight Is Great—Wells Fargo Case
- Identifying and Establishing Structured Reviews

Regularly Reviewing Performance to Manage the Business

With the rapidly shifting business landscape of today, measures and data need to be reviewed to ensure their continuing relevance so the organization is responsive to market and internal changes.

Reviewing measures is akin to standing on the scales when losing weight—it shows you the truth of your efforts. Precisely for this reason, some leaders prefer *not* to review the measures, as they can display bad news. Your strategy measures also reflect the long-term objectives of the business while leaders in many organizations focus on the short term, as this is where they are held accountable.

It takes discipline to defend your position every quarter while balancing the long view with quarterly performance.

It's even tougher when resources are allocated and goals are set for short-term performance. This is one of the main reasons an implementation loses traction and can fail.

> *The truth of the matter is that you always know the right thing to do. The hard part is doing it.*
>
> – General H. Norman Schwarzkopf, U.S. Army

> *Measures are the means for managing the*
> *implementation and the business. Without*
> *specific measures, leaders typically rationalize*
> *any outcome as they expected.*
>
> – Robin Speculand

How to Use Reviews

Instilling the discipline to manage the business using the BSC has to be a top-down initiative. When the CEO uses the BSC to manage the business, then so will their direct reports, and then their direct reports, in turn. People pay attention to what their immediate boss pays attention to.

Establishing regular, structured reviews is a disciplined best practice because it gives support while reinforcing key messages and objectives. It also ensures the right actions are taken, allows for changes, holds people accountable, and identifies opportunities to celebrate.

Ensuring the Quality of Your Measures

If the numbers reported are to be meaningful, the organization needs to have 100% confidence in them. If it does not, the lack of confidence can undermine the implementation. As technology improves and systems automate the gathering of analytics, this can increase confidence. Data gathered manually increases the opportunity for errors, takes time, may be unconsciously biased, and can undermine confidence in the numbers.

Effective analytics is a powerful enabler of ensuring quality of measures.

Ensuring Transparency

You may be tempted to limit what you share or sometimes to interpret the data creatively. Any sense of this among employees is likely to undermine their confidence in implementing the new strategy. You need to lead by example, and that includes behaving transparently.

Transparency in business means no hidden agendas or pre-conditions. It also requires the availability of all requisite information to support collaboration, cooperation, and collective decision making.

Aligning Rewards and Recognitions to Measure

When organizations tie pay and performance to strategy performance measures, it guides employees' actions, increases their engagement, and improves productivity.

By leveraging the measures to drive the right actions—the time and effort—employees become more inspired as their contribution is recognized and rewarded.

Start every leadership meeting with a review of the BSC as the first item on the agenda.

Best Practices for Using Measures to Manage the Business

Goal	To improve leaders' ability to use strategic measures to manage the business.
Implementation Challenge	In some organizations the leaders spend considerable time developing measures to track the performance of the new strategy but then don't use those strategic measures to make decisions and manage the business.
What Needs to Change	Fifteen measurement best practices enable you to understand how to use strategic measures to run the business.

These are 15 measurement best practices from organizations that have successfully implemented their strategy:

1. Translate your strategy into objectives.
2. Drive actions through measures.
3. Start leadership meetings with the Scorecard as item one on your agenda.
4. Address disconnects between what you say and what you measure.
5. Avoid using obsolete measures.
6. Adopt intangible and tangible measures.
7. Avoid feel-good measures.
8. Assess the complexity of the measures.
9. Recognize that statements are not measures.
10. Have confidence in the numbers.
11. Discuss the Strategy Scorecard with board members.
12. Use a weathercaster's style—first the measure, then the reason behind it.
13. Link pay to performance.
14. Use measures to inspire.
15. Follow A2B formula.

Let's examine each of these best practices.

1. Translate Your Strategy into Objectives

Strategy objectives are the critical, must-achieve, make-or-break organizational performance outcomes. Use a short sentence (e.g., build and leverage brand strength) that fits in the box for your Strategy Map. Set objectives to articulate what the strategy needs to accomplish. *Note: There is no right number of strategy objectives, just as there is no right number of measures.*

2. Drive Actions through Measures

Selecting the right measures and executing them is challenging because specific measures focus people on what to do. For example, as children, we adopted specific actions to gain pocket money; as adults, we adopt specific actions to earn bonuses. Be aware of the actions driven by the measures selected, and constantly review the difference they make.

3. Start Leadership Meetings with the Scorecard as Item One on the Agenda

At the beginning of every leadership meeting, discuss relevant Scorecard measures and determine the progress made. This keeps the execution on the leaders' radar, allowing them to take action as required. It also emphasizes what's important and where to allocate time and resources.

Creating the Strategy Map and Scorecard is relatively straightforward, but having the discipline to adopt them to manage the business can be challenging. Many organizations fail at it.

4. Address Disconnects between What You Say and What You Measure

Eliminate confusion around the execution of a new strategy as quickly as possible so people know what's expected of them.

Part of the confusion happens when leaders say one thing but measure something else. For example, in one organization, a strategy to improve customer satisfaction was set but no measure was attached to it. Instead, people were measured against the financial performance of the business, creating a disconnect. *In the long run, people take actions based on what leaders measure, not on what they say.* In this case, they took actions to increase sales and not to improve customer satisfaction.

These kind of disconnects happen all too frequently. Make sure your measures reinforce the strategy, the desired actions, and the instructions you give.

5. Avoid Using Obsolete Measures

Many measures used in organizations today are the wrong ones. They haven't been recently reviewed and changed and consequently are no longer relevant. Some leaders are guilty of using existing measures designed for an old strategy.

Any new strategy requires a regular process for reviewing and adjusting its associated measures.

6. Adopt Intangible and Tangible Measures

Most organizations track a disproportionate number of tangible versus intangible measures.

Interestingly, Apple is classified as a manufacturer by the US government, yet it has 500 stores worldwide. Its revenue comes mostly from selling products, with all of its production outsourced. It also offers iCloud-related services. Apple rents out servers, which allows it to easily add or reduce capacity.

7. Avoid Feel-Good Measures

Classic examples of feel-good measures are the number of people attending trainings and the number of Facebook *Likes*. Both measures are easy to capture, offer apparently tangible data, but simply aren't meaningful. Just because staff members have attended trainings doesn't mean they've adopted new competencies. And just because the organization has Facebook fans doesn't mean those fans are buying products. Effective measures would include an increase in the competency levels of people and the number of customers who purchased new products through Facebook promotions.

8. Assess the Complexity of the Measures

When identifying measures, what sounds like a good idea at the time can be hard to adopt when you scrutinize it further. After selecting a measure, ask, "What is the cost and what are the challenges in adopting this measure?"

When considering which measures to adopt, err on the side of caution and choose the simplest ones that work.

9. Recognize That Statements Are Not Measures

In reviewing its yearly planning methodology, leaders of a global pharmaceutical organization identified problems using cut-and-dried statements as measures. For example, they'd say, "We will sell our new product to doctors." This is a binary measure, something they will either achieve or miss, but that makes it an unhelpful measure of performance trends or a basis for improvements in subsequent years.

Compare this to saying you plan to run a marathon. The cut-and-dried measure is whether you do it or not. You don't know beforehand how prepared you are until you track the number of runs you do and over what distance. You might add other measures such as how many kilometers you run each week to gain endurance and how many times you work out to gain strength. These indicate your progress toward being ready to run a marathon.

A measure is expressed as an absolute number or a percentage, not a statement.

10. Have Confidence in the Numbers

To be meaningful, you must have 100% confidence in the numbers reported. If you don't, this fact will undermine the execution. As technology improves and systems gather analytics without any human intervention, having this confidence becomes easier. Data gathered manually increases the opportunity for errors, takes time, and can lead to a lack of confidence in the numbers.

11. Discuss the Strategy Scorecard with Board Members

Your board should never be surprised about what is happening in the organization. By regularly reviewing the Strategy Scorecard with board members, you make sure they are aware of the objectives and actions. They can then offer meaningful assistance and guidance.

12. Use a Weathercaster's Style—First the Measure, Then the Reason Behind It

Think about how the weather is reported on television. Weathercasters first report the temperature and then explain why that temperature will be accurate. In meetings, many leaders do the opposite; they explain the why and then report the measure. Reporting the numbers using the weathercaster's method helps you:

- Increase the impact of your presentation
- Avoid disruptive questions that aren't relevant to the discussion
- Set up the context for valuable discussions on what the numbers mean

13. Link Pay to Performance

When you tie pay and performance to strategy performance measures, it guides employees' actions, increases their engagement, and improves productivity. By leveraging the measures to drive the right actions—the time and effort—employees become more inspired, as their contribution is recognized and rewarded.

14. Use Measures to Inspire

What you measure is what people pay attention to. When striving for excellence in execution, measures are leveraged to inspire people to contribute at a high level. Ensure they know what's expected based on what's measured. They must also know what will happen if they reach the goal *and* what will happen if they don't.

15. Follow A2B Formula

When identifying and reporting measures, adopt the format A (current) to B (target). For example: A $268,000,000 to B $350,000,000 in 12 months (A is the current revenue, and B is the target revenue).

Lessons for Using the BSC

When adopted correctly, the BSC is not a tool for measuring strategy implementation but becomes a methodology for managing the business, changing the way, for example, that meetings and reviews are conducted.

A high percentage of organizations fail to adopt the BSC as a methodology for managing the business. Creating the Strategy Map and the Scorecard are relatively easy compared to changing the structure for managing the business.

Why the BSC Fails

More than 50% of the Fortune 500 have adopted the BSC but to various success. From examining the failures, we have discovered it fails for various reasons:

- A lack of executive commitment to adopting into the business
- Is not driven by the C-suite
- Too much emphasis is placed on the financial measures and not enough balance on the nonfinancial measures
- There are too many objectives defined and too many performance metrics being measured
- There's poor communication across the organization about how to use it

> *A successful Balance Scorecard program starts with the recognition that this is not a metrics' project; it's a change project.*
>
> – Robert Kaplan and David Norton

Strategy Office

To overcome the challenges of both adopting the BSC to manage the business and implementing the strategy, some organizations create a dedicated strategy office. The office ensures the organization has a balance in its approach and both a short-term and long-term perspective. It also ensures the organization adopts the discipline and best practices required to succeed while coordinating plans and communication.

Setting up a strategy office is not the right approach for every organization. Some leaders argue they need an additional focus on structure and discipline that a dedicated strategy office can provide. The opposing argument is that implementation is the responsibility of everyone, not only one office.

The answer to this question lies in your organization's approach to making implementation your own. To assist in the discussion, consider the following list of responsibilities for the strategy office.

- Connect the corporate strategy to the lines of business (e.g., communicate and explain what needs to be achieved)
- Report directly to the CEO
- Champion and support the development of the BSC
- Manage organizational alignment with the strategy by overseeing the BSC cascading
- Keep implementation on the leaders' radar e.g., influence meeting agendas
- Provide guidance and support throughout the implementation journey
- Ensure regular implementation reviews of the BSC are conducted
- Champion, standardize, and manage the measures on the BSC
- Prepare regular assessment meetings
- Ensure implementation governance is in place
- Share best practices and lessons learned across all lines of business
- Review the strategic landscape outside the organization for changes that impact the strategy

To successfully adopt the BSC into an organization takes discipline and hard work. It involves changing the way the business is managed from the core. It cannot be conducted at the peripheral and needs to, like any significant transformation, be driven by the C-suite. The senior leaders need to create a cascading effect of using the BSC to manage the business by leading by example when running a meeting.

A best practice is to start the leadership meeting with the review of the BSC.

Start the Leadership Meeting with the Review of the BSC

This sends a powerful message that it's number one on the agenda. It also has the benefit of creating a cascading effect down the organization—employees assist in preparing the content for the leadership meeting review and start to adopt the BSC because they see their boss using it. This then cascades down to their direct reports and so on.

Eight Is Great—Wells Fargo Case

How Wells Fargo Stole Customers' Money

A customer came into a Wells Fargo branch in the USA and explained that he was on Social Security disability benefits, was in the late stages of AIDS, and couldn't work. He could barely walk and talk. The Social Security benefit was all the income he had, and it was barely enough to pay for his rent and food.

He was being charged monthly fees because the amount he was getting from the Social Security was not enough to waive the $15 monthly fee on his account. The customer service rep approached his manager and reported it as an issue of the bank's social responsibility.

The manager's solution was to open the customer a savings account and make a $25 automatic transfer from the accounts that would waive the fees. The customer agreed because he could not afford to lose the $15.

A few months later a nice lady walked into the branch and explained her brother had died and she was there to claim the money from his account. The customer service rep received the death certificate and realized that it was the customer he had helped.

When he opened her brother's accounts, the customer service rep noted that the Social Security checks had stopped coming (because the brother had died) but the $25 transfer was still happening each month. This was putting the accounts into overdraft.

He kept looking at the computer and looking at her face and he didn't know what to tell her. This was fraud, but he could not report it if he wanted to keep his job!

The customer service rep became a whistleblower. This triggered an investigation to how Wells Fargo pushed for growth by elevating its profits over its legal rights of its customers. This then triggered responses from people across the nation validating employees and customers. This revealed the Wells Fargo cross-selling scandal.

- Following the global financial crisis, Wells Fargo was considered one of the safest banks, as it had less exposure to subprime lending. By 2014 it was the biggest bank in the world.
- Wells Fargo was the only bank that had its cross-selling ratio in its earnings report.
- The CEO's preferred tag line was "Eight is great"—meaning every customer should have eight cross-sell products.
- This single-minded target created an adverse culture.

The result of the CEO's "eight is great" initiative was that employees opened 3.5 million phantom deposits and credit cards without customers' consent in order to try and meet impossible sales quotas.

Ironically, new employees received one month training before they were introduced to the code of ethics, which included a guideline not to issue ATM cards to people who didn't request them, not to order credit cards for people who hadn't asked for them (or didn't need them), and never to open accounts without customers' consent.

In the morning huddle, before the branches opened, employees would be required to commit to a figure for how many accounts they would open that day. Managers would then check up to three times a day to see how many new accounts were opened. Staff constantly felt under pressure to deliver the numbers.

At the end of the day, employees were asked why they weren't making their goals. The regional office was calling four to five times a day asking how many new accounts had been opened. The bank's compensation scheme further encouraged employees to pursue underhanded sales practices.

Employees felt pressured to do whatever was required to deliver the target. If they complained to the human resources department about ethics, they were concerned they would be fired, which would make them an example to discourage others from reporting the problems.

- Employees started to open accounts without the full disclosure that was required by US law.
- Social security numbers were just made up.
- Credit cards were issued to customers without their permission.
- A nine-year-old customer had seven different accounts.
- Staff targeted customers who did not speak English.
- Customers were charged fees for accounts that they had not opened.
- Everyone was under peer pressure to open eight new accounts a day.
- The bank knew millions of illegal accounts were being opened and did nothing about it. They reported that the problem was limited to "a few employees"!
- Employees were fired for not meeting sales quotas, and when the disgruntled employees took Wells Fargo to court, the judge supported the bank's right to fire employees.
- Fired employees were blackballed from working in any part of the banking industry.
- 5,300 employees were fired over five years over this issue.

Well Fargo was one of the biggest banking scandals in history, right after new regulations established in the wake of the global financial crises were supposed to clean up banking!

- CEO John Stumpf was forced to resign but was not fired.
- Under his stewardship, the bank's market capital grew by $110 billion, and he left with a compensation package of $130 million!
- Wells Fargo paid over $4 billion in fines but makes about $20 billion a year.
- Wells Fargo paid $620 million to resolve lawsuits from customers and shareholders and spent years publicly apologizing.

No Wells Fargo employee has gone to jail over this.

In 2020, the government fined John Stumpf $17.5 million and barred him from the banking industry for life.

Eight Is Great—Key Lessons

- Employees respond to peer/culture pressures.
- Much of the language in the bank about caring for team members and customers was just about words and not lived out in the behavior of management.
- Internal controls need to be centralized.
- Whistleblowing employees who report wrongdoing need protection.

Identifying and Establishing Structured Reviews

Goal	To ensure the implementation is regularly reviewed by checking an implementation's performance against its objectives is the only way you know if a strategy is succeeding.
Implementation Challenge	Review is often poorly practiced among leaders in organizations. Why? There is the mistaken belief that once the strategy has been crafted, the leaders' work is mostly done and the implementation will take care of itself.
	Even today, many leaders still review their implementation only once or twice a year. This is a recipe for failure. By the time they conduct the reviews, small problems may have become large problems; the wrong actions may be being taken, causing damage to the organization; and it becomes harder to take corrective action to turn the organization around.
	One of the main challenges in implementation is to shift the dialogue from discussing operational performance to discussing both operations and strategy implementation.
What Needs to Change	When reviews are adopted as a business discipline, it can mean the difference between success and failure and becomes one of the strongest drivers of the implementation. Strategy implementation needs to be reviewed every two weeks in each business vertical and in its entirety every quarter. Every two weeks, departments should meet to discuss the implementation, and every three months, you and your fellow leaders should meet to review how the whole strategy implementation is performing.

Your organization's external environment (customer expectations, technology, economy) are changing continually and at an ever increasing pace, and your strategy needs to be adjusted accordingly. The implementation reviews are the enabler to track and identify the impact of changing conditions on the strategy and business. What was ideal for today will not always be suited for tomorrow.

As you start to implement, you move from theory to practice, from planning to action, and from concept to delivery. As the strategy is rolled out, you will realize that what sounded good in theory does not always work in practice, and you will need to adjust the strategy accordingly.

Another critical benefit of reviews is that when the organization sees the implementation being reviewed every two weeks in departments and quarterly by the senior leaders, they know that the organization is serious about the new strategy. Likewise, when employees see leaders meeting only twice a year on the strategy—they are likely to doubt the leadership's sincerity and commitment.

Strategy reviews are a two-hour structured meeting conducted regularly by leaders to track progress against the strategy objectives and measures.

By adopting regular reviews, leaders instill the discipline to ensure that the right actions are being taken and the right results are being achieved. They also provide a platform for reflecting on the overall strategy, holding employees accountable, and making adjustments.

The underlying principles of effective reviews are:

1. Transparency
2. Confidence in the Numbers
3. Responsibility for Taking the Action

1. Transparency

To avoid a lack of confidence in the implementation, leaders must make sure that there is transparency throughout the implementation process. During a period of transition from the old to the new strategy, employees can become unsure of what to do and may even feel nervous about their job security. To ensure transparency, information reported in the reviews must be clear and grounded in evidence. The content must be accurate, useful, and timely. The more open and frank the reviews are, the more efficient and effective they will prove in accelerating the successful implementation.

The 1998 Asian financial crisis dramatically emphasized the importance of transparency since it was the lack of business transparency in many of the affected countries that heavily contributed to a lack of confidence in their currencies.

2. Confidence in the Numbers

Reviews need to be both quantitative and qualitative. It's critical that the numbers reported are accurate. In any reviews, the numbers examined should be drawn from the Scorecard. If you don't have confidence in the numbers reported, you will challenge them and may start to doubt the basis for the whole implementation.

One way to increase confidence in the numbers is to use a Management Information System (MIS) that gathers the numbers electronically and reduces the opportunity for human error. Another effective practice is to record all the assumptions made *before* reporting the numbers (e.g., an assumption that the competitors' market share has remained static). Stating assumptions up front not only helps ensure confidence in the numbers but also reduces debate on how the numbers were calculated, rather than focusing on what they mean to the business.

3. Responsibility for Taking the Action

A key purpose of reviews is to ensure that those responsible for taking action do so. Employees know they are going to be held accountable. Leveraging reviews to hold employees accountable is one of the strongest best practices among effective leaders. An effective leader follows up with staff members to make sure they did what they said they were going to do. The review may start with an analysis of actions agreed at the previous review.

Review Objectives

There are 10 objectives to consider during a review:

1. Identify any changes in conditions and any changes required to the implementation.
2. Ensure effective implementation of action—track them and, more importantly, their impact.
3. Keep the implementation on the senior management's radar screen. There is only so much a leader can focus on. Regular reviews ensure that the strategy implementation remains part of the leadership's long-term focus.
4. Champion simplicity rather than overly complex information. Present all relevant information clearly and concisely.
5. Ensure the review and its objectives remain grounded in reality. Regular reviews help ensure that leaders check performance continually against objectives and adjust actions accordingly.
6. Identify any additional ideas that emerge as the strategy is implemented.
7. Introduce objectivity into the organizational culture. The discipline of regular reviews helps ensure that decisions are based on facts and data, as well as intuition.

8. Break down silos. Regularly reviewing and sharing information assists the organization in breaking down silos because leaders and staff improve their understanding of the operating environment, the bigger business picture, and the priorities of other departments.

9. Support continuous learning. Creating a platform for sharing success and learning from mistakes supports the organization's growth.

10. Facilitate long-term organizational success. Regular reviews are instrumental in guiding the organization.

The Five Components of a Structured Review

1. Review the deliverables.
2. Review the strategic landscape.
3. Assess critical success factors (CSF).
4. Document and discuss organizational learning.
5. Plan the next steps.

1. Deliverables

Reviews are designed to highlight the results of the implementation. Those presenting need to clearly explain what's happening (transparency), signal whether any actions need adjustments, and show how they will address future challenges. A simple color-coded spreadsheet showing the action items can reflect this process at a glance: green is on schedule, yellow is an alert to watch carefully, and red means trouble.

2. Strategic Landscape

Regular reviews provide the opportunity to examine boardroom trends that may affect the strategy. The strategic landscape review looks at such things as stakeholders, organizational changes, and environmental analyses. It allows leaders to keep an eye on the bigger picture and provides the platform for adjustment if the economy, market situations, or the competition change.

3. Critical Success Factors (CSF) Assessment

The CSFs establish the key drivers and challenges that will make or break an implementation, so it is imperative that they are reviewed to acknowledge any impending changes. For example, a common Critical Success Factor for an implementation is that leaders maintain focus and drive, and champion the implementation. The review checks to make sure that they are doing just that.

4. Organizational Learning

Throughout the process, all the teams involved should document and discuss key lessons as they are learned. As the implementation rolls out, different groups will experience different challenges. The quarterly review ensures cross-functional group learning so that mistakes are not repeated and best practices are adopted.

5. Plan the Next Steps

The review should record any changes to the implementation as:

- Additions—what new action steps need to be taken?
- Deletions—what should we stop doing?
- Amendments—what are the changes?

If required, new owners and deliverable dates may be set for each of the changes. Immediately after the review, a summary of the outcomes can be distributed to keep everyone informed.

Case Study

Mars

In their book Leading Culture Change in Global Organizations, *Daniel Denison, Robert Hooijberg, Nancy Lane, and Colleen Lief shared a story about how the leaders of the candy-making company Mars held a two-day meeting. The first morning, the meeting was held in Prague. After lunch, the team boarded a bus to Budapest where they met for the second day. Why waste time traveling to a second city?*

Along the way, the bus stopped at numerous stores so the leadership team could check how well their products were positioned on the shop shelves. This demonstrated powerfully how the organization's strategy was implemented in the field while reinforcing what was important. Clearly, it was more important to review the product placement physically with the leaders rather than to just discuss it in theory in a meeting room.

Successful strategic implementation results from periodic reviews of actions that ensure that the right results are being achieved.

> *He who smiles when something goes wrong has someone to blame it on!*
>
> – Richard Nixon

External Papers

- How Do You Measure Success In Digital? Five Metrics for CEOs, **McKinsey**

Video Links

- The 4 Disciplines of Execution, **Productivity Game**

SUSTAINING

Introduction

Sustaining is reviewing the strategy to ensure it's still adding full value.

- Reviewing Strategy Objectives and Measures
- Ensuring Reviews Become Part of the Organization's Culture
- Challenging Assumptions Made in Original Strategy

Reviewing Strategy Objectives and Measures

Some organizations treat measures and data static indicators and over time they become obsolete and thus actions can become obsolete. The measures and data must stay relevant by leaders reviewing constantly reviewing their significance.

Business is running at a faster pace than at any other previous time, and within just a few months the strategy and/or implementation may require adjustments.

Why Measures Need to Be Reviewed

Fast Food Chain Example

The outlet manager of a fast-food chain paid only lip service to many of the measures management adopted. This was because he knew the only measurement that management checked thoroughly was how much cooked chicken each outlet threw away at the end of the day—a measure they called Chicken Efficiency. The Head Office measure was aimed at managing costs by reducing the amount of uncooked chicken across outlets, but this was not the only outcome.

The outlet manager focused on keeping his Head Office boss happy. To reach the chicken efficiency target, he informed his service team to delay cooking any chicken until it was ordered by the customer. The result was customers had to wait over 15 minutes for their fast-food chicken! As customer wait time increased, customers' satisfaction decreased, and many stopped using the outlet.

Initially, management was happy, as the outlet was hitting its targets and had the best chicken efficiency across the whole chain. It was only later that they changed their minds when they saw sales dropping.

Bank Example

The CEO of a bank had just adopted a new strategy in an emerging market that had customer service at its heart. When asked what measures he was using to track organization-wide customer service, he did not have even one! He had no way of measuring the key component of the strategy.

Employees are smart—over the long run. They work on what gets measured, not on what leaders just talk about. The employees in this organization did not focus on improving service, as they were not measured against it. In the bank branches, they were measured on cross-selling of products, not customer service.

That meant this was what they focused on, and customer wait time steadily increased, creating an associated drag to customer satisfaction.

Bank staff would look at the next customer in the line and make a judgment as to whether there might be a cross-sell opportunity. If not, they would not serve them and wait until they saw a customer they liked. Not only was the bank failing to measure customer satisfaction, but the current measures were driving the strategy in the wrong direction.

Measures must support the strategy and drive the right actions, but in many organizations, this does not happen.

Within 90 days of launching the BSC, leaders should meet with the employees to discuss the new measures and review the impact on the business. Take the time to check what has changed and to recognize how employee behaviors have changed.

Meet as a leadership team to discuss your findings and to ensure the desired actions are being taken. Any disconnects or misalignment need to be discussed and resolved.

These two exercises should be repeated quarterly.

> *Excellence in implementation demands*
> *frequent and regular reviews.*
>
> — Robin Speculand

Regularly Reviewing Assumptions

Every six months, when the leaders are meeting to discuss the BSC, they should also step back and review:

1. The extent to which original assumptions are still valid
2. Strategic objectives to check whether they are still fully relevant
3. Obstacles in the implementation of measures and data in the organization

4.   Key factors in the successful implementation

5.   Improvements that can be made

Ensuring Reviews Become Part of the Organization's Culture

Goal	To instill the discipline of reviews into the DNA of the organization.
Implementation Challenge	Bridges research revealed that 85% of organizations spend fewer than 10 hours a month discussing their implementation. Even though leaders know what to do, they are still not doing it! Reviews need to become part of the fabric of the organization so that leaders are guided to conduct them as required.
What Needs to Change	The responsibility of instilling reviews into the DNA of the organization lies with senior leaders. What's crazy is that this only takes discipline. There are no budget requirements, no legal issues, and no additional resource requirements.

You need to be seen to do the right thing. The following example shows how some leaders and organizations have approached this challenge.

To adopt the discipline of regular reviews, one CEO held his regular operational reviews at a rectangular table. There, he expected his managers to represent the interests of their business. However, he held strategic reviews at a round table where he expected everyone to discuss what was best for the whole organization. The physical move to the round table reinforced that everyone had to contribute to the strategy and its implementation. It conveyed that each person's input was important.

Case Study

Alan Mulally, former CEO of Ford

In 2006, Alan Mulally became CEO of Ford during an extremely difficult time. The organization was on the brink of bankruptcy. By the time he left in 2014, he had turned it around.

When the organization was struggling, Mulally introduced the discipline of daily reviews to identify problems before they snowballed. He encouraged leaders to be open, to support each other, and to nurture personal accountability. The daily reviews shifted the culture of the meetings. For example, in Mulally's early meetings, all the reports showed the data in green (positive), yet the organization was losing millions. This was because the leaders were afraid to share the bad news. They were also concerned about their colleagues taking advantage of their poor performance. Mulally insisted the reviews be accurate; by doing so, he could start to successfully transform Ford.

Case Study

Singapore Air Force

Singapore Air Force (SAF) recently leveraged its regular reviews to change the culture around fighter jet near misses. Previously, personnel were discouraged from reporting these, as the culture was one of "don't tell." The Head of the Singapore Air Force transformed the approach because it contradicted the organization's strategic focus of embedding safety as a discipline.

Today, SAF takes the following steps when a near miss occurs:

- *Everyone in SAF is informed, and both bad and good news are shared.*
- *The focus is not on the individual but on the incident, so others can learn from it.*
- *Measures are in place to track key actions.*
- *The ground crew and air crew alike know the importance of reporting near misses.*
- *Every quarter, the chief attends the safety forum to discuss, review, and make positive changes to avoid future incidents.*

The aim is to hold people accountable to ensure the strategy is implemented successfully.

Ensuring reviews become part of the organization's culture changes the dialogue in the organization and specifically in meetings. They focus people on the strategy and its implementation—what it promises, how to adopt it, what actions to take, why it's important, what's working, and what's not.

Try adopting the following question to change the dialogue:

"What have you done this week to implement the strategy?"

By asking this question at the start of every meeting, you will put the strategy and its implementation where it should be, front and center. This is important, as individuals pay attention to what their immediate boss pays attention to.

Keep the review meetings short and succinct. Convening for more than two hours is a workshop, not a meeting.

Create a culture in which strategy check-ins become a habit just like people check-ins.

To ensure reviews become part of the organization's culture, they can be woven into the fabric of the organization by holding different types and length of reviews every week, biweekly, quarterly, and annually.

Weekly—short questions from an immediate boss demonstrate not only the importance of the strategy being implemented but also taking the right actions. It tells people they'll be asked how they are progressing against the actions they plan to take, how they will be held accountable, and allows for support and coaching.

Biweekly—longer reviews across business verticals ensure people in the organization have the discipline and are taking the right actions. They allow for immediate corrective action and support such as allocating resources and reinforcing the right actions.

Quarterly—strategic implementation reviews, which are in depth, involve the top leaders and invited employees. They encapsulate the discussions and actions from the biweekly reviews across all the business verticals and provide a summary of the progress being made throughout the organization. They also might identify flaws in the strategy that need correcting as they collectively examine the feedback from the biweekly reviews.

Annual—leadership reviews set aside a time, one or two days, to reflect on performance, share best practices, define lessons learned, and embed changes across the whole organization. They bring together the key players in the implementation and present opportunities to celebrate successes.

1.	2.	3.	4.
Weekly question from immediate boss	*Bi-weekly* reviews across every business vertical	*Quarterly* strategic implementation review	*Annual* leadership review

Figure 28.0: Regular Reviews

If you as a leader don't pay attention to the implementation, then neither will your people.

Questions for Reviews

Weekly	Biweekly	Quarterly	Annual
What have you done this week to implement the strategy?	Which strategic objectives are you focused on and what actions are you taking to implement them?	What have we done in the last 90 days to implement the strategy?	What have we achieved in the past 12 months?
Is the work you're currently doing adding value to the new strategy?	What mistakes have been made from which we can learn?	Are we providing the right resources?	What has changed in our strategy, and what is the impact on the implementation?
Are the actions you're taking today driving the implementation forward?	From the Strategy Scorecard, which measures are performing well and what concerns are outstanding?	Are people taking the right actions to deliver the strategic objectives on which we are currently focused?	What mistakes have we made?
What support do you need in order to succeed?	What should we stop doing?	What are our successes?	What lessons have we learned?
	What are we doing right?	What should we stop doing?	What more can we do to support our people?
	What is being communicated about the implementation?	What assumptions have we made and were they accurate?	What was successful that we should keep doing?
	What are our recent successes?	What has changed in our strategic landscape?	What are the best practices we can share?

What support do you need to succeed?	What can we do to be more effective as a team?	What can we celebrate?
What needs to change in our current approach to the implementation?	What needs to change in our approach?	
When we meet again for our next review, what key achievement(s) will you aim to share?	When we meet again for our next review, what key achievement(s) will you aim to share?	

> *Sometimes, I think my most important job as a CEO is to listen for bad news. If you don't act on it, your people will eventually stop bringing bad news to your attention, and that is the beginning of the end.*
>
> — Bill Gates, former CEO, Microsoft

If you only review your strategy once a year, your whole landscape could have changed; think of Nokia or Kodak!

Challenging Assumptions Made in Original Strategy

You need to ensure the assumptions made in the crafting of the strategy remain relevant throughout the implementation.

- If the assumptions are no longer relevant, then the impact may be minor or they may be devastating on the strategy implementation.
- After about six weeks, half the assumptions made on a strategic decision are forgotten if they are not revisited. Leaders may be making decisions on unreliable information, causing damage to the organization.

- Assumptions are factors that are considered true, real, or certain during the strategy planning.

Over time, assumptions made in the strategy discussions need to be revisited to check for relevance, as strategic assumptions form an identical, underlying foundation for the strategy. Typical assumptions are made around markets, competition, customers, resources, and profitability.

> *Decisions previously made are filed in our minds with "emotional tags" that influence future reviews of any previous decision or a decision on a related issue.*
>
> – Andrew Campbell, Jo Whitehead, and Sydney Finkelstein

Asian Hydro-Electricity Example

One Asian hydro-electricity corporation built a number of facilities based upon two strategic assumptions: that there would always be glacial melt waters, and that there would be a predictable monsoon season each year. Neither of these strategic assumptions are now valid.

> *No plan survives contact with the enemy.*
>
> –Tom Kolditz, retired brigadier general

> *What we anticipate seldom occurs; what we least expect generally occurs.*
>
> – Benjamin Disraeli, former UK PM

As we tend to forget assumptions, it's important we make the effort to write them down when they are discussed and review them regularly to make sure they're still relevant.

Questions to consider during the implementation include:

- What has not gone as expected?
- What new technology has emerged?
- What has shifted in customer expectations and needs?
- Have any new competitors entered our market?
- What will change in the workforce over the next three to five years?
- Are the resources available?

External Papers

- AI Is Revolutionizing How Companies Manage Transformations
- How AI will evolve for machine-assisted Strategy Execution

Video Links

- Alan Mulally, former President and CEO Ford Motor Company & Boeing, **Antonio Nieto-Rodriguez**

IMPLEMENTATION QUIZ QUESTIONS

1. Too many leaders start off with the right intentions, but somewhere between thought and actions they lose focus and commitment. To maintain focus and commitment organizations should?

   A   Allow leaders to identify their own measures for their own business

   B   Check on leadership performance once a year

   C   Dictate to employees exactly what needs to be done

   D   None of the above

2. A best practice is to break strategy into objectives. This is important in tracking performance because?

   A   Breaks the implementation into deliverable components

   B   Creates more specific measures

   C   Generates better discipline across the organization

   D   All of the above

3. Strategy Maps are a powerful one-page visual summary of the strategy. Organizations can leverage Strategy Maps to?

   A   Demonstrate the relationship between different strategy objectives

   B   Substitute measures with objectives

   C   Ensure Strategy Maps are only shared among leaders for security

   D   Never adjust or tweak the Strategy Map

4. The odds of successfully implementing a strategy that isn't regularly reviewed are slim to none. Organizations can leverage reviews to?

   A   Reinforce the right key messages

   B   Ensure the right actions are being taken across the organization

   C   Reinforce the right discipline

   D   All of the above

5. A best practice is to conduct regular reviews of the implementation. To ensure reviews are effective, organizations should?

   A   Emphasize the importance of being open and honest

   B   Constantly move forward with not looking back at mistakes

   C   Don't keep records so as people do not fear the meetings

   D   Always accept the assumptions made when planning this strategy

6. It is essential for organizations to identify the right measures to track the performance of the implementation. This is essential within an organization because?

    A   Measures drive behaviors

    B   Leaders are able to manage the business not just measure it

    C   Assists in articulating the right actions for employees to take

    D   All of the above

7. In addition to identifying the right measures, leaders also need to consider their complexity. This is because?

    A   The more complex they are, the more significant they are

    B   The more complex they are, the more costly they are

    C   The more complex they are, the more important they are

    D   The more complex they are, the more attention leaders will pay to them

8. The Balanced Scorecard has become an established measurement and management tool within organizations. To ensure its successful adoption, organizations should?

    A   Keep the Balanced Scorecard only among the top leaders to avoid leakage to competition

    B   After creating the Balanced Scorecard, recognize that it does not ever need to be adjusted

    C   Consider translating the Balanced Scorecard into a visual dashboard

    D   Develop annual budgets independently of the Balanced Scorecard

9. Organizations need to regularly review measures to ensure their relevance. To instill the review discipline, organizations should?

    A   Encourage leaders to defend their position every quarter for balancing the long view

    B   Encourage leaders to recognize that measures are a means for managing the implementation

    C   Ensure leaders are conducting reviews on the implementation at least quarterly

    D   All of the above

10. The creation of a Strategy Office is used by some organizations to oversee the implementation. A key responsibility of a Strategy Office is to?

    A   Take full control of the strategy implementation

    B   Impose what needs to be done

    C   Champion and guide the organization

    D   None of the above

Answers to the quiz questions can be found on page 314 in the Appendix.

Appendix

STRATEGY
IMPLEMENTATION
INSTITUTE

Answers to Quiz Questions

Ch 2: Leadership Excellence Answers

1	C
2	B
3	B
4	D
5	A
6	B
7	A
8	B
9	B
10	D

Ch 3: Value Creation Answers

1	A
2	D
3	B
4	C
5	A
6	B
7	C
8	C
9	D
10	D

Ch 4: Business Model Answers

1	D
2	B
3	C
4	C
5	B
6	A
7	A
8	A
9	C
10	D

Ch 5: Culture Evolution Answers

1	C
2	D
3	B
4	D
5	C
6	D
7	D
8	D
9	D
10	B

Ch 6: Stakeholder Management Answers

1	A
2	C
3	A
4	A
5	D
6	D
7	B
8	D
9	B
10	D

Ch 7: Employee Engagement Answers

1	D
2	D
3	D
4	D
5	A
6	D
7	D
8	B
9	D
10	C

Ch 8: Track Performance Answers

1	D
2	D
3	A
4	D
5	A
6	D
7	B
8	C
9	D
10	C

Index of Figures

Board of Advisors

The founders, Robin Speculand and Antonio Nieto-Rodriguez, are guided by a high-profile board:

- **Rita Gunther McGrath** is a best-selling author, a sought-after speaker, and a long-time professor at Columbia Business School.
- **Mark Langley** is the president & CEO of the Project Management Institute (PMI) through 2018 and is currently an independent consultant, advising associations, private sector firms, and individuals on critical and emerging business issues.
- **Francisco de Miguel** is a Spanish national who joined the multinational Van Leer Group in 1968 and has held several managerial positions. In 1998 he was appointed strategic business manager for Van Leer's operations in Latin America. He joined the executive board of Van Leer in 1995.
- **Dr. Tony O'Driscoll** is global head of Duke CE Labs and lecture fellow at the Fuqua School of Business.
- **Lori Figueiredo** is Asia Pacific's leading learning strategist and founder of Syzygy Solutions Pte Ltd.
- **Patricia Enslow** was a managing director of Credit Suisse and the chief marketing officer in the Asia Pacific Division, based in Singapore. Patricia joined Credit Suisse from UBS in October 2016, where she was head of marketing for Wealth Management, Asia Pacific.
- **Vaughn Richtor** is the former CEO of ING DIRECT Australia and CEO Challenger and Growth Countries—Asia, ING Group.

Become a Strategy Implementation Professional

In an increasingly complex and rapidly transforming world in which implementation capabilities are anxiously required by organizations, the online certifications course and Fellowship ensures you're qualified to meet the demands.

The Strategy Implementation Professional (SIP) is rapidly being recognized as the gold standard in certification within this field. This is an online self-learning blended course, built around the seven stages of the Strategy Implementation Road Map©.

Developed by strategy implementation experts, the online certification course is based on rigorous standards and ongoing research to meet real-world needs of organizations. With the Strategy Implementation Institute certification behind your title, you'll have a skill set deeply appreciated by many organizations and a recognized qualification that will increase your career progression opportunities.

The Institute works in association with APMG International to increase competencies and recognition of implementation professionals. We have jointly developed the Strategy Implementation Professional—SIP—certification, the first global credential of its kind. Two years after being a certified SIP you can apply to become a Fellow of the Institute.

Become a Fellow of the Institute

The Fellowship is the highest and most prestigious recognition from the Strategy Implementation Institute (Institute) for practitioners in the field of strategy implementation. "Fellows of the Institute" have successfully:

- Demonstrated a passion in the subject
- Proven the skills they have learned as a Strategy Implementation Professional—our online course and certification
- Exhibited a desire to continuously learn and develop

Recognition as a Fellow of the Institute enters you into an exclusive club of not only Fellowships of the Institute but also among the few leaders globally who have the skills and experience to successfully implement strategy. Recipients are accomplished leaders from a broad range of fields who have had the vision and passion to make significant and lasting contributions to the strategy implementation profession, community, and the Institute.

Implementing strategy is a rare and highly appreciated skill set that sets apart the most influential and successful leaders in business.

The Fellowship is a significant part of the Institute's purpose to develop implementation professionals around the world. A core criteria for becoming a Fellow is that you have:

1. Learned the skills as a Strategy Implementation Professional (SIP)
2. Been a certified Strategy Implementation Professional for a minimum two years

The Strategy Implementation Professional and Fellowship titles are being globally recognized as the highest standard in strategy implementation certification.

For more information visit here:
www.strategyimplementationinstitute.org/fellowship/

Connect with us at: info@si-institute.org

Made in the USA
Las Vegas, NV
16 September 2024

94958666R00195